History Matters

Patriarchy and the
Challenge of Feminism

J U D I T H   M .   B E N N E T T

Manchester University Press

First published in 2006 by
University of Pennsylvania Press
Philadelphia, Pennsylvania 19104-4112

First published 2006 in the United Kingdom by
Manchester University Press
Oxford Road, Manchester M13 9NR, UK
www.manchesteruniversitypress.co.uk

British Library Cataloguing-in-Publication Data
A catalogue record for this book is available from the British Library

Library of Congress Cataloging-in-Publication Data
Bennett, Judith M.
  History matters : patriarchy and the challenge of feminism / Judith M. Bennett.
    p. cm.
  Includes bibliographical references and index.
  ISBN-13: 978-0-8122-3946-1
  ISBN-10: 0-8122-3946-6 (cloth : alk. paper)
  1. Women—History. 2. Women—Historiography. 3. Feminism—Historiography.
4. Feminist theory. 5. Patriarchy. I. Title.

HQ1121.B424 2006
305.42072'2—dc22

                                                                    2006044716

ISBN 0 7190 7565 3 *hardback*
EAN 978 0 7190 7565 0

14 13 12 11 10 09 08 07 06   10 9 8 7 6 5 4 3 2 1

For Susan Porter Benson (1943–2005)
Unmatched in political courage, generosity of
spirit, intellectual integrity, and sharp wit

Contents

Chapter 1
Introduction: Feminism and History

I first came to feminist history in the 1970s as a way of reconciling my two full but contrary identities at the time. In one, I was a lesbian feminist, absorbed by activism at home and in the streets. In the other, I was a studious medievalist, training under the guidance of male professors, most of them priests, at the Pontifical Institute of Mediaeval Studies. Radical feminist by night, medievalist by day; feminist history brought my two selves together. As I recall, the reconciliation was less than perfect. Among some feminists I felt awkward about the elitism of my education, the snottiness of my diction, and the maleness of my chosen profession. And at both the Pontifical Institute and the University of Toronto I encountered a steady stream of students and professors who dismissed feminist history, not to mention abortion rights, lesbian self-determination, and the other struggles that nourished my political soul. But there was one aspect of the reconciliation that was always a perfect fit: I never doubted that my work as a historian was important work for feminism. In the 1970s it seemed crystal clear that one of the battlefronts of feminism was women's history, where feminists—both in the academy and outside it—were reclaiming a lost past in their research, empowering students in their teaching, and using historical insight to inform feminist strategy.

This book seeks to recover some of the clarity of that 1970s ideal of a seamless union of history and feminism—and to add depth to it. In the thirty years since I first pulled a history book off the shelves of the Toronto Women's Bookstore, the history of women and gender has developed into a recognized academic field, institutionalized in departments, conferences, journals, and presses, and mature enough to participate in the creation of such newer fields as lesbian history and the history of masculinity.[1] Feminism, even though it has waxed and waned in popularity, has also grown immensely, its theories becoming more sophisticated and inclusive and some of its tenets now realized in the legal codes, educational curricula, and everyday values of some nations; in the 1990s, for example, sexual equality was enshrined in the constitutions of the emerging states of Namibia, South Africa, and the Czech Republic. Yet, although both history and feminism have grown stronger over these decades, the relationship between them has weakened. Women's history once shone as a critical battlefront of the feminist struggle, but today it is often considered irrelevant: feminist media include much less history than they once did (such once-regular venues as the "Lost Women" column of *Ms.* magazine and the "Archives" section of *Signs: A Journal of Women in Culture and Society* are now themselves "history"); much feminist theory is remarkably uninformed by historical insight; and, most worrying of all, some young feminists cavalierly reject the utility of the past, proclaiming proudly that "we don't much remember."[2] I *want* to remember; I think that the achievement of a more feminist future depends on such remembrance; and I believe it is the particular job of feminist historians to ensure that those memories are rich, plausible, and well-informed.[3]

I first began expressing my concerns about an eroding relationship between "feminism and history" in an article of that title published in 1989. In the years since, I have learned from the generous suggestions of readers and audiences, refined my thinking, and continued to reflect in print on developments in feminist history. This book borrows from some of these past publications but in ways that will often be unrecognizable. I have drawn my thoughts together here into a new argument about the depoliticization of women's and gender history, the loss of historical depth in feminist scholarship, the critical perspectives afforded by a long view of the history of women and gender, and the importance of studying what I call a "patriarchal equilibrium." In this process of rethinking and revision, I have formulated some new ideas and text, and I have also sometimes freely self-plagiarized from previously published articles. *History Matters: Patriarchy and the Challenge of Feminism* addresses some subjects entirely new to my process of historiographical reflection, and it also provides, compared to any of my individual articles, a more coherent and thorough statement of my hopes for feminist history.[4]

In tackling the major issues of this book, I can speak, of course, only from my own experience and expertise. I teach in the United States, where I was born to non-immigrant and middle-class parents of European descent and where I retain the privileges of citizenship; I pursued my graduate studies in Canada; I now spend a few months of each year in England, the country whose medieval history is the subject of my academic research. My perspective is, in short, profoundly Anglo, in American terms, or Western, in world terms. These are the intellectual traditions within which I work and from which I draw most of my observations.

Although my examples will be largely taken from European history, my working assumption has been that the issues raised here are of general relevance to feminist historians. My familiarity with non-European branches of women's history is necessarily more limited, but what I know of the pursuit of women's history in other world regions—particularly the United States, Latin America, Africa, Australia, and China—suggests that, in these areas, too, feminist history is challenged by depoliticization, present-mindedness, and inattention to long-term continuities. Such challenges do, of course, play out differently in the histories of specific regions and times, and I certainly do not mean to imply that the history of European women should serve as a paradigm for histories of women elsewhere. Instead, I hope that readers of this book will consider both the European peculiarities of my concerns and the general trends of which Europe is merely one example of many.

Even for Europeanists, much of the historical information in this book will be new, for I draw the bulk of my examples from my own field of *medieval* women's history. Most historians of women, Europeanists or not, are unfamiliar with the history and historiography of the European Middle Ages. My focus on medieval evidence speaks directly to this book's contention that feminist history should be more attentive to premodern eras. In "getting medieval," I have endeavored not to dwell unnecessarily on medieval arcana and to offer examples that are clear, accessible, and to-the-point, even for readers unfamiliar with early Europe.[5] I hope that readers will, in turn, open themselves to these earlier histories, thereby expanding their temporal perspectives on feminist history while also thinking in comparative ways about women's history, broadly conceived. This is not a book on medieval women's history; this is a book in which every incursion into the history of women is intended to help us think more generally about history, patriarchy, and feminism.

One last caveat. I have been told that anyone who begins a sentence with "we" is starting to deceive her (or his) audience, and I know that there are many circumstances that separate me from the diverse feminist historians who will, I hope, read this book. By using the first-person plural, I mean to evoke our common feminist interest in the past, not to claim a common subjectivity. My evocation is practical and strategic, and it seeks to extend to "feminist historians" the implications of Iris Young's smart argument that we can conceptualize "women" as a serial collective, as formed by shared circumstance rather than common attribute or identity.[6] Feminist historians are a sort of serial collective, too. We work in many national and institutional settings; we work on many subjects and centuries; we are both teachers and students; and we work with tape recorders as well as trowels, in archives as well as streets. Feminist history is different everywhere—it has been, for example, especially influenced by socialism in Britain, shaped by Marxism in China, interested in women's culture in the United States, allied with sociology in Brazil, and fractured by "women" versus "gender" in Japan.[7] These sorts of differences are a rich strength of women's history, and they need not divide us. In writing this book for feminist historians, in other words, I have seen myself as part of a diverse collectivity of feminist women and men who share a common interest in studying the past.

The argument of this book builds steadily from problem to solution to elaboration. The next two chapters lay the foundation by outlining the challenges that women's history—a term which I will use as a shorthand for "women's and gender history"—faces in the twenty-first century, specifically a waning of feminist connection in history (Chapter 2) and a waning of historical depth in feminism (Chapter 3). Chapter 4 suggests a way of approaching these problems—that is, by attending more to the history of a "patriarchal equilibrium" whereby, despite many changes in women's experiences over the centuries, women's low status vis-à-vis men has remained remarkably unchanged. The fact of this patriarchal equilibrium presents, in my view, a critical feminist problem that only historians—and, indeed, only *feminist* historians who take a *long view* of women's past—can unpack. The next two chapters offer in-depth illustrations of how deep historical study can enrich feminist understandings of women's work (Chapter 5) and lesbian sexualities (Chapter 6). The book is wrapped up with a chapter that adds a new twist—the challenges of textbooks and classrooms—to viewing women's history from a distance and with feminist intent. And a brief conclusion offers some final and (I hope) stirring thoughts.

Feminism has come a long way since the 1970s. As I look back now, I am amazed by some of the "truths" I then held dear, embarrassed by the differences among women I then overlooked, and ashamed by some of the ways in which my certainties then oppressed other women.[8] But I remain as confident now as I was then that history is critical to the feminist project, that history provides feminist activists and theorists with long-term perspectives essential to building a better long-term future. I hope this book will help us think more explicitly about what *sorts* of feminist history can best aid feminist struggles in the twenty-first century. In the 1970s, feminists often turned to history for inspiring stories about great women who had triumphed over adversity and accomplished marvelous deeds. Today, feminists still mostly see history, when they turn to it at all, as an ever-expanding list of positive and encouraging role models: such women as Rosa Parks, Eleanor Roosevelt, Simone de Beauvoir, Susan B. Anthony, and, for those who take a longer view, Elizabeth Cady Stanton, Sojourner Truth, Olympe de Gouges, Mary Wollstonecraft, and perhaps even Christine de Pizan.

These women are certainly important parts of the feminist past and their inspiration does important work in the feminist present, but I seek in this book to encourage a more substantive integration of history and feminism, one that turns to history for *strategy* as well as inspiration. To my mind, the strategic lessons of women's history are more sobering than encouraging. Stirring tales of strong women who accomplished marvelous deeds against great odds may build self-esteem and confidence, but women's history, especially when viewed across many centuries, can also stimulate feminist outrage and revolutionary fervor. To whet your appetite for the long view, here is one example taken from the pages that follow: in fourteenth-century England a female wage-worker earned, on the average, 71 percent of male wages; in Great Britain today women earn roughly the same—75 percent of the annual wages earned by men.[9] There are many ways to qualify this bald comparison and I will do just that in Chapter 5, but surely this "sticky" wage gap offers good information for feminists to think through. The feminist potential of this particular sort of women's history—focused on feminist issues, aware of the distant past, attentive to continuities, and alert to the workings of patriarchal power—is the subject of this book.

Chapter 2
Feminist History and Women's History

In 1405, Christine de Pizan, an Italian humanist who spent most of her life in France, set out to rebut the misogynistic literature of her time. Crafting what was to become the first major feminist tract in the Western tradition, Christine de Pizan turned, again and again, to the feminist promise of history. In *The Book of the City of Ladies,* she described a city populated with the great women of the past—Queen Esther, who saved the Jews; the Sabine women who solidified peace between the Romans and their neighbors; Clothilda, who brought Christianity to the Franks; and of course, the Virgin Mary and various other notable female saints. By focusing on the accomplishments of these admirable women, Christine de Pizan used women's history to demonstrate the grievous errors of those who lambasted the female sex as inherently weak and evil. She also turned to these historical women to inspire ordinary women in her own day: "My ladies, see how these men accuse you of so many vices in everything. Make liars of them all by showing forth your virtue, and prove their attacks false by acting well." In the hands of Christine de Pizan, history was a feminist tool for celebrating women's past accomplishments, rebutting the accusations of those who maligned women, and urging women to greater goals.[1]

Some six hundred years later, probably no one would consider *The Book of the City of Ladies* an ideal example of feminist history; its tone is too polemical, its sources too mythical, its perspective too elitist, and its examples too much in the mode of "women worthies." But Christine de Pizan inaugurated a tradition of feminist history that has long endured.[2] In the centuries since she wrote, some of our greatest feminists have found inspiration in history (think, for example, of Elizabeth Cady Stanton and Simone de Beauvoir), and some of our greatest historians have been motivated, at least in part, by feminism (Catherine Macaulay, Eileen Power, and Mary Beard are a few classic examples). In the 1970s, the link between feminism and history was simultaneously broadened and deepened. On the one hand, the feminist media—not only in the "Lost Women" column of *Ms.* magazine but also in a proliferation of such free-standing publications as *Witches, Midwives, and Nurses*—exposed the feminist public to the outrageous omissions of history as it was then taught in schools and universities.[3] On the other hand, in the halls of academe itself, feminist scholars began to rewrite the past, so that history not merely included women but also tussled substantively with topics of importance to the feminist agenda. So, for example, Sheila Rowbotham traced the history of socialist women in her 1972 book *Women, Resistance and Revolution*; a few years later Linda Gordon added a historical voice to the feminist struggle for reproductive rights with her *Woman's Body, Woman's Right*; and two years after that, Joan Scott and Louise Tilly tackled the complex history of women's work in *Women, Work, and Family*.[4] These early works were often produced in a heady mixture of activism and writing; thus, for example, Sally Alexander researched the sweated work of nineteenth-century women by day and advocated better conditions for cleaning staff by night. In such a context, as Sara Evans has recently noted, the questions of feminist history were easy to formulate: "We just started taking the questions from our own activism and applying them to the past."[5]

Today, women's history (I will explain shortly why I use this as an umbrella term for "women's and gender history") reaps the benefits of the feminist offensive of the late twentieth century, having matured into a field of intense research, writing, and teaching throughout the world. We now have departmental positions in women's history (in some cases even chaired professorships), undergraduate majors and graduate fields, programs on several continents that offer master's and/or doctoral degrees (there are some seventy such programs in the United States alone), regular conferences and prizes for articles and books, an international association, and three journals dedicated just to the English-language side of the field.[6] As women's history has grown, it has also expanded into gender history and helped to give birth to new subfields, especially the history of men and masculinities and the history of sexualities. Although it is in the United States in particular that a flexible university system has most thoroughly accommodated women's history, all world regions have been touched—both intellectually and institutionally—by the remarkable advance of women's history.[7] Christine de Pizan's pioneering plunge into the feminist possibilities of the past has now grown into an institutionalized field of historical teaching and research.

All this is cause for celebration. But there is cause for caution too. Women's history is stronger than ever before, but its links with feminism have weakened. This withering partnership with feminism poses a major challenge to women's history in the twenty-first century. This chapter and the next examine the two parts of that withering—here, the slow eclipse of feminism within history and, then, the truncation of historical consciousness within feminism. But, first, I would like to lay out some history, clarify some concepts, and define some terms.

Feminism

Feminism cannot claim sole credit for the phenomenal growth of women's history in the late twentieth century. In part, feminist historians were able to build on related disciplinary developments that redirected historians away from "great men" and toward ordinary people. In Britain, for example, many feminist historians emerged from traditions of Marxist and socialist history; in France, Christiane Klapisch-Zuber and others found some support for their study of women's past in the traditions of the Annales School;[8] and in the United States, the methods and subjects of what was then called the "new social history" proved amenable to women's history. The advance of women's history was also aided by the extraordinary expansion of higher education after World War II; when universities began to accommodate more women as both students and professors, the curriculum changed accordingly. And in part, the growth of women's history was spurred by complementary advances in the histories of other neglected groups, especially the roughly simultaneous expansion of African American history in the United States. But these factors played supporting rather than initiating roles. As reported by women's historians from across the globe in 1991, feminist advocacy was the chief impetus for the expansion of the field in the 1970s and thereafter.[9]

This is a proud legacy, but it has been undermined by decades of assaults on feminism, assaults that have grossly misrepresented what feminism and its corollary, feminist history, really are. To my mind, feminism is simply the conviction that women, like men, should be afforded the opportunity to realize fully their humanity.[10] Simple as that. Yet, not so simple, for feminism has been slandered, smeared, and saddled with so many canards that many people who today agree that women should be afforded full human rights nevertheless avoid calling themselves "feminists," much less "feminist historians." What exactly do feminists believe?

FEMINISM AND "WOMEN"

In our postmodern world, feminism's focus on the category "women" is easily ridiculed as naive and old-fashioned. The notion that there exists a distinct category of "women" lies at the foundation of feminism, but it has now proven to be a cracked foundation. Thanks to Denise Riley, Judith Butler, and the lived critiques of transgender and transsexual people, the old confidence that "women" can be clearly identified by bodily characteristics no longer stands. Thanks to Audre Lorde, Elizabeth Spelman, Chandra Talpade Mohanty, and the ongoing critiques of women marginalized in the dominant discourses of feminism, the old confidence that "women" constitute a transcendent sisterhood that somehow bridges such differences as class, race, religion, sexuality, and world region also no longer stands.[11] As Jee Yeun Lee recently put it, "These days, whenever someone says the word 'women' to me, my mind goes blank. What 'women'? What is this 'women' thing you are talking about? Does that mean me? Does that mean my mother, my roommates, the white woman next door, the checkout clerk at the supermarket, my aunts in Korea, half the world's population?"[12] There is, in other words, no stable subject—no coherent thing called "women"—at the heart of either feminism or feminist history.

Yet, as Toril Moi has refreshingly argued, "we do not have to believe that the word 'woman' always carries heavy metaphysical baggage."[13] Feminists continue to talk about "women," and I will do the same throughout this book. My reasons are threefold. First, the epistemological arguments of Riley, Butler, and others might be compelling, but they have limited practical resonance. As Riley herself has noted, it is perfectly feasible to acknowledge that "women" do not really exist "while maintaining a politics 'as if they existed'—since the world behaves as if they unambiguously did."[14] In other words, "women" is a slippery concept in theory, but in practice it usually acts as a stable category—for its time and place—that can critically determine a person's life chances. This practical categorization of "women" matters today, and it has mattered in the past; it is therefore a proper subject of feminist thought and feminist history. Please note my caveat "for its time and place"; the category "women" does not have a practical meaning that transcends all other categorizations, but it does have practical meanings in specific contexts. Second, in dealing with the differences that fracture the category "women," I find useful Mary Maynard's distinction between universalizing (which suppresses differences) and generalizing (which seeks patterns among differences). The former is to be avoided; the latter is critical to both the feminist project and historical writing.[15] Third, to my mind, differences among women present not insurmountable obstacles but instead strategic opportunities. Rather than building walls between women, the articulation of difference is leading to greater understanding, better coalitions, and a stronger unified—but not unitary—category of "women."[16]

Feminism also does not dictate, as some people sometimes believe, that there is anything inherently "womanly" about women. Some feminisms have argued that women are more moral than men, or more maternal, or more pacific. Others have so emphasized victimization that it can seem a basic female trait. But these are branches of feminism, not the main trunk. Feminism's chief observation about women is also its motivating force: women's relative disadvantage vis-à-vis men. Almost every girl born today will face more constraints and restrictions than will be encountered by a boy who is born today into *the same social circumstances as that girl.* As a feminist, I consider this a wrong that should be righted. The disadvantages that women today face vary considerably, especially by class, race, religion, sexuality, and world region, yet, despite these variations, the general characteristic of female disadvantage remains. This disadvantage does not, however, cast women as hapless victims. Women's history has shown, again and again, that women have not been merely passive victims of sexual inequality; women have also colluded in, undermined, survived, and sometimes even benefited from the presence of patriarchy. Benefited from patriarchy? Certainly. In fifteenth-century Europe, an elite woman like Christine de Pizan was able to increase the coin in her purse by employing women instead of men because, as one medieval handbook advised, "a woman will work for much less money than a man would take."[17] In most societies today, well-off women do the same, paying other women low wages to clean their houses, watch their children, and paint their nails.[18] There is no doubt in my mind—or, I think, the minds of most other feminists—that the oppression of women can have endured so long and in so many places only thanks, in part, to women's collusion in the oppression of women.

FEMINISM AND DIFFERENCE

Some feminists have sometimes been inattentive to other social inequalities, such as those created by class, race, religion, sexuality, and world region, but this inattention is no more inherent to feminism than maternalism and victimization are inherent to "women." Of course, when someone speaks as a feminist, she or he is speaking from the conviction that women's lives could and should be improved, but this does not preclude similar convictions against racism, class privilege, heterosexism, and the like. Indeed, compared to proponents of other liberation ideologies, feminists usually have been and still are relatively attentive to inequalities created by such other factors as class and race. If you doubt this, I invite you to compare, for example, the treatment of class in any women's history journal to the treatment of gender in any labor history journal. As Gisela Bock advised in the late 1980s, feminist historians have worked long and hard to see the relation of gender to other sociocultural relations as a matter not of "competition" (does class matter more than gender?) but instead of as "one constituent factor of all other relations."[19]

FEMINISM AND MEN

Yes, some feminists have sometimes blamed men, as men, for women's plight, but most feminists recognize that sexual inequalities are not solely rooted in male antipathy. Few feminists "hate men." Feminism's central insight that women are generally disadvantaged does not thereby mean that women and men cannot interact in happy, fulfilling, and meaningful ways. Of course they can. But as Sally Alexander and Barbara Taylor put it long ago, "all this loving and needing and solidarising [does not mean] there is no general structure of sexual antagonism."[20] Although it has thus far proven difficult to convince many men that feminism is in their interests too, I emphatically believe this is the case. So, too, does an ever-growing group of feminist historians—mostly men, but also some women—who are subjecting masculinity to historical study. For just one example, Michael Roper's work on the psychic and emotional lives of male managers in twentieth-century Britain is explicitly framed by the feminist need to better understand the "glass ceiling" against which women in business still so often bump.[21]

FEMINISM WORLDWIDE

Western feminism once reflected only the circumstances of women in the West, particularly in its espousal of an individualist ethic that ill-suited some women in other world regions. As a result, some people who have supported feminist goals have eschewed the label "feminist" and preferred such other terms as "women's rights" or "womanist."[22] Yet feminism did not originate in the West, nor has it been a Western phenomenon of little resonance for women in other parts of the world; as Antoinette Burton has emphasized so concisely, women in early twentieth-century India, Iran, Turkey, Egypt, Japan, China, and Latin America were advocating for women's rights just as were suffragists in Europe and the United States.[23] All these feminisms were and are not the same, but all share the core conviction that women, like men, should be able to realize fully their humanity. Even though feminism has been unfairly stereotyped as a single sort of Western, individualistic feminism, women's rights advocates worldwide have continued to claim the term as their own and put it to their own uses. For example, in Afghanistan, the Revolutionary Association of the Women of Afghanistan (RAWA) not only courageously fights for women's rights but also readily labels its founder a "feminist," and in Africa, more and more activists are embracing a feminism of their own making. Some women's rights organizations—the U.S.-based MADRE, which works with sister organizations in Latin America, the Caribbean, Africa, and the Middle East, is one example—still usually avoid the term "feminist." [24] But feminism has never been a Western-only phenomenon and is not so today. Instead, its worldwide impact is evident everywhere: in the presence of women from ninety-five countries at the 2002 Women's World Congress in Uganda, in the thriving United Nations Development Fund for Women (UNIFEM), in the ratification by 162 nations of the Convention to Eliminate All Forms of Discrimination against Women (CEDAW), and in the proliferation of feminist NGOs.

Feminism itself has a fraught history that is, at once, admirable and abominable. Feminists have sometimes heroically tackled male supremacy, speaking strongly in the face of ridicule and hostility. But feminists have also sometimes horribly linked their own struggles to the elitist, imperialist, racist, and heterosexist agendas of their day, as, for example, did some nineteenth-century white feminists in the United States and their middle-class counterparts in Britain who objected to the extension of suffrage to black and working-class men, respectively. Today, feminism boasts a myriad of contemporary meanings and movements, of which the two most fundamental divides are long-standing. The first distinguishes between those who seek *equality* with men (and hence an eventual erasure of sexual difference) and those who seek to maintain sexual difference but establish *equity* between the sexes.[25] The second distinguishes between feminist thought and feminist activism, a divide that has broadened in recent decades as academic feminism has drifted away from its activist moorings. But these two divides are just two of many, for the feminism on which feminist historians draw is an extraordinarily rich, varied, and contested tradition. For Barbara Smith, feminism is "the political theory and practice to free *all* women; women of color, working-class women, poor women, disabled women, Jewish women, lesbians, old women—as well as white, economically privileged, heterosexual women. Anything less than this vision of total freedom is not feminism, but merely female self-aggrandizement."[26] For Joan Scott, feminism is "a site where differences conflict and coalesce, where common interests are articulated and contested, where identities achieve temporary stability—where politics and history are made."[27] For Charlotte Bunch, feminism is "an entire world view or *gestalt*, not just a laundry list of 'women's issues.'"[28] None would recognize herself in caricatures of feminism as essentializing women, or ignoring other social inequalities, or hating men, or bewailing women's victimization, or addressing only Western concerns, and all root their feminism, as I do, in *advocacy on behalf of the full humanity of women*. We might argue about how to best accomplish that advocacy and where it might lead us, but at a fundamental level, feminism really might be as simple as that.

Feminist History, Women's History, Gender History

All historians of women are not ipso facto feminist historians. When William O'Neill published his history of U.S. feminism in 1969, for example, he forthrightly denied any feminist sympathies. "I have avoided the question of whether or not women *ought* to have full parity with men," he wrote, opining that "since we do not know what genuine equality would mean in practice, its desirability cannot fairly be assessed."[29] In the 1980s, modern European women's history was briefly rocked by a controversy over purported feminist "betrayals" of and "threats" to women's history.[30] And in 1996, Helen Jewell sought to distance herself from feminism in her survey of women in medieval England, claiming that it would be a mistake to start "from a modern feminist perspective which may not be transferable to the Middle Ages."[31] Such explicit disavowals of feminism are not common in the writing of women's history, but others have sought to distance themselves from feminism in more subtle ways. As Joan Scott has noted, for example, the shift in the 1980s from "women" to "gender" was fueled in part by a search for "political acceptability."

Because "gender" had an apolitical cast, it was often preferred to the more threatening "women."[32] This remains true today. Bernard Capp, reacting in 2004 to a feminist critique of his *When Gossips Meet*, recently averred that he prefers "gender history" for the supposed "plurality of perspectives" that it allows.[33]

This discomfort with feminism partly springs from our profession's discomfort with owning any political perspectives at all. Some historians aspire (naively, in my view) to reaching god's-eye truths about the past, and some worry (unnecessarily, in my view) that politically inspired scholarship imposes a "pattern ready-made" on the past.[34] History is not, of course, simply "the past," and historians are not, of course, unbiased reporters or god-like observers who simply reveal the past "as it really was." This "positivist" aspiration has served more to disguise than to suppress the politics of historians.[35] All recovery of the past entails interpretation, so that no matter how assiduously a historian might seek to let the past speak, he or she unavoidably speaks alongside the historical record. Few historians today embrace pure positivism, but it lingers in our profession's continued discomfort with the mingling of history and politics. Today, mainstream political approaches are readily cast as apolitical history, whereas histories associated with such liberation movements as feminism are caricatured as ahistorical politics. It raises few eyebrows, for example, that the changing political culture of the United States has dramatically recast the 1492 voyage of Columbus; the heroic epic that I learned as a schoolchild in the 1950s is now rightly told in the more sober light of the devastation that European contact brought to Native Americans. But many eyebrows are still raised over feminist history, because of the enduring assumption that historians inspired by feminism "distort the evidence and the conclusions to support modern feminist ideology."[36]

Let me be clear in response: feminist history does not entail distorting evidence and twisting conclusions. As a feminist historian, I respect the possibilities and limitations of my sources; I strive to approach the dead and different people of the Middle Ages with what Ruth Roach Pierson has called "epistemic humility"; and I would never manipulate my research findings to suit any conclusions ready-made.[37] Yet I am, like all historians, more than a reporter of facts newly discovered; I am also an interpreter of the facts as I see them. My work necessarily reflects my feminist politics, just as the interpretations of all historians reflect their political views: that is, feminist politics informs the questions that frame my research (for example, encouraging me to turn to history for insights into why women today

are generally paid less than men); it shapes some of the methods with
which I approach my archival work (for example, teaching me to be
more aware of differences among the women I encounter in my documents); and it inspires, too, some of the implications I draw from my
conclusions (for example, suggesting to me that women's persistent
economic disadvantages might be integral to patriarchies, past and
present). Feminist historians might be more forthright about their
politics than are other historians, but this political—one might call
it "moral"—dimension is as old as the profession itself. Almost two
thousand years ago Tacitus taught that the first duty of historians was
to help people remember "virtuous actions" and to abhor "evil
words and deeds."[38] To accomplish this, historians *must* exercise judgment (what *is* virtuous? what *is* evil?). These judgments will differ, of
course, with the politics and subjectivities of historians. As Adrienne
Rich has put it, "Feminist history . . . is, indeed, as the department
chairmen and the deans of liberal arts suspect, political. So, of course,
is the history of white men, as told by themselves, political, having to
do with the retention of power."[39] Some historians embrace the politics of history and others shun it, but whether we like it or not, history
is always and already inflected by politics. This political edginess is
one of history's greatest attractions, inspiring countless generations
to try to learn from the past in order to build better futures. This is
the hope of feminist history, too.

If we may relax, as I think we should, about the *politics* of feminist
history, what, then, about its *subject matter*? "Feminist history" (history
informed by feminist politics) is sometimes taken to mean the "history of feminism" (history of the people, movements, and ideas that
have sought to improve women's lives); the two are best kept distinct.[40] Feminist history is not strictly equivalent to women's history.
After all, as we have just seen, there are some historians of women
who reject the feminist label. The two are tied by a strong recursive
link, since so many readers assume that any study of women is ipso
facto feminist, but the link can be undone either by explicit authorial
disavowal (as above) or by more subtle historical practices (which I
will explore more fully below). There are also some feminist historians who work on topics unrelated to women, gender, and sexuality.
Gabrielle Spiegel, for example, is certainly a feminist, but her published work has focused mostly on history-writing, both in the Middle
Ages and today. Similarly, Karen Halttunen is a feminist whose work
on the intellectual life and culture of the nineteenth-century United
States ranges far from "women's history." I am grateful to Spiegel,
Halttunen, and others who take their feminist politics into more tra-

ditional areas of historical inquiry, for it would be foolish and counterproductive to confine feminist approaches to women's history alone. Yet I focus here on feminist history within the field to which it has given birth and shape: the history of women.

Nancy Hewitt has recently introduced me to the initials WGH, a handy stand-in for "women's and gender history." I have been tempted to use these initials throughout this book, for in writing about women's history I mean to include gender history. The relation between women's history and gender history is long, complex, and fraught, but the two share much more than the small distinctions that divide them. Before feminism, "gender" was a humble grammatical term that signified nothing more than an inflection—masculine, feminine, or neuter—given certain nouns and pronouns in some languages. "Sex" meant the categories of male and female, but it also, rather awkwardly, denoted sexual activity. Because gender provided a more polite (that is, less tinged by sexuality) signifier of differences between women and men, feminists began in the 1970s to replace "sex" with "gender"—so that the "sexual division of labor" became the "gender division of labor" and "sexual differences" became "gender differences." As a lawyer writing briefs for the U.S. Supreme Court, Ruth Bader Ginsburg began to use "gender" when a secretary advised her, "I'm typing all these briefs and articles for you and the word sex, sex, sex, is on every page. Don't you know those nine men [on the Supreme Court], they hear that word and their first association is not the word you want them to be thinking? Why don't you use the word 'gender'? It is a grammatical term and it will ward off distracting associations."[41] In much the same way and at about the same time, "gender" also began to signal a more professionally acceptable approach to history. I took advantage of this myself, defending a dissertation in women's history in 1981 but using "gender" in its title because it seemed likely to be more palatable to my examiners.[42]

By that time, "sex" and "gender" had also begun to develop entirely different connotations among feminists, especially feminists in the academy: "sex" indicating biological differences between women and men, and "gender" indicating the ways in which societies elaborate on those biological differences. Hence, a baby girl was understood to be of the female *sex*, but her pink attire indicated her female *gender*. This definition of gender as "a social category imposed on a sexed body" has both defined contemporary feminism and troubled it.[43] Antifeminists hate the distinction; see, for example, a papal letter of 2004 which emphatically reaffirmed the preeminent importance of biological distinctions between women and men, asserting that a focus on the social construction of such differences undermines families, heterosexuality, the authority of the Bible, and Catholic faith.[44] But some feminists now question the distinction, too, arguing that it gives too much weight to biological absolutes by implying that human bodies always provide two sexes clearly distinguished by genitalia, chromosomes, or other somatic markers. They can point to cases of indeterminate "sex" at birth when physicians and parents make social decisions about the sex/gender of an infant—social decisions that are then surgically imposed on the infant's body. They can also point to the indeterminacy of "sex" in the history of the West, especially as seen in Thomas Laqueur's exploration of how an ancient understanding of a one-sex human body (women and men sharing a single type of body) has been replaced by a modern view of human bodies differentiated into two sexes.[45] Thus, even "sex" itself is "gender"; *all* distinctions between female and male are created; and feminist usage has begun to circle back to the early days of the 1970s when one term signified much the same as the other, *except* that now both terms signify socially constructed differences of female and male.[46]

What a muddle! One solution might be to revert to "sex" alone. "Gender" has proven difficult to translate into many languages; until the 1980s, feminists managed to differentiate between biological and social constructions without the aid of "gender"; and the term has never firmly taken hold except in the English-speaking world.[47] But because sex/gender clearly differentiates aspects *thought to be* biological from those *thought to be* social, it still has practical use.[48] Even more important, feminist historians simply cannot do without "gender," because the term has taken on a life of its own within our field. When the journal *Gender and History* was launched in 1989, its editors stressed the new journal's feminist stance, its firm commitment to "the recovery of women's past experiences," and its interest in "addressing men and masculinity as well as women and femininity."[49] This expansion of the field of vision to include men, masculinity, and relations between women and men was not entirely new (very few women's historians had ever studied women in isolation from men), but it was newly emphasized. The editors also spoke about gender as a "symbolic system," an insight that drew on the theoretical inspiration of Joan Scott. In an immensely influential article published in the mid-1980s, Scott argued that feminists should move from looking at the *causes* of the social construction of gender to the *meanings* of gender, particularly gender's use as a metaphor in human relations and activities. Arguing that gender is a "primary way of signifying relationships of power," Scott sought to bring women (or really, gender) into traditionally male areas of history. Because, for example, women rarely wielded political power in Western societies, political history had remained largely untouched by the history of women; but, Scott argued, gender was present in the rationales, languages, and discussions of politics, even if women themselves were not. To Scott's mind, this discourse-based approach promised to transform history, for it subjected *all* historical subjects—not just women—to gender analysis.[50] Scott was also influential, a few years later, in Denise Riley's epistemological assault on the coherence of the term "woman," and a few years after that, Scott herself argued that "experience" has no material foundation and is instead constructed through language.[51]

Scott's advocacy of gender history represented the fulfillment in feminist history of the literary turn in the late twentieth century. Her vision of feminist history argued that we no longer needed to examine just women's lives or even just the social construction of female and male; we could look everywhere—even at such traditionally prestigious and "male" historical subjects as politics, intellectual discourse, and economics—for gender used as a "primary way of signifying relationships of power." In the 1940s, Jack Hexter had excused the absence of women from history by asserting that women were simply not in the places that mattered, that "through no conspiracy of historians, the College of Cardinals, the Consistory of Geneva, the Parliament of England, and the expeditions of Columbus, Vasco de Gama, and Drake have been pretty much stag affairs."[52] Scott's formulation offered us a much-needed response; even if women were not present on these occasions, gender was.[53]

The turn to gender history has terrifically enhanced the field of women's history, particularly by encouraging us to explore the construction and contestation behind many seemingly "natural" ideas about women and men. Thanks to our focus on the play of gender, women's history now boasts entirely new areas of inquiry: the study of gender as performance; the examination of the many genders that fracture the bi-gender paradigm of female and male; the tracing of gender's power in discourse generally; the history of masculinities. And gender history's greater focus on *meanings* has also yielded rich harvests. Nan Enstad's study of working-class women's popular culture in the early twentieth-century United States, for example, has shown how both contemporaries then and historians since have mistaken "women with pretty hats for women with empty heads." Enstad's work has restored political meaning to seemingly frivolous consumer behaviors, a lesson as useful in negotiating the world today as it is for understanding past worlds.[54]

Today, the relation of "gender history" to "women's history" is exceedingly varied. In Britain, "gender history" can still retain, for a scholar like Bernard Capp, a pleasant whiff of political disengagement from feminism. In Japan, "gender history" has quite the opposite resonance, signifying a more explicitly feminist approach to traditional historiography.[55] In the United States, "gender history" is strongly associated with Scott's cultural turn and is even seen by some as entirely superceding an old-fashioned and out-of-date "women's history."[56] Yet in terms of global connections, women's history still rules the day; of the thirty-two national committees associated with the International Federation for Research in Women's History, only one (Swedish Women and Gender Historians) uses "gender" in its self-description.[57] To my mind, the best relation between the two emphasizes what they share more than what might differentiate them. Yes, some women's history is distinct from gender history, and yes, some gender history is not women's history, but the overlap is very, very strong; although many of us might choose to differentiate ourselves as "historians of women" or "gender historians," I think most of us are reasonably comfortable with the identity of "women's and gender historians." I *like* the shorthand WGH, but it would prove an inelegant style to use throughout this book, as would the wordier "women's and gender history." So I ask you to understand "women's history" in this book as broadly including gender history. "Women's history" works best for thinking about feminist history across national divides; it has a stronger feminist connotation, at least in the English context from which it arose; and it has the advantage of priority, of being a sort of mother—not a single mother, but a co-parenting mother—of gender history, the history of masculinities, and the history of sexualities.

The Politics of Women's History Today

In the 1970s, feminist historians in the United States and elsewhere built the academic practice of women's history while working within a largely male profession, most of whose members were either nonfeminists or antifeminists. In this hostile environment, feminists demanded not just that the profession accommodate more women more fully but also that women's history be integrated into mainstream history.[58] Just as few historians then welcomed a feminist politics that challenged the fundamental presumptions of their private lives, so few welcomed an approach to history that criticized their profession and sought to transform it. Yet this little-welcomed women's history has won the day. We might argue about whether or not women's history has fully "arrived," but it is undeniably established as a permanent part of the historical profession in the United States and some other parts of the world. How has this happened? How has a feminist project won such a large place in nonfeminist academia? At least part of the answer is that the feminism of women's history has been diluted and muted. Academic success has walked hand-in-hand with political co-optation.

This dilution is partly a natural consequence of a new movement growing older and, indeed, maturing. Feminist history has changed from its early days when issues were starkly clear, agendas were straightforward, and most everyone was "on message" into a field that is more subtle, but also more fractured, complex, and co-opted.[59] Fair enough. Also fair enough is the relocation of our feminist energies from communities to universities. Many feminist historians share the often unanticipated, sometimes distressing, and nevertheless ineluctable experience of watching personal energies seep away from community-based activism and pour into university-centered labors. Feminist successes are themselves partly to blame. As more students have studied feminist topics, as more universities have sought to improve the status of women, and as more women have entered the professoriate, those feminists lucky enough to possess secure appointments are mentoring more students, serving on more committees, writing more tenure letters, and running more interference on more complaints of harassment and "chilly climate."[60] The rightward turn of the United States has also required that feminists there respond publicly to well-funded attacks on affirmative action, feminist studies, academic freedom, and even publicly funded education per se.[61] Let no one doubt that there is good feminist work—good, old-fashioned feminist activism—being done in the halls of academe.

Good feminist work is being done in women's history, too, but the force of feminism in the field seems to be slowly waning, perhaps particularly in the context I know best—that is, among women's historians who work in the United States, albeit not necessarily in U.S. history. As women's history has gained institutional sanction in the United States, some of us have succumbed to pressures to produce studies that are palatable to our nonfeminist colleagues—studies that avoid hard feminist questions and that appear more mainstream. And as feminism itself has matured, changed, and survived media assault, some of us have turned away from explicit feminism. I am not alone in sensing this shift away from feminism, but it is a harsh charge to make against fellow historians of women and a charge that is difficult to prove without ad hominem examples. One less personal symptom of the trend is the *language* of women's history, as it has been and now is practiced. When women's history was a nascent and marginalized activity, its founding mothers wrote freely and often about patriarchy and women's oppression. In 1975 Gerda Lerner wrote straightforwardly:

For most of historical time, woman is oppressed not through her reproductive sexuality—that is, through the need of society to assign most of a woman's adult lifespan to tasks of child-bearing and child-rearing—but through the devaluing of such activities by men as they institute organized society. Women are oppressed also through sexual exploitation, as manifested in the rape of women of the conquered group by the victors, the rape of women of subordinate classes by the masters, in the millennia of organized prostitution, and in the constant pressure on single women to make marriage and family service their main career. Women as a group are oppressed through the denial to them of access to educational opportunities on an equality with men and, finally, through the denial to them—for longer than to any other group—of political representation and power in government.[62]

By the 1980s we were already speaking less forthrightly than this, replacing "oppression of women" and its implication of male agency with the more neutral "subordination of women." This shift was subtle and even unconscious, much like the turn in the 1970s from "sex" to "gender," but Lerner herself characteristically examined her own changing lexicon. In 1986, she reported that she preferred "subordination of women" to "oppression of women" because the latter term, in her view, problematically implies male agency, an absence of female complicity, and "the consciousness of the subject group that they have been wronged." I'm not convinced by her arguments, but neither my preference for "oppression" nor hers for "subordination" carries much weight today. [63]

Instead, both have almost disappeared in favor of still milder terms, ones that do not even specify which sex (or gender) is disadvantaged: terms like "gender hierarchy," "gender inequality," and "gender imbalance." These are the sorts of phrases that predominate, for example, in articles published from 2001 through 2004 in the three major English-language women's history periodicals—*Journal of Women's History, Gender and History,* and *Women's History Review.* When I surveyed these articles, I began by looking for the keyword "patriarchy" and its derivatives.[64] In the 1970s and 1980s, historians of women readily talked about "patriarchy"; today, it is barely whispered. Of the nearly three hundred articles in my survey, not one title directs readers' attention toward "patriarchy," "patriarchal," or any other variant forms. Not one. Seventeen abstracts use such terms, but usually for description, not analysis—that is, the authors note, in passing, that patriarchal values prevailed in Wales, or rural areas, or the antebellum U.S. South. In several of these cases, "patriarchy" refers only to its restricted meaning of fatherly authority over wives, children, and other domestic dependents. Only two abstracts promise direct, analytical engagement with patriarchy: Joanne Wright's investigation of Hobbes's attack on the "theory of patriarchalism" and Laura Gowing's argument that "competitive relations between women [were] functional to patriarchal order."[65] What about the possibility that the authors in my survey pay attention to patriarchy but just do not use the word? I found that only one in four abstracts alludes (in even the slightest ways) to the truncated opportunities for women that are at the root of feminist politics. Of this minority, most simply take this inequality as a given; few treat it as a matter worthy of investigation; and almost all characterize "patriarchy/women's oppression/women's subordination" in much more genial and inoffensive terms. Some use phrases that obfuscate who is advantaged over whom (for example, "gender order" and "gender hierarchy"), and others use terms that so emphasize difference as to eclipse inequality (for example, "gender differences" and "fault lines of gender"). We once often talked frankly about patriarchy and women's oppression; we now tend to talk smoothly about gender hierarchies and gender differences.

As our language has shifted, so, too, has our thinking. Some of our best historians of women continue to publish hard-hitting feminist analyses. No one could reasonably complain, for example, that Amy Richlin's articles fail to bring feminist concerns to bear on Roman sources, or that Ruth Karras's study of medieval masculinity is inattentive to the feminist implications of the subject, or that Julie Hardwick's examination of notaries ignores the everyday work of patriarchy among the families of early modern Nantes, or that Dorothy Sue Cobble's book on "labor feminism" does not rewrite how we can think about recent U.S. feminism.[66] I have chosen these few examples from among many possibilities, for many women's historians certainly continue to publish self-conscious, politically engaged feminist work. But as others before me have noted, women's history seems to be losing its feminist edge: deferring unnecessarily to male authority, dwelling overmuch on biographies of unusual women, taking a sharp cultural turn away from social and material considerations, attending more to diversity than to the power differentials, and allying with a history of masculinity that is developing in surprisingly problematic ways. I do not wish to repeat here what others have already said or to dwell on these difficulties, but it seems useful briefly to review each concern.

Since the 1990s, Catherine Hall, Kathleen Canning, Judith Newton, and others have commented on a tendency in some women's history to defer to male authorities and overlook the earlier intellectual work of feminist scholars.[67] As Hall put it in a review of books by Riley and Scott, "some of the insights attributed to post-structuralist theorists have been thought in other ways by feminists. We did not need post-structuralism to develop gender as a category of analysis—rather it emerged out of years of work both with texts and in consciousness raising groups."[68] Postmodernists have been singled out for criticism; but I think this practice extends as well to many sorts of theoretically inflected women's history. Within certain academic contexts, this citational strategy makes good sense: it reflects the male-ness of traditional philosophy, psychoanalytic theory, and historical epistemology; it emulates a standard rhetorical strategy of building arguments on the authoritative statements of "great men"; it builds from high theory drawn on philosophical premises (for example, Jacques Derrida on difference) rather than middle-range theory drawn more on empirical insight (for example, bell hooks, Alice Walker, Valerie Amos, and Pratibha Parmar); and it might even encourage more faculty to read such articles, assign them in classes, and cite them.[69] But these practices of reference are nevertheless problematic: they obscure the accomplishments of female scholars; they defer to men whose works either ignored women (for example, Michel Foucault) or problematically considered women (for example, Jacques Lacan); and they reinforce the age-old assumption that abstract intellectual work is the work of men. No one is objecting to the just recognition of men's important contributions to feminist history. Medieval women's history, for example, owes a great debt to the advocacy of David Herlihy in the 1960s and to the insights since of such historians as Stanley Chojnacki and Jeremy Goldberg; their work is quite rightly cited by feminist medievalists all the time.[70] But let us beware of the *needless* evocation of male authority and consequent suppression of female authority. Women's history should enhance, not diminish, the intellectual reach of feminist scholarship.[71]

Our recent swing toward biography also raises new challenges. In the 1970s, feminist historians, armed with the then-dominant methods of social history, eschewed the study of great women and sought to understand, as best we could, the daily constraints and choices of ordinary women in past times. Inspired by Natalie Zémon Davis, who urged us in 1976 to move "from Women Worthies to a worthier craft," we worked with intransigent documents—tax lists, court records, censuses, business accounts, and the like—to reconstruct the ordinary lives of peasant women in medieval Europe, working women in early modern towns, and women of the nineteenth-century working classes. [72] By the 1980s, some of us, discouraged by the tedious and table-ridden tendencies of social history, were turning to the new genres of collective biography and microhistory, and Davis's own *Return of Martin Guerre*, published in 1983, was one critical inspiration.[73] Since then, we have moved confidently back to the possibilities of biographical approaches; again, Davis herself exemplifies the trend, by offering *Women on the Margins* in 1995, a study of three seventeenth-century women—a merchant, a nun, and a naturalist.[74] Now, in U.S. women's history, as Gerda Lerner has recently counted, about one-fourth of all books, articles, and dissertations are adopting a biographical approach.[75] Biography is no longer a genre confined to elite lives alone—as Laurel Ulrich Thatcher's *The Midwife's Tale* illustrates—but it is especially suited to privileged, articulate people who left archives deemed worthy of preservation.[76] Are we in danger of tilting women's history too far back toward women worthies?

A similar challenge is posed by the cultural turn in women's history, especially by our efforts to unpack the complex meanings of gender.[77] Many of us are now focusing more on representations of past lives than on lived experiences, more on the performative creation of gender rules than on the effects of male power, and more (in this context, too) on well-documented outstanding individuals than ordinary people. Both published studies and dissertations now regularly detail for us, on the one hand, how newspapers, advertisements, plays, films, music, poems, and other media have constructed, represented, and manipulated gender, and, on the other hand, how various individuals and groups have understood, changed, and transgressed gender rules. These studies have shifted women's history away from concrete, accessible histories and toward analyses that can be abstract in both subject matter and exposition. The hard lives of women in the past; the material forces that shaped and constrained women's activities; the ways that women coped with challenges and obstacles—all these things sometimes disappear from our histories of the contradictory and contested meanings of gender. And as with biography, our reliance on cultural texts necessarily refocuses our interests either on those privileged few who have left articulate remains or on a recent past accessible through oral histories or modern media. Many feminist histories inspired by the cultural turn combine scholarly excellence and political engagement. Gail Bederman's study of manliness and civilization, for example, forces us to think in new ways about the close partnership of racism and sexism.[78] But in sheer quantity, they could be swamping women's history.[79] When Joan Scott issued her clarion call for gender analysis, she located the "radical potential of women's history" as lying in the complementary study of *both* gender constructions *and* women's experiences.[80] This is certainly the best way forward.

I also share the concerns of Linda Gordon and Lise Vogel that current feminist approaches sometimes promote "an uncritical discourse of pluralism, a celebration of diversity."[81] There is absolutely no doubt that attention to differences among women is promoting better, more subtle, and richer women's history.[82] By unpacking the differences elided by the umbrella term "women," we are seeing old subjects in new ways; Jane Mangan's examination of indigenous, African, and Spanish women in the markets of colonial Potosí is one recent example.[83] We are also adding such factors as sexuality, religion, marital status, and world region to the original trinity of "race, class, and gender"; thus, for example, never-married women have come into the foreground thanks to Elizabeth Heineman's study of twentieth-century Germany and Amy Froide's work on early modern England.[84] And we are edging our way toward again recognizing the ties that bind women, despite differences; Nancy Hewitt's recent *Southern Discomfort*, a study of the shifting, self-conscious, and strategic identities of Latin, Anglo, and Black women in Tampa a hundred years ago is one outstanding example.[85] But difference-talk still sometimes functions as an end in itself, a celebration of diversity that urges us more to respect difference than to resist the inequalities that can arise from it. And while we must certainly continue to examine differences among women and the ways in which some women have oppressed other women, we also must not stop examining the ways in which men-as-a-group have oppressed women-as-a-group. As with the cultural turn, a *both/and* approach works best here; as exemplified by Deborah Gray White's study of the class, racial, and gender dynamics of black women's associations in the twentieth-century United States, feminist history works best when it juggles *both* differences among women *and* differences between women and men.[86]

Last, the history of masculinity has, thus far, proven a mixed blessing. It has the potential to be one of the most radical offshoots of feminist history, applying to past times the feminist premise that maleness and masculinity are changeable, contested, and, quite simply, constructed. Men, too, have a gender, and the history of masculinity, a virtually unexplored terrain before 1990, has since developed into an innovative field in which feminists—both female and male—cast inquiring gazes on male identities, male anxieties, and the ideological bases of male power. Yet, as Toby Ditz has recently traced with humor and care, this new men's history is too often "occluding women and downplaying men's power over women." Men's history tells us that masculinities have been complex, fraught, diverse, and ever-fragile, but in its inattention to men's gendered power over women, it often "risks replicating the oppressive omissions of conventional history." Interestingly enough, Ditz's solution—that men's history should be pursued within a foundational understanding that "the gender order pivots on men's access to women"—seeks to redeem the postmodernism at the heart of gender history with a hefty dose of anthropological structuralism.[87] I hope we will see more such histories in the future.

Some of these worrisome trends in women's history reflect the growing pains of a field that is more crowded, more diverse, and more engaged in more historical endeavors than it once was.[88] The burgeoning market for materials on women is partly met by popular products that uncritically celebrate women's past; in my own field, for example, lavish wall calendars picturing medieval women appear annually, and books like *Uppity Women of Medieval Times* have sold so well that we can now also buy *Outrageous Women of the Middle Ages*, as well as new volumes for uppity and outrageous women in other places and times. On a much more academic level, enthusiasm for women's history is met in part by important projects of recovery—that is, again using medieval women as my example, published texts of saints' lives, editions of women's writings, descriptive biographies of female saints, queens, and heroines, and densely empirical histories of individual nunneries or religious orders. These books offer exceedingly useful information about medieval women, but their purpose is to recover that information, not to tackle difficult questions about the sexual dynamics of power within medieval society. And women's history has so diversified that a lot of relevant work is not in "women's history" per se. Kate Haulman has recently found, for example, that although few dissertations in U.S. history are focusing specifically on "women's history," almost two-thirds include some consideration of men, women, and gender.[89] I think we can fairly expect to find more feminist influence in the former than in the latter.

Our efforts on behalf of another undoubted feminist objective—

that is, integrating women, gender, and sexuality into traditionai torical fields—have also diverted us a bit from foundational femin questions. The challenges of "mainstreaming" women's history have been historiographic as well as historical—that is, focused on influencing debates in history as well as the content of history. In the 1970s Joan Kelly urged us to write women's history with an eye to transforming the foundational practices—description, periodization, and explanation—of history.[90] And in the 1980s, Louise Tilly reminded us that we need to be able to answer colleagues when they ask such questions as, "Now that I know that women were participants in the French Revolution, what difference does it make?"[91] Textbooks have been the focus of much feminist mainstreaming, and I will later (Chapter 7) describe what my own ventures in this regard suggest about the challenges and compromises of improving the surveys that introduce so many students to history. Feminist mainstreaming happens through research, too. For example, Caroline Bynum's examination in *Holy Feast and Holy Fast* of the spiritual practices of female saints, especially as they pertained to food, fasting, and eating, is firmly situated within the traditions of women's history.[92] Moreover, like Joan Brumberg's *Fasting Girls*, it offers a historical perspective on the eating disorders among young women that so trouble the contemporary West.[93] But Bynum's book is more than this, for written with authority, based on deep research, and argued with verve, it has also re-visioned and re-invigorated a traditional field. No one can now fairly ask, "Now that I know that female mystics often undertook pious fasting, what difference does it make in the history of medieval religion?" Among other things, it makes the difference that we now see "the body" as not opposed to "the soul" in medieval religious practice but instead profoundly intertwined with it; in Bynum's words, medieval ascetics "were not rebelling against or torturing their flesh out of guilt over its capabilities so much as using the possibilities of its full sensual and affective range to soar ever closer to God."[94] Packed with such insights, *Holy Feast and Holy Fast* is now required reading for any student of medieval religion. An array of other women's history books are now equally essential in their allied fields. For just one more example, I doubt that anyone can now study the expansion of railroads in the nineteenth-century United States without taking into account Amy Richter's *Home on the Rails* and Barbara Young Welke's *Recasting American Liberty*, which both place gender front and center in their stories of how this technology changed a nation.[95]

Not surprisingly, women's history in this mainstreaming mode rarely focuses on the oppression of women. I do not mean to imply

r, Welke, and others naively assume that the women
oppressed, for they most certainly recognize this
y take women's oppression as a given, they nei-
mics of male power nor critique it, and their
s thereby almost disguise it. Mainstreaming works
mind, as a *supplementary* tactic for feminist history, not as
ain strategy. Yes, we should contribute, as Tilly put it, "to general
questions already on the historical agenda," but we should not do so
at the expense of marginalizing issues integral to women's history.[96]
After all, most historical fields are male-centered and male-defined; if
we uncritically accept their questions as our questions, we ignore
Mary Beard's wise caution against taking man as the measure of historical significance.[97] And in any case, a well-nurtured feminist historiography is a critical element in building a women's history that can
meet other historical fields on level ground. What most sustains wom-
en's history, in short, is a historiography of its own.

Fortunately, we have such a historiography, and it now shapes our
field around two issues in particular. Since the 1980s Joan Scott's
advocacy of the study of gender as a "primary way of signifying relationships of power" has galvanized many historians of women, and
so, too, has the study of difference in women's history deepened our
field, especially complicating our understandings of relationships
among women. But we need a third pole supporting the broad tent
of feminist historiography, for it is appropriate that feminist history
should work also to historicize the thorny problem of women's
oppression. The study of patriarchy is surely a native ground of feminist history, a subject to be analyzed and unpacked, not ignored or
taken as an obvious fact. I do not propose that historians of women
stop liaising with other fields of history, or cut short their searches for
the many meanings of gender, or quit studying the historical intersec-
tions of race, class, gender, and other related factors. But these
inquiries are best accompanied, as I will argue more fully in Chapter
4, by a return to the feminist heartland of critiquing and opposing
the oppression of women. *Why and how has the oppression of women
endured for so long and in so many different historical settings?* I hope we
will more fully incorporate this question into the historiography of
women's history as it develops in the twenty-first century.

As Bonnie Smith has shown so devastatingly well, the profession of
history is inherently hostile to feminist approaches. When history took
root in nineteenth-century universities, it was built on a dismissal of
so-called amateur history associated particularly with women writers,
and it celebrated both masculine conquest in the archives and manly

dispassion in historical writing. The practices of history have changed a great deal since Leopold von Ranke described unread documents as "so many princesses, possibly beautiful, all under a curse and needing to be saved." But, as Smith notes, our discipline even today retains a masculinist ethic in which "talk about the oppression of women by men" inevitably sounds "minor, amateurish, overemotional, and uncritical."[98] When historians of women began to challenge the history establishment in the 1970s, especially in the United States and Great Britain, the clarity of our outsider status helped us negotiate this silencing of feminist talk. It was scarcely a surprise, then, if the gatekeepers of academic history ridiculed, dismissed, and ignored our voices. But as we have established a place within the sanctums of history, we have muted our feminist voices. In a discipline in which any talk about patriarchy sounds "minor, amateurish, overemotional, and uncritical," we are often choosing to talk about other things.

Our discussions of these other things have contributed to the feminist project in substantive and valuable ways. The feminist project in women's history is enriched by archive hounds who sniff out hitherto ignored information about the lives of women in the past; it is extended by mainstreamers who bring women and feminist analyses into the discourses of other historical fields; it is deepened by gender historians who analyze the powerful play of genders in the past; and it is strengthened by those who trace how the category "women" has been both fractured and constructed by difference. Thus, in an ironic twist, even our avoidance of talk that might strike colleagues as "minor, amateurish, overemotional, and uncritical" has had positive feminist effect, for it has helped us establish an institutional place for women's history within a hostile discipline. In making our voices heard within the broader conversation of history, women's history has calmed down, behaved, *and* been rewarded.

I would like to hear more feminist talk in women's history, to hear our voices more raised, more angry, and more often speaking about how the past can inform the politics of feminism. But if women's history speaks in these ways, will other feminists hear it? Women's history has largely lost its feminist audiences, partly because of changes in feminist movements, partly because of the publishing malaise of academic history generally (the production of piles of print that only a few dozen people read), and partly because too many feminists in other academic disciplines have no time for history. Feminist activists and scholars, once so steeped in history, have lost interest in the past. It is to the implications of this eroded historical vision within feminism that I now turn.

Chapter 3

Who's Afraid of the Distant Past?

In 1979, Judy Chicago premiered *The Dinner Party,* an exhibition of a grand banqueting hall that celebrated women of the past. Visitors to the first showing in San Francisco walked on a floor of porcelain tiles inscribed with the names of 999 great women from history; in the center of the floor, they found a triangular table with place settings for 39 diners; and at each place-setting, they could examine a celebration in ceramic and cloth of a woman from the past; starting with Primordial Goddess, these place settings took visitors, in a steadily ascending incline, through Hypatia, Eleanor of Aquitaine, and Sojourner Truth to Virginia Woolf and Georgia O'Keeffe. As Christine de Pizan had done in *The Book of the City of Ladies,* Chicago's exhibition celebrated great women of the past, this time in porcelain, cloth, ceramic, and paint. And like Christine de Pizan, Judy Chicago's historical vision was a long one; the 13 settings on the first side of the table moved visitors from prehistory through the classical era; the second side began with Marcella, an influential early Christian who died c. 410, and ended with the learned Anna van Schurman (d. 1678); and the last 13 settings covered the three most recent centuries, ending with the then still-living O'Keeffe. The project, which began in 1974 and involved more than two hundred artists, subsequently toured on three continents. It was, for its time, a hugely influential and well-publicized feminist cultural event that sought, in Judy Chicago's words, to "tell women's history through women's crafts."[1]

Today, women's history reaches many more people in the United States than ever before, particularly through the well-organized efforts of the National Women's History Project (NWHP), which promotes attention to women's history, especially in secondary schools and especially during March, officially designated by the U.S. Congress as Women's History Month. Each year, the NWHP produces a poster that, like the works of Christine de Pizan and Judy Chicago, offers up specific women worthies for admiration. The women celebrated in recent renditions of these NWHP posters are a remarkably contemporary bunch. Of the 11 women featured in 2003, the most "historical" died in 1964 (Rachel Carson) and most of the rest were still living. In 2004, 8 women, all living, were singled out for attention. And in 2005, the occasion of its twenty-fifth anniversary, the NWHP produced a poster detailing 143 former honorees, of whom 126 had lived in the twentieth century and 46 were still alive. Only 17 had died before 1900, and not a single honoree had died before 1800. Even by the standards of the relatively truncated history of the United States, the women's history of these posters is remarkably foreshortened.

The contrast between the deep historical vision of *The Dinner Table* and the shallow vision of the NWHP posters is the subject of this chapter. It is a contrast that reflects my own lived experience, watching women's history swing toward the present during the last thirty years. But the contrast can also be demonstrated by hard facts and figures. In the 1970s, when I was a young feminist, the distant past was integral to the ways in which we critiqued the present day and envisioned a better future. When I walked into the Toronto Women's Bookstore, conveniently located midway between the university where I studied and the feminist cooperative where I lived, I found on its shelves a feminist scholarship in which long-past eras—the Middle Ages, the ancient Mediterranean, even prehistoric hunting and gathering societies—were critical parts of the enterprise. Think, for example, of *Witches, Midwives, and Nurses*, published in 1973, a history of women healers by Barbara Ehrenreich and Deidre English that began in fourteenth-century Europe, segued easily to the American medical profession, and concluded with seven points for feminist revision of the contemporary health system. Or think of Joan Kelly's electrifying 1977 essay that posed the question "Was there a Renaissance for women?" that has been subsequently repeated for many other eras of history.[2] When I began to read the new journals for feminist scholarship that first appeared in the University of Toronto library in the 1970s, I found there, too, that the distant past was downright central. In the first four years of *Signs: A Journal of Women in Culture and Society* (1975 through 1978), I read four articles on premodern topics (that is, anything before 1500 CE), four articles on the early modern era (that is, 1500–1800), and seven articles that stretched across multiple eras. The nineteenth and twentieth centuries were not neglected— they merited twenty-three articles—but modern history was well balanced by early modern, premodern, and transhistorical perspectives.[3] I also took pleasure in the "Archives" section of *Signs*, a treasure trove of primary sources that stretched as far back, in those first years, as Hippocrates. And when I started going to the Berkshire Conferences

TABLE 1. CHRONOLOGICAL COVERAGE IN WOMEN'S HISTORY JOURNALS, 2001–2004

Topics by era	Gender and History	Journal of Women's History	Women's History Review	Totals	Percentage
Modern (c. 1800–present)	74	81	96	251	87
Early modern (c. 1500–1800)	14	8	8	30	11
Premodern (before 1500)	4	2	1	7	2
Total	92	91	105	288	100

Note: This count focused on research articles; reports on archives, forums, memorials, and other such miscellanea were excluded. Also excluded were seven articles whose chronological sweep defied categorization. If an article evenly spanned two eras, I placed it in the earlier one.

on the History of Women, I found that they too had more papers than I could possibly hear about ancient and medieval women.[4]

No more. Today, *Signs* is a fatter journal than in the 1970s but one with many fewer pages for history and virtually none for history before the modern era. In 2004, not a single historical article was included in the four issues of *Signs*; in 2003, three historical articles made the cut, two on suffrage and one on Quakers in the eighteenth century; and in 2001 and 2002, six historical articles were published, *all* on the twentieth century. The "Archives" section itself is long gone; after sporadic appearances in the 1990s, it disappeared after 1998. The Berkshire Conferences have gotten bigger, too, but the proportional space they offer to papers on the distant past has fallen dramatically in the last two decades. Moreover, although since 1989 we have had English-language journals devoted entirely to research on women's *history* (as opposed to the women's *studies* journals that began in the 1970s), these women's history journals publish shockingly little history of a past more distant than two hundred years. As Table 1 shows, in the first four years of the twenty-first century, the three major English-language journals in women's history—*Gender and History, Journal of Women's History*, and *Women's History Review*—have published 295 articles of which 7—yes, 7—deal with women's history before 1500. The situation is actually even more acute than these data show, for the modern history represented in the first row is mostly *contemporary* history: the twentieth century alone accounts for well over half of all articles.

This march toward the present in women's history has not been created by a lack of research or teaching about the world before 1500—indeed, quite the contrary. In the early 1970s, there were just a dozen or so scholars in North America publishing on premodern women; today, there are hundreds of professional historians in the United States and Canada who work on women in premodern times and places—especially the ancient Mediterranean and the medieval West, but also premodern China, Japan, and India, the early Americas, and Africa before European contact. For example, the Society for Medieval Feminist Scholarship today boasts more than a thousand members worldwide, produces a twice-yearly journal (*Medieval Feminist Forum*), and nurtures a variety of online bibliographic resources, including the spectacular Feminae: Medieval Women and Gender Index (http://www.haverford.edu/library/reference/mschaus/mfi/mfi.html). The study of women in early eras of human history is flourishing, but not within women's history generally, where it is now outside the mainstream of what matters. In the 1970s, there was not a great deal of premodern women's history being written, but that little bit was very much part of the broad and inclusive new field of women's history. Today, premodern women's history is a flourishing field, but little known to modernists. In many venues, "women's history" has effectively come to mean "nineteenth- and twentieth-century women's history."[5]

In this chapter, I explore how we have reached this troubling circumstance and why we need to move beyond it. As a medievalist, I would of course be delighted if more feminists read more medieval history, but my point is not merely ego driven. I believe that modern history is impoverished by inattention to the premodern past and that feminism is impoverished by an inattention to history. By broadening our temporal horizons, we can produce both better feminist history and better feminist theory.

Don't Know Much about History

I was introduced to history by teachers who believed that their work ended at the point when living memory begins. But since World War II, many historians have felt differently, and now the twentieth century—most of it well within living memory—has become *the* major field of historical research, both in women's history specifically and in history more generally. The historians' past, for better or for worse, is now as recent as yesterday. This shift toward the present has not yet occasioned much self-reflection among historians, and its causes are doubtless more complex that I can cover here. But in the interest of opening a discussion among feminist historians, I will offer some figures and suggest some causes.

"Old Europe." In a quintessentially U.S. statement, Donald Rumsfeld thus characterized France and Germany in the midst of the international debate in 2003 that preceded the Bush administration's aggression against Iraq. To Rumsfeld and many others in the United States, "old" is inherently bad and "new" is inherently good. In part, the presentism of U.S. culture stems from the simple fact that most U.S. history is, after all, modern history. In part, however, it also grows from a resentful sense that most history before 1776 harkens back to a tradition-bound, elitist, European past, a past that has been properly replaced by the dynamism of U.S. democracy and multiculturalism. In this worldview, any history before 1800 seems largely irrelevant, as epitomized in Henry Ford's famous statement, "History is more or less bunk . . . the only history that is worth a tinker's damn is the history we make today."[6]

This presentist view might be quintessentially U.S., but it is not uniquely so. In the same year that Rumsfeld coined "Old Europe," Charles Clarke, then British education secretary, reportedly opined, "I don't mind there being some medievalists around for ornamental purposes, but there is no reason for the state to pay for them."[7] Yet Clarke's comment circulated in a different cultural milieu from that of Rumsfeld. Few in the United States were bothered by the "old" of Old Europe, whereas Clarke's slur generated a furor in the British press, prompting a not quite believable denial and eventually a strong statement of support for medieval studies. British and other national cultures might be edging toward presentism, but the move is especially strong in the United States. Since it is within the United States that feminist scholarship has particularly flourished in the past thirty years, I therefore posit as the first likely culprit in the tilt toward the present of women's history the ahistoricism of my own national culture.

A second suspect is rather more surprising: the historical profession itself, not just within the United States but also internationally. For members of a profession devoted to the study of the past, historians are now remarkably uninterested in most of it. When historians worldwide congregate every five years at the meeting of the Comité International des Sciences Historiques/International Committee of Historical Sciences (CISH), we mostly discuss the nineteenth and twentieth centuries. We do the same in the United States at the annual meetings of the American Historical Association (AHA). As

TABLE 2. CHRONOLOGICAL COVERAGE AT RECENT HISTORY CONFERENCES[8]

Topics by era	CISH Conference (2005)	AHA Conference (2005)
Modern (c. 1800 +)	75% (216)	75 % (445)
Early modern (c. 1500–1800)	10% (31)	18.5% (109)
Premodern (before 1500)	13% (40)	6.5% (38)
Total	287	592

Note: The CISH data are taken from the online program (http://www.cishsydney2005 .org/) as posted in February 2005; I counted papers in the three categories of round tables, major themes, and specialized themes. The AHA data, taken from the printed program, include sessions of affiliated societies but exclude nonresearch sessions devoted to such matters as pedagogy and professional development. I counted only papers whose titles (or session context) indicated their chronological coverage, and if a paper equally spanned two eras, I placed it in the earlier one.

Table 2 shows, when we gather in these venues to talk about history, we mostly talk about the history of the past two hundred years.[9]

History's own lack of historical depth is relatively new. As Lynn Hunt has noted, "history" in the United States and Europe little more than a century ago was mainly *ancient* history.[10] It is only in the last few decades that twentieth-century history, once "consigned to the province of journalism," has entered the historical mainstream and taken it by storm. In Hunt's view, the new hegemony of what she calls "short-term history" is especially linked to identity politics. Perhaps so, although I suspect that the information explosion (and hence, the explosion in primary sources), the decline of secondary training in classical languages, and the challenges of writing global, rather than national, histories have also contributed to the trend. Even as individuals, many historians tend to creep toward the present, perhaps because ever-better sources beckon us to move forward in time; my own research started out firmly rooted in the early fourteenth century but has now ranged as far forward as the late sixteenth century. In any case, it seems likely that a second cause of the relentless modernity of women's history might be, quite simply, the relentless modernity of the practice of history in general.

I hesitate to blame the victim, but ancient and medieval historians might constitute a third collective culprit, for those of us who work in these earlier eras have somewhat detached ourselves from the historical discourses that now largely exclude us. Ancient historians long ago withdrew into the discrete, interdisciplinary world of classics, a withdrawal so complete that it is now rare to find historians of Greece and Rome in history departments (at least, in the United States, Canada, and Britain); they reside instead in departments of classics. In the United States, the major annual meeting of classicists—the conference of the American Philological Association—has long clashed with the annual meeting of the American Historical Association, thereby ensuring that ancient historians must annually decide whether they are classicists or historians. Enclave-building in medieval history lags just a bit behind. Medieval historians are still usually housed in history departments, but their intellectual energies often lie in cross-appointments to medieval studies programs and in the many conferences and journals that allow medievalists to speak to no one but themselves. I think it is fair to say, for example, that most medievalists in the United States think more about publishing in *Speculum* than in the *American Historical Review.*[11] This interdisciplinary bent explains how ancient and medieval women's history can be flourishing but nevertheless eclipsed within women's history generally: studies of women before 1500 are mostly shared in conferences, journals, and books whose intended audiences are classicists or medievalists, not historians.

Make no mistake: there are considerable benefits to the interdisciplinary and multidisciplinary work of classics and medieval studies. Their graduate programs provide vital technical training, often not otherwise available, in such matters as philology, languages, and codicology, and their journals are willing to publish extended technical discussions that would not find an audience in history-only periodicals. It immeasurably enriches ancient and medieval history that its practitioners talk so much with scholars of ancient and medieval literature, art, philosophy, and archaeology. But it is regrettable when ancient and medieval historians therefore communicate less with historians of more modern centuries, neither submitting articles to history journals nor offering papers at broadly conceived "history" conferences. It is also worrisome that these premodern enclaves seem to have created a segregation that is dangerously comfortable to both sides. Many classicists and medievalists, eager to be freed from the supposed taint of modern concerns, are content to withdraw into their interdisciplinary encampments. Many modernists, tired of a distant past that seems more "a site of pedantry and antiquarianism" than one of stimulating inquiry, are content to be freed from sustained contact with colleagues they regard as elitist, effete, and out-of-touch.[12]

If I am right that these three factors—a presentist culture, especially in the United States; history's tilt toward modernity; and the partial segregation of ancient and medieval historians—are encouraging a more contemporary approach to history, they still cannot

TABLE 3. CHRONOLOGICAL COVERAGE AT RECENT HISTORY AND WOMEN'S HISTORY CONFERENCES[13]

Topics by era	CISH Conference (2005)	AHA Conference (2005)	IFRWH Conference (2003)	Berkshire Conference (2005)
Modern (c. 1800–present)	75%	75%	80% (183)	88% (521)
Early modern (c. 1500–1800)	10%	18.5%	11% (26)	9% (51)
Premodern (before 1500)	13%	6.5%	9% (21)	3% (16)
Total	287	592	230	588

Note: For full CISH and AHA data, see Table 2. The counts for the IFRWH and Berkshire conferences exclude nonresearch papers and papers whose chronological content could not be determined by title or session. If a paper equally spanned two eras, I placed it in the earlier one.

explain why this approach is particularly pronounced within women's history. Table 3 compares chronological coverage at the CISH and AHA historical conferences with coverage at the most recent meetings of the two major triennial conferences of women's history, the 2003 meeting of the International Federation for Research in Women's History and the 2005 Berkshire Conference on the History of Women.

As this table shows, most historians study the last two hundred years (about 75 percent of the time, to judge by CISH and AHA programs), but if we are historians of women, we are even more firmly oriented toward recent times (as much as 88 percent of presenters at the Berkshire Conference). Why should women's history be particularly afflicted by this tilt toward the present? I suggest that at least three factors *specific* to women's history might be inclining our field toward its current state: the loss of a premodern golden age; the present-mindedness of feminist scholarship outside the discipline of history; and the challenges of broadening women's history beyond a mere history of women in the West.

In the 1970s, premodern women had an established place within the narrative of women's history, a place whose foundations had been set in the nineteenth century by two very different books: Jakob Bachofen's *Mother-Right* (1861) and Friedrich Engels's *The Origins of the Family, Private Property, and the State* (1884). Both argued that early societies were much better for women than later ones. For Bachofen, matriarchal societies had prevailed until the "male principle" was asserted in classical times. For Engels, the sexual equality of early societies waned once the rise of private property inspired men to control women's sexuality and limit women's work. When feminists began to advocate for women's history in the 1970s, these narratives of a past golden age provided both intellectual support (Engels was a particularly credible authority) and political inspiration (if women were once equal, they could be equal again). They also placed early women at center stage, for prehistoric, ancient, medieval, and early modern women *had* to be integral parts of a feminist historical narrative that traced how the primordial equality of women and men was slowly undermined by modernity and particularly by the advent of capitalism. This was a story told in a host of popular books in the 1970s, and it was a story that shaped professional history as well: Gerda Lerner's *The Creation of Patriarchy* remains its most authoritative articulation.[14]

This narrative renders the distant past highly relevant to feminists and intensely inspiring. Even today, feminists can read popular books, attend public lectures, go on packaged tours, and buy statuary and jewelry that evoke the memory of this once glorious matriarchal (or, at least, sexually egalitarian) past. Yet academic women's history has abandoned this understanding of the past, and rightly so. In the 1990s, grand narratives lost their appeal within history, especially under the weight of postmodernist critique, and this particular grand narrative also crumbled under the weight of empirical research in women's history. Many cultures have myths of ancient days when women ruled, but these myths are just that—myths. With lessons that are misogynistic rather than feminist, these tales warn of the horrors of female power (and its just overthrow) rather than tell of an authentic past. Cynthia Eller has cogently revealed the ahistoricity of matriarchal myths, and ancient and medieval historians have steadily chipped away at the notion that these premodern (and precapitalist) eras were somehow relatively golden for women.[15] As we will see in the specific case of women's work in Chapter 5, the golden age theme stills crops up in professional women's history, but more as a vestigial remnant than as confident narrative. Bachofen and Engels no longer rule, at least in the academic side of women's history, and with them has declined the place of early women within the field. We now have a distant past that is more historically plausible but less inspiring and less self-referential: a distant past that is more distant and, therefore, more easily ignored.

At the same time as we have been abandoning the golden-age myths that once gave such prominence to the distant past in women's history, some of our feminist colleagues in other disciplines have been abandoning women's history altogether. In the developing years of feminist scholarship, women's history was in the forefront of the field—defining issues for research, contributing to feminist theory, and convening some of the first university-level courses on women. History now seems to have lost that leadership role, yielding partly to present-focused social sciences and partly to the new frameworks of feminist literary criticism. Feminist scholarship is exceedingly diverse, and some feminist scholars continue to draw on historical insights, but among younger scholars, as Jennifer Manion has put it, "it is no secret that cutting edge feminist scholarship is more likely found in literature and American studies than history."[16] Jane Newman has similarly reported that history has almost no purchase at all among some feminist academics. This is not just a matter of young postfeminists proclaiming that they live in the present, look to the future, and do not care to remember the past. It is also a matter of feminist teaching and scholarship. In women's studies programs in the United States, most feminist teachers and students now assume that "the most recent is also the best." They are replacing the old grand narrative with its inversion; instead of a lost golden age that feminists can work to recover, the past is now caricatured as a wretched abyss from which today's feminists have luckily escaped. In women's studies classrooms, history has little place (why bother with an abyss?), and the relevant past begins no earlier than 1945. Worse yet, this tiny slice of the past is flattened so as to create a passive reflection of today's feminism. Hence, to use one of Newman's primary examples, Simone de Beauvoir now functions in many women's studies courses as the first feminist, flawed in many ways but nevertheless taking the brave baby steps that have led to the supposed triumph of feminism in women's studies classrooms today. Aside from the ways in which this approach ignores Christine de Pizan, Mary Astell, Mary Wollstonecraft, John Stuart Mill, Harriet Taylor Mill, and many others in the Western tradition who publicly criticized the gender rules of their own times, this treatment of Beauvoir also misrepresents both her intellectual context and her book *The Second Sex*, which has, as Newman notes, "the dubious distinction of being one of the most often invoked, yet recently most seldom read, of the 'founding texts' of Western feminism."[17]

When the 1940s are the distant past and the relevant past begins in the 1960s or 1970s, the study of anything earlier becomes politically suspicious. As Newman puts it, there now resides within women's studies an "implicit claim that reaching back before these years [that is, before the 1960s] can represent nothing other than antiquarian—and potentially politically incorrect—knowledge projects."[18] Women's history, once the queen of feminist scholarship, is now its whipping girl. This hostile-to-history environment might explain the eclipse of historical studies in such feminist journals as *Signs*. It also might encourage our women's history journals to devote so much space to the recent past; the contemporary world is, quite simply, the only past that has credibility with many of our feminist colleagues. If a colleague in women's studies picks up the November 2004 issue of *Gender and History*, she can pass painlessly over an article on violent masculinity in medieval Normandy, quickly over articles on the early twentieth century, and then feast on articles that address our contemporary world—women and violence in El Salvador since 1992, legislative efforts to control domestic violence in India in 2002, and the artistic vision of the very-much-alive South African artist Clive van den Berg. By making our history more contemporary, we might be accommodating to the contemporaneity of feminism today. Or, as Kate Haulman has phrased it, the practices of women's history today suggest that the recent past is "not of greater scholarly worth, but seemingly of greater political import."[19]

I am least confident about my last factor, but I want also to raise the possibility of a symbiotic connection between our expanding awareness, since the 1980s, of non-Western histories and our waning attention to the West's distant past. In the 1970s, "sisterhood" tripped easily off our tongues, and virtually all women's history concerned Europe or North America. I think it is possible that the historical tunnel vision of that time made it easier for us to look farther down the tunnel—only European and North American history, to be sure, but more of it. Today, the histories of women in Europe and the United States still dominate women's history, but our field extends to many more world regions than it once did. Between 2001 and 2004, 20 percent of articles published in the three major English-language women's history journals dealt with non-Western history, particularly the histories of South Asia, Africa, and Latin America.[20] I am not sure what ideal proportions would be, but this is certainly progress, albeit not parity. Much the same can be said for attention to difference, especially difference inflected by race and ethnicity (16 percent of articles) and class (24 percent).[21] All of us have stories of how reading more widely in women's history has enriched our specific research. For my own ongoing work on never-married women in medieval England, I have learned, among others, from Joanne Meyerowitz's studies of young, unmarried women in early twentieth-century Chicago, Jean Allman's analysis of spinsters in colonial Asante, Janice Stockard's work on "sworn spinsters" in the twentieth-century Canton Delta, and Laurel Cornell's exploration of why there are no spinsters in Japan.[22]

By raising the possibility that this expansion in spatial breadth might be tied to a contraction in temporal reach, I do not want to revive the "class versus gender" debates of earlier decades in a new "non-West versus early West" rendition. This is not an either/or situation; we need *both* more non-Western history *and* more early history (and sometimes, of course, we get both at once). If the former has expanded at the expense of the latter, neither is to blame; instead, the elephant in the room looks to be the history of the modern West whose dominance over both seems to have yielded little ground, if any. For history generally, I will offer only an anecdote, but it is one that many colleagues in ancient, medieval, or early modern history will confirm; in the United States today, many departments are expanding their few positions in non-Western history, contracting their few positions in pre-1800 Western history, and leaving unscathed the bulk of their appointments in the history of the modern United States and modern Europe.[23] For women's history specifically, the trend since the 1970s can best be discerned in *Signs*, which not only has *less history* than it once did but also *different sorts of history*: proportionately less pre-1800 Western history, less history that crosses over several eras, and more non-Western and global history.[24] Only the predominance of the modern West has stayed constant and, indeed, expanded a bit. The raw numbers are small (thirty-eight history essays in 1975–78 and only nine in 2001–4), so my findings are suggestive, not probative. The proportions shown in Figures 1 and 2 tell the story most clearly.

Among the history articles still published in *Signs*, the modern West thrives, and the space once occupied by the West before 1800 is now taken by non-Western and global histories. Women's history might best be served, I submit, by rather less modern West and rather more room for both the non-West and the premodern world (non-West as well as West).

I wonder if this juggling happens within our brains, too. Attending to difference, as essential and incomplete as it is, is also *challenging*. For a historian of working-class women in nineteenth-century London it must often seem much more important to know about nineteenth-century histories of imperialism, colonialism, class, and race than to know about working women in, say, seventeenth-century London. Historical knowledge is not a zero-sum game, but there are limits to the materials any one of us can juggle, and when hard choices have had to be made, juggling the difference of the distant past might

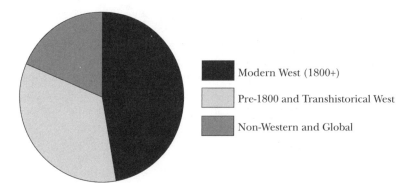

Figure 1. History coverage in *Signs,* 1975–1978

often be giving way to juggling differences that have more contemporary resonances. Such a subtle shift is easier to suggest than to demonstrate, for it happens within our heads—the subjects we choose to study and the ways we choose to study them—rather than in any public venue. But I suggest that each of us ask ourselves whether we might be, as our intellectual imaginations range more widely across the world and deal more deftly with differences among women, slacking in our attention to the past that precedes the era we study. As our vision grows more panoptic, are we failing to look down the tunnel?

Women's History from a Distance

Clearly, history has a "distant past" problem. All historians should better attend to the past before modernity and defend its relevance in the present day. Otherwise, as Lynn Hunt has noted, the central irony of our creep toward the present might become that it "put[s] us out of business as historians."[25] As teachers and scholars of history, we are challenged by the study of the past, informed, amused, personally fulfilled, professionally rewarded, and, in a move that distinguishes historians from antiquarians, we seek better to understand our present circumstances by reference to the past. In our willing obeisance to the hermeneutic powers of the past, we seldom—as best I know—set temporal limits on that power. If studying the 1950s illuminates our contemporary world, then so, too, does studying the 1850s, the 1750s, the 1650s, and so forth. If anyone understands the importance of the past as an ever-receding horizon, we historians do.[26] For feminist historians, the imperative to turn more deeply toward the past is particularly compelling, for if we examine feminist

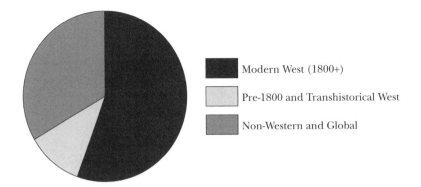

Figure 2. History coverage in *Signs*, 2001–2004

issues from a distance, we can produce not only better women's history but also better feminist theory.

Modern women's history is persistently marred by an extensive series of myths about women in the world before 1500. There was no childhood or adolescence in the European Middle Ages, right? Wrong.[27] Little affection between wives and husbands? Wrong.[28] No effective birth control before 1500? Wrong.[29] No sexual identities? Wrong.[30] No advocates for women? Wrong again.[31] In all these cases (and there are many others), the distant past is understood by modern historians as the antithesis of whatever it means to be "modern." If companionate marriage is a quintessentially modern trait, then medieval marriages *must* have lacked love; if the presence of sexual minorities is quintessentially modern, then there *must* have been no sexual identities in premodern times. Ancient and medieval historians have built cottage industries around revealing the foolishness of these myths in well-researched books and articles. But the rebuttals are remarkably ineffective: among modernists, these myths still prosper, even decades after they have been demolished by credible scholarly research.

Silly stereotypes like these have no place in women's history or history generally. The women and men who lived long before us were not profoundly "other" in awful or admirable ways; they were like us in some ways and different from us in others. Our history will be better if we attend to these past lives with the same attentiveness we bring to such factors as class, race, religion, sexuality, and world region in the present. Yes, one of the great pleasures of the historian's craft is to see the era we study (whatever era it might be) as ipso facto a time of unique and earth-shattering change. Yet this is a dangerous pleasure, one that falsely reifies the distant past and also limits our ability to understand more recent history. I offer substantive support for this point in the chapters that follow: Chapter 4 investigates long-standing continuities in the history of women that were not broken, as so many feminist historians think, by the advent of modernity; Chapters 5 and 6 explore how we can enhance feminist scholarship by looking across the great divide of modernity, using the examples of women's work and female sexuality, respectively. Chapter 7 examines the pedagogical usefulness of the distant past. Let me here briefly illustrate the benefits of a temporally expanded women's history from the entirely different angle of "women and the state," a subject of such importance that all three English-language women's history journals have recently devoted special issues to it.

State-building is one of the basic markers of modernity, distinguishing, in the traditional telling of Western history, medieval realms and fiefdoms from modern nation-states. This makes "women and the state" a hard case for incorporating the distant past. The *Women's History Review* chose a focus that precluded pre-1800 contributions altogether: women's suffrage in Britain.[32] The topics of the *Journal of Women's History* ("Women and the State") and *Gender and History* ("Gender, Citizenships, and Subjectivities") were more inclusive, and the introductions to these issues promised articles that stretched "across the world and time" and encompassed "different time periods and locations."[33] Yet more was promised than delivered; all three journals presented "women and the state" as a topic firmly bounded by the temporal confines of modernity. This is unfortunate, for both the special issues themselves and their individual contributors could have better understood critical aspects of "women and the state" if they had looked earlier than 1800. I offer three specific examples: women and citizenship, the private political power of some women, and the development of feminist thought in the West.

Before Europe had nation-states, it had cities, citizens, and customs of citizenship that are highly relevant to feminist understandings of the history of women and the state. In northern Europe during the later Middle Ages, for just one example, men admitted to the "freedom" of a town or city acquired a host of privileges and duties: immunity from local feudal authorities; access to the town's military protection and social services; economic privileges in urban markets; and the obligation to obey, support, and participate in town government. Known as *Bürger* (German), *Poorters* (Dutch), *bourgeois* (French), or burgesses, these men usually acquired citizenship by birth (a son could follow his father), by trade (membership in certain guilds could automatically confer the town's freedom), or by redemption (paying a fee). Women, too, could acquire the freedom of a town, usually by birth, redemption, or marriage (a wife of a citizen was often ipso facto a citizen), but women were "passive citizens" whose rights were more economic than political; although female burgesses shared the protections and rights of other citizens, they did not participate in city elections or serve in city offices.[34] Yet female burgesses (sometimes styled "freewomen") enjoyed privileges that were often denied others, male as well as female, because many towns extended their freedom only to the wealthiest men and women.

This premodern history is directly relevant to a problem with which several contributors to these special issues grappled—that is, the relation of women to citizenship in modern states. In the *Journal of Women's History*, Kif Augustine-Adams studied how Argentinian women in the late nineteenth century were "dependent citizens" whose marriages to foreigners de facto expatriated them; in *Gender and History*, Brigitte Studer examined a similar practice that created "contingent national belonging" for women in twentieth-century Switzerland.[35] This so-called marriage rule has a complex modern history that has played out differently in a variety of national contexts, but it is not, as Studer suggests, "an invention of the administrative state in the late eighteenth and the nineteenth century."[36] As Martha Howell has shown, medieval cities also worried about marriages of female citizens with male noncitizens and similarly sought to subsume the wife's status into that of her husband: the foreign-born wife of a freeman acceded to his freedom, but the foreign-born husband of a freewomen did not automatically do the same.[37] In medieval towns, the issue was tied up with civic rights, residence, and household governance; in modern states, the issue has been more inflected by racism and nationalism; but in both, the reigning assumption was that a wife's citizenship followed that of her husband. There need not be a direct, lineal link between citizenship in fifteenth-century Lille or Cologne and citizenship in Argentina in 1871 and Switzerland in 1941 for this enduring assumption to be interesting, relevant, and worthy of incorporating into modern histories of women's citizenship.

The public sphere seems as much a part of modernity as the nation-state, so much so that women's public participation in the state—through suffrage, salons, and women's organizations—is mostly treated in these special issues as equivalent to political voice.[38] But women's history before 1800 can remind us that a great deal of political life happens on informal, personal, and private levels from which women of the powerful classes have been rarely proscribed. The early Tudor court was once studied in public terms that replicate, in an early sixteenth-century context, the publicity that seems so basic to modern politics: monarchs, parliaments, and bureaucracies studied through the proclamations, statutes, and orders they generated. But Barbara Harris's analyses of aristocratic women in Tudor England have given us a new take on "political" that emphasizes its informal, personal sides—the politics of marriage, the politics of seemingly casual socializing, the politics of gift giving and token-exchange, the politics of patronage and kinship, the politics of influence.[39] The "Tudor court" will never look the same again, but neither should our understandings of politics, writ large. Given the long-standing private influence of women in European monarchies, it is unlikely to be the case, as one article claimed, that in nineteenth-century France "elite women gained unprecedented access to political life."[40] Catherine de Medici would have smiled at this notion. And it is a mistake to be so mesmerized by the modern public sphere that we fail to recognize the continuing power of women's private influence in modern states, even democratic ones. We need only think of the private powers of such women as Eleanor Roosevelt and Lynne Cheney or the accession to public office of such well-born or well-wed women as Indira Gandhi, Eva Peron, Hillary Clinton, and Benazir Bhutto to realize that private empowerment is still an important aspect of "women and the state" that the essays in these special issues obscure.

The history of feminist thought is littered with forgotten premodern advocates for women. Gerda Lerner has argued that the critiques of Christine de Pizan and others like her were so effectively silenced that, until the eighteenth century, each subsequent generation had painstakingly to recreate feminism, with no awareness of the insightful labors of those who came before.[41] If so, surely we should not replicate these gaps in our own histories of feminist thought—that is, surely we can trace the often-broken trail of feminist thought without adding new breaks of our own. One article in these special issues argues that two men—John Stuart Mill and Giuseppe Mazzini—profoundly shaped suffragist thought in late nineteenth-century Britain. This is fair enough, but it is not fair to claim, as the author does, that it is from Mill—and hence, only after 1869—that feminists learned "the fundamental insight that the source of tyranny was in the home."[42] Feminist writers before Mill had pointed this out, and perhaps even more to the point, as Sarah Hanley has shown, women's public protests against what she calls the "family-state compact" in support of male right had created a long-standing, sophisticated, public, *and* popular discourse against domestic tyranny on which Olympe de Gouges and others drew almost a century before Mill published his treatise.[43] From a short view, John Stuart Mill can appear central to suffragists' understandings of domestic tyranny, but from a distance, Mill and other late nineteenth-century feminists appear as part of a long tradition of objection by women—in action as well as in thought—to the twinned domestic and political tyrannies of men. Perhaps there was a break in this tradition—that is, perhaps Mill had to reinvent this particular feminist idea—but if so, it is the historian's task to acknowledge the broader context, to see what Mill and the suffragists who read him could perhaps not see, and to seek explanations for their foreshortened vision.

These three special issues looked at women and the state in geographical contexts that ranged from Latin America and North America to India, Australia, and (predominantly) Europe. This rich world feast delighted and informed my reading of the volumes, but the meager consideration of the distant past left me unsated, with less food for thought about women and the state than a longer temporal view would have provided. I hope this example, which could be multiplied ad nauseum, can gently remind us of the value of looking more deeply into the past. I am not suggesting that feminist historians abandon the nineteenth and twentieth centuries to plunge into the pleasures of studying the world before 1800, but I am suggesting that, no matter what era we might study, we can better attend to that era's own past. Our common commitment to the peoples and societies that have gone before us is, after all, what makes us feminist historians, as opposed to, say, feminist sociologists or feminist political scientists. Given our professional commitment to the importance of the past in the present, I hope we can agree that women's history will be improved if we do not assume that the "usable" past really starts about 1900, or, generously, 1800, or indeed, whenever "our" period starts.

Let me put this another way. The people who lived in the past are not us, and their difference from us compels our attention as much as those differences that we daily encounter such as class, race, religion, sexuality, and world region. As a student of women during the European later Middle Ages, I must attend to the differences that fractured the meanings of "woman" and the experiences of women in fourteenth-century and fifteenth-century Europe—especially social status, marital status, sexual status, legal status, religion, and region. But I must also attend to the past contexts of these women—the thirteenth and twelfth centuries, to be sure, but also their more distant pasts, such as Latin antiquity and early Christianity—in order to understand what was new and not-new in the world in which they lived. I cannot start afresh in 1300, for if I did, I would misunderstand their lives and their histories. We will produce better, richer, wiser women's history, if we attend, at least a bit, to the past histories of the past times that we study.

Feminist Theory from a Distance

Feminist historians have a second good reason to attend to the distant past—that is, the critical role of history in the creation of feminist theory. "Feminist theory" casts a wide net, from activists whose "theory" is also "strategy," to postcolonial and psychoanalytic theorists, to feminist theories that are so epistemologically based that they almost become, as Mary Maynard has put it, "theory about theory."[44] Whether strategic, middle-range, or highly intellectualized, good theory grows from temporal depth, as illustrated most immediately by Bachofen and Engels, both of whom viewed their chosen problems from the distance provided by thousands of years of human history. Their theories relied mostly on history-as-legacy, on history as a story that links us with past peoples and societies from which we are supposedly descended. This sort of history has less purchase now than it did in the nineteenth century, and it is especially hard to sustain in feminist scholarship, where attention to difference has rendered absurd the notion that the situation of women today somehow descends from any single past.

We once readily assumed this to be the case. For example, in 1893, Frances Buckstaff, who would later serve on the board of regents at the University of Wisconsin, published what might be the first piece of feminist medieval history in the academic tradition, an article arguing that the legal rights of married women in England declined with the Norman conquest of 1066. Toward the end of her essay, Buckstaff briefly reviewed the later English history of these disabilities, then traced their legislative survivals in many parts of the United States, and finally concluded with this observation for her U.S. audience: "It is not the purpose of this monograph to discuss the present state of married women's property. But I have called attention to it in order to remark the curious fact that the Norman dower of one-third the real estate, which superseded the community of property of our Anglo-Saxon forefathers, is still the rule eight centuries later in a large number of the laws of a race which has no prouder name for itself than Anglo-Saxon."[45] Buckstaff's easy equation of "United States" with "Anglo-Saxon" was common in her day, but it did not accurately describe her world. Wisconsin, home to Native Americans as well as Europeans, was then predominantly populated by people of German, Irish, and Norwegian descent. Buckstaff's perspective might be a little more justified by the legal context of her work (there remains even today a thick web of English antecedent in U.S. law), but even there notions of lineal descent are hard to defend. History-as-legacy is especially easy to illustrate in U.S.-based studies of European histories, but it haunts all history, especially nationalist history, even today.

For feminist theory, a different sort of history is optimal, history-as-temporal-comparison. Joan Scott has judged that "simply comparing data about women did not get us very far."[46] I disagree. It has taken us far, and it will take us further still, especially if we seek to build feminist theory that, in the words of Charlotte Bunch, "grows out of and guides activism in a continuous spiraling process." Seeking to demystify theory and root it in feminist practice, Bunch has described theory as a four-stage process: (1) *description* of what exists, (2) *analysis* of why it exists, (3) *vision* of what should exist, and (4) *strategy* of how to achieve that vision.[47] Feminist historians have a great deal to contribute to processes such as these, especially in terms of description and analysis. Surely, for example, feminist efforts to crack equal pay barriers can be advanced by recognizing that women's wages in comparison to men's have been remarkably stable over many centuries. As I will show in Chapter 5, the wage gap in England seems to have emerged with the advent of wage labor, and it has fluctuated for centuries within a limited range, with women paid—on medieval manors, in early modern towns, on eighteenth-century farms, in nineteenth-century factories, and in twentieth-century offices—about one-half to three-quarters the wages of men. We do not need comparative history in the scientific mode to render an observation like this useful to feminist strategists and theorists.[48] But we do need longer temporal vision. The major U.S.-based advocacy group on the wage gap, the National Committee on Pay Equity, begins its history of the issue in 1932 and hopes to solve the problem through legislation requiring that wages be based on job not job-holder.[49] Claudia Goldin, the U.S. economist who has commented most substantively on the wage gap, confines her analyses to the modern economy and pins her hope for eventual wage parity on the "economic progress" of technological change, education, white-collar occupations, and the like.[50] The long history of the English wage gap suggests to me that legislation and economic progress are likely to be short-term solutions, at best, and that the elimination of wage differentials will require more fundamental human change. As this instance shows, history-as-temporal-comparison can have an effect on feminist theory that is both sobering and radicalizing.

It is, of course, important for feminist theorists to undertake cross-cultural comparisons as well as temporal ones, to look beyond privileged world regions and people, to see, for example, how women's work has been remunerated beyond the West or among the poor or among sexual minorities. But in the creation of feminist theory, our vision best takes in *both* the contemporary world in all its variety *and* past worlds, too. For some insights, we perhaps do not need to go much further back than the last century. The gender politics of Western nations after the two world wars of the twentieth century might suffice, for example, to caution us about conservative reactions following times of extraordinary opportunity for women. Other insights, however, require a longer view. The wage gap is one example, for it presents one sort of challenge if viewed from the confines of the modern economy, and it looks entirely different if viewed across centuries and across, therefore, a variety of economic formations. Women and citizenship is another example. The seemingly modern challenges of female citizenship take on different meanings when we recognize that citizenship was also an incomplete status for women in the Athenian polis, the Roman republic, the cities of medieval Europe, and the Italian city-states. In both these instances—and there are many others—the striking conundrum is the persistence of a practice of sexual inequality, mutatis mutandis, in many different places and times. If feminist history can unpack these historical persistences, feminist theory will benefit.

In this contribution of history-as-temporal-comparison to feminist theory, history before 1800 has a challenging but critical role to play. The challenge springs from the simple fact that the distant past is most often a privileged past, a past whose study is especially liable to be understood by feminists, as Newman has noted, as "antiquarian" and "politically incorrect"—endeavors.[51] It is no accident that the wage gap can be tracked back to the 1300s in *English* records, or that we know so much about women and citizenship in the great polities of the *Western* tradition, or that, if I were more skilled, I would draw further examples from the Tang and Song dynasties of *China*. It is also no accident that we know a lot more about aristocratic women eight hundred years ago than we do about women among the peasantry, and more about peasant women than about the landless poor.

To the winners belong the archives, and to the archives flock the historians. Feminist historians of premodern societies are finding remarkable materials in these archives, materials that tell us much more about the lives of humble people—peasants, poor, and prostitutes—than we once expected. We are also using old sources in new ways, uncovering new sources, and turning to methodologies, such as archaeology, that allow us to rely less on the survival of the written word. But the feminist turn to the distant past will always and already entail histories that privilege some world regions over others, the wealthy over the poor, and the powerful over the disempowered. Although we can work against this, we cannot escape it, and we have no choice but to make use of the distant past wherever we can find it. Whatever we think of ancient Rome or the Song dynasty or medieval England, their archives are among the relative few that allow us to undertake the sorts of temporal comparisons feminism needs.

This archival challenge is worth meeting for two simple reasons: the theoretical insights generated by early history and the theoretical benefit of the sheer distance of the distant past. Historians of women in the Middle Ages, for example, have developed certain specialties about which they speak with particular authority to *all* feminist scholars. Are you interested in female sexuality? If so, you will learn a lot from Karma Lochrie's exploration of medieval sexualities unshaped by modern heteronormativity.[52] Are you researching women within Christian traditions? If so, you will benefit, no matter the time or place of your research, by reading Caroline Bynum and other medieval historians who have opened up new ways of understanding one very distinctive expression of female spirituality.[53] Are you worried about how to teach male-authored texts in feminist ways? If so, I suggest you learn about Jane Burns's subversive readings of "bodytalk" in the predominantly male canon of medieval literatures.[54] Are you studying prostitution? If so, you should have your brain twisted a bit by Ruth Karras's argument that medieval prostitution was more about promiscuity than sex-for-money.[55] Are you interested—as were the authors in the recent special issues—in gender and political power? If so, you need to read not only Martha Howell's work on citizens in medieval towns but a variety of other scholars whose studies of medieval queens and queenship have provided some of our best analyses yet of how class can—and cannot—trump gender.[56]

As these examples suggest, all of us can benefit from reading more deeply into the past. Each and every one of us need not abandon the twentieth century and embrace the Middle Ages, and, indeed, if we did, the historical vision of women's history would become truncated in another worrisome way. But all of us can think more wisely about women's history by reading across temporal divides. It helps to search out the specific earlier histories of the specific subjects we study, and thus, to pick up on my earlier example, historians of working-class women in nineteenth-century London can certainly benefit from delving into histories of working women in London's earlier centuries, as well as from attending to nineteenth-century histories of imperialism, colonialism, class, and race. It helps perhaps even more to read eclectically, familiarizing ourselves with the best, most illuminating, and even most provocative histories that each era has to offer. This is why I think it is so important for journals and conferences in women's history to take in a broader temporal range than is now the case. These venues encourage all of us to dip into histories outside our specialties, and I hope that, in the future, they will do more to facilitate the access of historians of modern women to the latest developments in women's history before 1800.

Finally, as all historians know, the passage of time provides new perspectives, clearer understandings, and more measured analyses—this is why we pride ourselves that history is more dispassionate than journalism. In a subject as personally fraught and politically freighted as women's history, the distance of the distant past is especially useful. This is true in the classroom where students can more frankly discuss abortion, wage inequities, and homosexuality in the fourteenth century than in the twenty-first century; it is also true in the making of theory. What we cannot yet see in, say, the twentieth century, we can sometimes see more clearly in, say, the fifteenth century. After all, it was Martha Howell working on medieval cities—not any of the authors or editors of the three recent special issues on "women and the state"—who reached the general conclusion that female access to citizenship might be linked to the extent to which citizenship was "equivalent to access to rule."[57] When citizenship in Howell's cities conferred little political access, women were citizens; when citizenship was equivalent to political power, women were excluded. This a hugely important insight, one that is painful to acknowledge in our own time but easier to see in past times. As a U.S. citizen, I have had ample opportunity to ponder Howell's observation in the past few years: the shredding of the electoral process in Florida in December 2000; the inauguration in January 2001 of a president not elected by popular vote; and the commitment in 2003 of U.S. soldiers to a war then opposed by the majority of U.S. citizens. Perhaps citizenship— such a prized achievement for U.S. women some eighty years ago— now has much less political meaning. This is a possibility historians of the twentieth century will have to answer, but it was raised by contemplating the distant past. For the insights that our own distance from a subject can bring, if for no other reason, the distant past has much to offer feminist theory.

Judy Chicago's vision of women's history in *The Dinner Party* was temporally deep but flawed. In a feminist twist on history-as-legacy, she turned to past times for foremothers with whom she could readily identify. She searched for these foremothers mostly within Western culture, and as suggested by the slowly ascending height of the banquet table, she understood their collective story as one of gentle progress for women. Worst of all, Chicago eschewed the advice of professional historians. She sought out skilled embroiderers, ceramicists, and other artists, but when she needed information on the women to be honored in the exhibition, she asked a painter to head a research team that "with no research skills and little scholarly background" trekked off to the library to look for books on women.[58] We do not want to return to this sort of feminist exploration of the distant past.

But we do need to return to the distant past. The master narrative of Western history tells of great chasms that separate one era from another—Rome and medieval Europe divided c. 500 CE; medieval and early modern c. 1500; ancien regime and modern c. 1800. These chasms partly reflect genuine historical transitions, but they have been deepened far beyond their natural contours by the repetitious power of a master narrative. That we pause at these chasms and seldom traverse them into the more distant past is a problem for all history, but it is a particular threat to feminist history, which, when confined to the modern, is sapped of interpretative power. As we'll see in the next chapter, the chasms of the master narrative particularly obscure what any master would not want us to see—continuities of patriarchal power that feminists need to explore and understand. Feminist history requires more than the short view and so, too, does the achievement of a more feminist future.

Chapter 4

Patriarchal Equilibrium

In women's history, the distant past tells a story of enduring patriarchy, a story that poses two challenges to our field. The first challenge is the long-standing and baffling job of locating the historical origins of patriarchy. From J. J. Bachofen and Friedrich Engels in the nineteenth century to Gerda Lerner in 1986, the search for the origins of patriarchy has been compelling and inconclusive.[1] It has not been a fruitless search—we have learned a great deal—but it is doomed in both conception (there was almost certainly no single original site of patriarchal power) and execution (the sources are too fragmentary for firm conclusions). The second challenge is posed by the seeming ahistoricity of patriarchy. If patriarchal power is a feature of all historical societies, then what can historians have to say about it? Or worse yet, perhaps the persistence of patriarchy betrays it roots in biological imperatives that are outside the purview of history altogether. If patriarchy is everywhere, where is its history?

This chapter argues that patriarchy does have a history, one that is inherent to the feminist project of women's history. Patriarchy might be everywhere, but it is not everywhere the same, and therefore patriarchy, in all its immense variety, is something we need to understand, analyze, and explain. If we have the courage to make patriarchy—its mechanisms, its changes, its forms, its endurance—a central problem of women's history, we will write not only better history but also history that speaks more strongly to central feminist concerns. The partnership of feminism and history has withered in recent years, but the venture of historicizing patriarchy breathes new life into the relationship. As I see it, the study of patriarchy is properly as central to women's history as is the study of capitalism to labor history or the study of racism to African American history. To move patriarchy from the margins of women's history to a more central position, this chapter begins with patriarchy per se, then examines the need to confront the continuity at the heart of patriarchy, and ends with a case study—of women in the English brewing industry between 1300 and 1700—that introduces the analytical concept of a "patriarchal equilibrium."

Patriarchy

In modern English, the term "patriarchy" has three main meanings. First, it can refer to the ecclesiastical power of men recognized as Christian leaders, particularly within the Greek Orthodox tradition; hence, the archbishop of Constantinople is commonly known as the patriarch of that church. Second, "patriarchy" can denote the legal powers of a husband/father over his wife, children, and other dependents. In seventeenth-century England, this confined-to-the-household definition of patriarchy was extended into political theory in an argument, popularized by Robert Filmer's *Patriarcha*, that the power of kings derived from the power of fathers.[2] Filmer's extension-by-analogy has been much repeated and elaborated on, and it has created an understanding, still found among some social scientists, of patriarchy as a form of government in which male heads of household rule over lesser males and all females. Despite its analogous extension to the state, this second meaning of "patriarchy" has usually remained limited to domestic, familial contexts; today, it is better expressed by such words as "patriarchalism" or "paternalism." The third meaning of "patriarchy," which I adopt here, broadly draws on feminist critiques of male power. As Adrienne Rich has defined it, patriarchy is "a familial-social, ideological, political system in which men—by force, direct pressure, or through ritual, tradition, law, and language, customs, etiquette, education, and the division of labor, determine what part women shall or shall not play, and in which the female is everywhere subsumed under the male."[3] Or as Allan Johnson has more recently defined the term, "Patriarchy is *not* simply another way of saying 'men.' Patriarchy is a kind of society, and a society is more than a collection of people. As such 'patriarchy' doesn't refer to me or any other men or collection of men, but to a kind of society in which men *and* women participate. . . . What is patriarchy? A society is patriarchal to the degree that it promotes male privilege by being *male dominated, male identified,* and *male centered.*"[4] When feminists at rallies chant, "Hey, Hey, Ho, Ho, Patriarchy's Got to Go," we are not talking about the ecclesiastical structures of Greek Orthodoxy or about a specific form of fatherly domination within families, but instead about a general system through which women have been and are subordinated to men. As Sylvia Walby has succinctly put it, patriar-

chy is "a system of social structures and practices in which men dominate, oppress and exploit women."[5]

This understanding of "patriarchy" is justified not only by its com-
monsense feminist usage but also by the fact that it is the *best* available
term to denote the system variously described by Rich, Johnson, and
Walby. "Male dominance" and "male supremacy" suggest not only
that such systems rest in biological differences but also, through anal-
ogy with such terms as "white supremacy," that patriarchal institutions are strictly equivalent to racist and other oppressive institutions
(the most striking divergences derive, of course, from the impractica-
bility of segregating women and men as thoroughly as has sometimes
been managed for people of different races, classes, and religions).
"Sexism" suggests mere prejudice. "Oppression of women" and "subordination of women" fail to convey the full complexity of systems in
which many women have colluded and from which some women have
benefited. "Patriarchy" also has the significant asset of being a single
word with straightforward adjectival and adverbial forms. As long as
we use a phrase like "male dominance," we will slip into using
roughly equivalent phrases like "male supremacy" or "male domination," and such a multitude of terms will lead to unclear thinking and
unclear writing. And, finally, "patriarchy" helps to re-orient our work
toward more explicitly feminist purposes, simply because, as we saw
in chapter 2, it comes with a sharp political edge. "Patriarchy"
focuses the mind, and in so doing, it can recharge feminist history.

To many people, talk of "patriarchy" goes hand in hand with
attacks on men, as men. I fear some readers will be thinking at this
point, "Oh dear, here comes the part where she blames it all on
men." And others might have quite different hopes, anticipating,
"Oh good, now she's going to prove that it is all the fault of men." I
intend to satisfy neither group. Men are certainly implicated in patriarchy; some men have vigorously supported its tenets and institutions, and most others have benefited from its power. But not all men
have gained equally from patriarchal structures, and some men—for
example, homosexual men in many societies—have suffered directly
from patriarchy and misogyny.[6] In any case, women have not been
innocent of collusion with patriarchy; some have supported it, some
have benefited from it, and most have raised their daughters and sons
to conform to it. In suggesting that we investigate patriarchy more
fully, then, I am not advocating a simplistic history of misogynistic
men oppressing virtuous women.

The term "patriarchy" is also sometimes associated with a feminism that falsely elides differences among women by assuming that white, middle-class, heterosexual women can speak for all women. The differences that have fractured the category "women" in the past and still fracture it today (for example, those based on race, class, marital status, sexual orientation, and world region) are differences signified by vast imbalances of power, and in suggesting that we focus some attention on the problem of patriarchy, I certainly do not intend either to ignore or to replicate these inequalities. "Patriarchy" is not a concept confined to the West nor used only there; for example, some of the most forthright recent uses of the term have occurred in studies focused on South Asia.[7] Similarly, recent studies in African American women's history have laid open not only the oppressive racial frameworks within which African Americans have had to live but also the patriarchal concerns that could trouble racial solidarities; for example, Michele Mitchell has traced how African American activists in the post-Reconstruction era "considered it critical that women radiate inviolable modesty, that men embody controlled manliness, that couples marry and establish patriarchal households."[8] As explained in the specific case of "women" in Chapter 2, if we seek general observations rather than universalizing statements, I believe we can cautiously deploy such categories without obfuscating difference. As Chandra Talpade Mohanty recently put it, "[D]ifferences are never just 'differences.' In knowing differences and particularities, we can better see the connections and commonalties because no border or boundary is ever complete or rigidly determining."[9] Like Mohanty, I seek to balance the particular and the general, to appreciate difference while seeing common ground, too.

Patriarchal constraint constitutes a central part of that common ground. It is no accident that when Ida Blom and her colleagues ambitiously set out to write a women's history of the world in the 1990s, they could agree on only one common theoretical framework: patriarchy.[10] Keeping in balance *both* the relationality inherent to differences among women *and* the relationality inherent to differences between women and men, feminist historians can work to develop new ways of considering how the history of women—as *women*—has been different from the history of men, as men. In late medieval England, for example, some women had more wealth or higher status than some men; some women wielded more political power than some men; some women enjoyed racial or sexual privileges denied to some men. But within each group of men and women—whether the group was structured by commonalties of class, race, ethnicity, or whatever—women as a group were disempowered *compared to men of their group.* Peasant women held much less land in their villages than did peasant men; townswomen did not enjoy the same benefits of guild association as did their fathers, brothers, and husbands; and women of the landed classes did not sit on privy councils, serve as justices of the peace, or attend parliament. The disempowerment of women vis-à-vis comparable men in late medieval England had specific late medieval, English components, but it is possible to study patriarchy in that time and place without thereby obscuring differences among women and without eliding or denying other inequalities. Most theorists of patriarchy insist, in fact, that systems of sexual oppression are closely imbricated with other systems of human oppression, such as imperialism, racism, feudalism, capitalism, and heterosexism. "Dual systems theory"—which in the 1970s and early 1980s attempted to synthesize feminist critiques of patriarchy with socialist critiques of capitalism—is just one example.[11]

Patriarchy has often been understood in simplistic terms. My students sometimes talk about "The Patriarchy," which always evokes for me a committee of white-haired men, nastily scheming to keep women in their place. Not so, of course. The concept of patriarchy might be singular, but its manifestations certainly are not. Examining the historical workings of patriarchy entails writing the many histories of many patriarchies—of its many forms and the many systems through which it has thrived. Sylvia Walby's work on modern England provides some critical help here. Her distinction between *forms* of patriarchy (that is, overall types of patriarchy) and its *degree* (that is, the intensity of women's oppression) frees us to examine patriarchy without being bound by problematic quests for progress. And her articulation of six *patriarchal structures*—mode of production, paid work, the state, male violence, sexuality, culture—provides an example of how to break the seeming monolith of patriarchal power into analyzable units. Walby traces a transition, in modern English history, from a "private patriarchy" which flourished in the mid-nineteenth century to a "public patriarchy" which has since replaced it. Her specific patriarchal forms, degrees, and structures might apply only to modern England, but her overall approach is not so limited.[12] Patricia Hill Collins's work is also helpful in thinking about patriarchy in more complex ways. Her notion of a "matrix of oppression" critically melds different oppressive systems; although her arguments are based on the specific dynamics of race and gender relations in the modern United States, they are more broadly applicable.[13] "Patriarchy" is not yet a fully analytical concept, in part because historians and others have insufficiently studied it. But in time, I hope that we might be able to distinguish various sorts of historical patriarchies, particularly as they have interacted with various socioeconomic systems; we might someday be able to distinguish analytically, say, "preindustrial patriarchies" from "capitalist patriarchies" from "socialist patriarchies."[14] I do not, however, look ahead toward any grand theory or metanarrative of patriarchy; to my mind, "patriarchy" is a concept that focuses feminist study and strategy, not a single system and not, as one historian recently phrased it, a "principle."[15] Patriarchal power might be a fact of recorded history, but this power is not solitary; our job is to understand the many varieties of patriarchy that have so successfully supported its adaptation to so many different historical circumstances.

Just as patriarchy is improperly understood as "The Patriarchy," so, too, are women misconceptualized as passive victims of its power. Women have certainly suffered under patriarchy, facing ideological, institutional, and practical barriers to equitable association with men (and indeed, with other women). But women have also colluded in, undermined, and survived patriarchy. The history of patriarchy is not, therefore, a history of men; it is also a history of women as survivors, resistors, and agents of patriarchy.[16] Women's agency is part of the strength of patriarchy; as Margaret Ezell has argued for seventeenth-century England, the very endurance of patriarchy must be explained, in part, by the "very looseness of its structure," which insured that "conditions were not intolerable to the point of open rebellion for the majority of women in their everyday lives."[17] And the linking of women's agency to women's vulnerability (as in, for a modern Western example, the "freedom" of women to walk the streets at night and their vulnerability in such environments to rape) is a crucial part of patriarchal endurance; we must examine the patriarchal ideologies and realities that have assured women that there is safety in protected subordination and danger in vulnerable freedom.[18]

In understanding women's agency within patriarchal regimes, Deniz Kandiyoti's concept of "patriarchal bargains" is key. Kandiyoti has shown how women strategize within the constraints of any patriarchal regime, creating opportunities for themselves, changing patriarchal systems, and even playing out "implicit scripts that define, limit, and inflect their market and domestic options." The "bargain" of "patriarchal bargain" is not necessarily a "good buy," but it both creates strategic opportunities for women and invests women in patriarchy. Thus, for example, a young woman will endure the dispossession of living as a daughter-in-law in her husband's family because she anticipates that she will someday be a mother-in-law, possessed of adult sons, property, and control over the labor of daughter-in-laws. In this form of what Kandiyoti calls "classic patriarchy," an older woman is subordinate to men but exercises substantial power over younger women, giving her a strong reason to maintain the patriarchal status quo.[19] Kandiyoti developed the concept of "patriarchal bargains" by contrasting sub-Saharan Africa and the Muslim Middle East, and many scholars have since put her concept to good effect in those contexts.[20] But those of us who work on women's history in other world regions will find it applicable, too; "patriarchal bargains" might help us, for example, to better understand why so many women were opposed to the Equal Rights Amendment in the late twentieth-century United States.

Antifeminists have often argued that male dominance is unavoidable, locating the roots of patriarchy in biological differences or functional imperatives. Feminists know otherwise; we know that patriarchy is contingent, constructed, and subject to change. We know, as Zillah Eisenstein has put it, that "the reason patriarchy exists is because a nonpatriarchal sex-gender system could exist if allowed to."[21] Yet unless feminist scholars historicize patriarchy by studying its many variants, it will remain a bugbear for feminists, an ignored but ever-present specter that suggests (however falsely) that the oppression of women is natural and ineradicable. The power of patriarchy in our lives today partly rests, in other words, on our failure to understand how it has worked in past times. So long as we are afraid to name patriarchy and to study its workings historically, we will understand our current circumstances inadequately, and the lives of women and men will be twisted by the perverse strengths of patriarchal institutions. Historians of women need not "go on endlessly repeating and proving the obvious, that is to say, the grossly unjust treatment that women have received over thousands of years at the hands of males."[22] But it is the special task of historians of women to investigate *the forces behind this obvious fact*—that is, to explain how the oppression of women has endured for so long and in so many different historical settings. This problem—the problem of historicizing patriarchy—has inspired considerable disquiet among historians, but our feminist politics demand that we address it.[23]

Confronting Continuity

In order to address patriarchy as feminist historians, we must first come to grips with continuity. The tension between continuity and change is perhaps the oldest and most productive of historical themes. At the center of eighteenth-century debates about Edward Gibbon's *The History of the Decline and Fall of the Roman Empire*, it remains powerful not just in studies of Rome but in most historical fields. In the twentieth century, the balance between continuity and change shifted slightly, as new historical approaches and subjects placed special emphasis on continuity. Seeking to downplay event-based history, Fernand Braudel and other historians in the *Annales* school began in the 1930s to stress the structural continuities of economy, society, and environment. By the late twentieth century, this emphasis on continuity began to seep into many fields, reshaping once-sharp breaks into more measured trends; for example, historians of religious reform in sixteenth-century Europe now emphasize gradual change and continuity with medieval practices. To the social historians, family historians, and historians of women who began to produce so many innovative sorts of history in the 1970s, this renewed emphasis on continuity also made good sense. Most readily agreed, for example, that the lives of European women were more influenced by slow-moving structural changes (such as the industrialization of the European economy) than by events (such as the publication of Mary Wollstonecraft's *A Vindication of the Rights of Woman* in 1792).

Nevertheless, change exerts a powerful narrative force over women's history. Events might often seem less important than long-term structural shifts, but historians of women still frequently focus on significant moments of seeming transformation in women's status, particularly on seeming advances or declines in women's status. As a result, we sometimes highlight "transformation" when the more important story may be about "continuity." I will unpack one such example in the next chapter—the assumption among many historians that women's work was more valued in preindustrial Europe than afterward. This is an old belief, much repeated even today; our two most recent interpretations of women's work in Europe's industrial revolution tell us that "[i]ndustrialization brought about the subordination of women in many realms of production" and that changes in this period "not only subordinated women's work, but contributed to identifying women as not workers."[24] The approaches of Deborah Valenze and Deborah Simonton are new in many ways, but they build on a familiar story about women nurtured by traditional economies and harmed by industrial ones. This story masks important continuities. To be sure, women's work in Europe has changed in many ways since 1300; today, European women work more often for wages than did their medieval predecessors, they more often travel away from home to a separate place of employment, and they also accrue welfare benefits through their work that would have been unimaginable to medieval women. But these changes have not transformed the work status of women, compared to men; today, as in 1300, "women's work" in Europe is still relatively low-status, low-paid, and low-skilled. This judgment rests on a critical distinction between *changes* in women's experiences on the one hand and *transformations* in women's status on the other. To my mind, there has been much change in European women's experiences as workers over the last millennium, but little transformation in their work status in relation to that of men.[25]

"Transformation" is the accepted or even canonical story; "continuity" is troublesome, worrisome, and even dismissible. In 1993, the Berkshire Conference on Women's History was entitled "Transformations: Women, Gender, Power," a title so innocuous and unproblematic that most participants probably never thought twice about it. Would we have thought twice (and even more) if the conference had instead been headlined as "Continuities: Women, Gender, Power"? I think so, and I think we need to discuss more actively and more explicitly *why* one title is so much more palatable than the other and *how* our preference for history-as-transformation might limit our ways of seeing the past lives of women.[26]

Historians of women have long written about the status of women falling or rising in certain times or places, but the "status of women" is a slippery concept that tends toward an overgeneralization of which feminists are justly skeptical. It is also haunted by subtle ideological practices that use "women's status" as a sort of litmus test of civilization. In the nineteenth century, Europeans claimed cultural supremacy over colonized peoples by, among other things, imagining that European women enjoyed higher status than did women in India, Africa, the Americas, or, indeed, any place other than Europe; more recently, the Bush administration has similarly deployed the "status of women" as part justification for its aggression in Afghanistan and Iraq. These are serious liabilities, but the desire to trace advances and declines in the status of women over time remains a fundamental part of our field. In the 1970s Joan Kelly added new power to what was already an old practice of judging the rising or falling status of women.[27] Kelly began by looking critically at the fit between women's history and traditional history, arguing that the periodization of the former inverted the periodization of the latter. As Kelly put it, "what emerges [from women's history] is a fairly regular pattern of relative loss of status for women precisely in those periods of so-called progressive change." A year later, she provided a historical example in her classic essay "Did Women Have a Renaissance?"

Kelly's negative answer to this question has been much revised and reconsidered, but her overall vision—of an often-inverted synchronization between the history of women and traditional history—has waxed strong in both research and teaching. Some fields of women's history have adapted to Kelly's formulation less enthusiastically than others. As Sandra Greene has pointed out, historians of women in Africa have consistently traced continuities between the precolonial and colonial periods; in the context of an Africa once misunderstood as having no substantive history before European contact, the continuity of indigenous practices is now deployed by historians "as a form of agency on the part of African societies."[28] And as Valerie Traub has noted, lesbian history, often motivated by a search for "historical foremothers," has been driven by "the logic of temporal continuity."[29] In women's history more generally, however, almost every great divide in the traditional historical narrative seems to have provoked Kelly-inspired assessments of how that divide affected women's status for better or worse. In European women's history, for example, we have considered how women's status was affected by the Christianization of the ancient world, the rise of capitalism, the Renaissance, the Reformation, the industrial revolution, the French Revolution, the Russian Revolution, and so on.[30] In most cases, the possibility that the status of women was not transformed is not even considered. We seem to assume that these turning points *must* have affected women's status, leaving to us the straightforward task of weighing the transformation. In so doing, we strive for an overall assessment—women's status getting better or getting worse—instead of considering the possibility that, despite change, shift, and movement, the overall force of patriarchal power might have endured. To use the terms proposed by Walby, we seldom consider how during these great divides, the *forms* of patriarchal power might have changed more than its *degree*.[31]

Karen Offen has suggested that this drumbeat of change, change, and more change is characteristically modern, because it is a simple fact of history that "historical change relentlessly accelerates . . . as we reach modern times."[32] The hoary myth of an unchanging premodern world underpins modernism, but, in fact, change pulses as strongly through premodern histories as modern ones. For example, medievalists have produced a large literature assessing how the status of women was transformed with the developments that created the so-called high or central Middle Ages. Inverting traditional historical assessments of this era, scholars have argued that many apparent "advances" associated with the eleventh and twelfth centuries actually hurt women. Because women were more reliant than men on informal and family-based modes of influence (the argument goes), the seeming improvements of the central Middle Ages—the consolidation of feudal monarchies, the papal reform and associated monastic movements, the rise of universities, and the relative pacification of feudal society—created a more formalized and public power structure from which women were increasingly excluded.[33] Before this central medieval watershed for women, there were (according to Jo Ann McNamara and Suzanne Wemple) "few restrictions on the power of women in any sphere of activity," but afterward (according to David Herlihy) "the social position of the medieval woman seems in some ways to have deteriorated."[34] In this instance as in many others, historians of women have accepted the traditional chronology but inverted it. We have synchronized transformations in women's status with major historical turning points, even though we have found regress for women in the midst of seemingly progressive historical change.

In college classrooms where women's history is now regularly taught, history-as-transformation also remains an effective and compelling theme. Most textbooks in women's history provide a periodization that marches women in time to traditional history (so that even if women and men "move" in different directions, they "move" at the same time), and most teachers also emphasize the turning points that are critical to the traditional narrative.[35] Apart from the occasional awkward "How's that any different from today?" most students accept this history as both sensible and convenient. We might struggle with college students to get them to give up whiggish notions of women's steady progress toward emancipation, but we do not have to struggle to convince them that the status of European women was different before and after the French Revolution, before and after the upheavals of 1848, or before and after World War I. These sorts of transformations are even more readily assumed in our undergraduate classrooms than they are in our research.

The critical question is *why*. As students, we are trained to have skeptical and inquiring minds. And as teachers, we constantly hear questions from students that force new ideas on us. Yet at the center of our work as historians of women lies the rarely questioned assumption that the history of women is a history of transformation in women's status—for better at some times and places, and for worse at others. I believe that we see women's history in such transformative terms for at least four very good reasons: because of the development of the field; because of the structure of the discipline of history; because of the particular influence of feminism in the academy; and because of our own lived experiences. Each of these factors compels us to put aside troublesome ideas about history-as-continuity and to seek out histories that emphasize transformation. Together, their power is largely silent and unacknowledged, and all the more powerful for that. In the hope of moderating their influence over our visions of the past, let us look each in the eye.

CONTINUITY AND WOMEN'S HISTORY IN THE 1970S

To begin with, the emphasis on history-as-transformation seems to spring partly from the development of the field of women's history. Our field's origins are usually traced back both to historians and intellectuals of past generations (such as Eileen Power, Simone de Beauvoir, and Mary Beard) and to feminist advocates of the recovery of women's past in the 1970s (such as Gerda Lerner, Joan Kelly, and Sheila Rowbotham). These scholars have certainly been very important in the development of women's history, but the field also grew from other sources that have critically shaped our ability (or *in*ability) to consider continuities in women's past. Like many feminists who came of age in the 1970s, my first taste of women's history did not come from Eileen Power or Gerda Lerner or other distinguished feminist scholars; my first taste came from popular feminist formulations—from such sources as the "Lost Women" column of *Ms.* magazine, Elizabeth Gould Davis's *The First Sex*, and Barbara Ehrenreich and Deirdre English's *Witches, Midwives, and Nurses*.[36] These popular formulations of women's history were often essentialist, finding their explanations for women's oppression in biological differences between the sexes. They often portrayed women as passive victims, overlooking not only women's agency but also women's collusion in sexual oppression. They also often took falsely universalist perspectives, assuming that the experiences of white, middle-class, heterosexual women could speak for all women. Most importantly, they emphasized continuity, a sisterhood between the oppressed women of the past and the oppressed women of the 1970s. In these ways, some of the first women's history produced in the 1970s raised issues about long-term continuities in women's status, but raised them in very problematic ways.

As women's history began to gain an academic foothold over the course of the 1970s (particularly in the United States), these early popular formulations that emphasized continuity, oppression, victimization, and a universal sisterhood were put aside in favor of a more professional scholarship that synchronized the history of women with the history of men.[37] Kelly's model of an inverted synchronization between women's history and traditional history provided a critical guide. Kelly explicitly challenged some of the basic assumptions of traditional history, but she did not fully reject its periodization; Kelly sought to change *evaluations* of great divides, not the idea of transformation per se. In other words, she accepted the notion that there was a turning point called "the Renaissance," she assumed that this Renaissance affected women as much as men, and she sought merely to argue that the Renaissance affected women in different ways than it affected men. Indeed, Kelly quite explicitly rejected the possibility that major historical transformations might *not* have affected the status of women in substantial ways and that therefore women's history should be periodized differently (in terms of both chronology and criteria) from mainstream history. For Kelly, a distinct periodization for women's history would have been essentialist (that is, it would have tied women's history in a biologically deterministic way to women's bodies), logically inconsistent (that is, it would have inverted what Kelly called the "causal sequence" of history), and isolating (that is, it would have separated women's history from the mainstream of historical work).[38]

Kelly's ideas spoke, I think, to the need of feminist historians in the 1970s to create an academically acceptable and useful history of women. She certainly spoke to my needs as a graduate student then seeking legitimacy for my work on peasant women in medieval England. Thanks to Kelly, I came to understand that my project was to provide the women's angle on medieval peasant society, to fit women into the hitherto male-dominated history of rural economy and society. In the last few decades, therefore, I and most other historians of women have accepted a periodization that marches women's history in time to traditional history, emphasizing the same turning points that are critical to the traditional narrative. We have tried to answer, for our own times and places, that question Louise Tilly passed on to us from a colleague, about what difference it made that women were participants in the French Revolution.[39] And in whatever era we have examined—in European history, whether we have looked at ancient, medieval, early modern, or modern women—we have tended to see that era within a framework of transformation in women's status.

CONTINUITY AND HISTORICAL PRACTICE

If history-as-transformation was partly formed by a necessary reaction to some early popularizations of women's history as it took shape in the United States in the 1970s, it has also been supported by the basic practices of history itself. In graduate school, most historians are prepared for one straightforward mission: find change and explain it. To be sure, historians are not blind to continuity, and the balance between change and continuity provides one of the great seesaws of historical writing and teaching. Thus, for example, the English historian Geoffrey Elton saw the year 1485 as inaugurating a Tudor revolution in government, a dramatic break with England's medieval past.[40] But many English historians have seen 1485 as little more than a convenient moment in dynastic history, an easy place to break the gradual shift from medieval England to its Tudor-Stuart successor. And others have subjected the core assumption behind the 1485 waypost—that English culture and society were profoundly transformed between c. 1300 ("medieval") and c. 1700 ("early modern")—to steady assault. Lee Patterson, David Aers, and other literary critics have shown that two shibboleths of modernity—historical consciousness and individualism—so misrepresent cultural continuities that, as Aers has put it, "it is thus time to put a self-denying ordinance on claims about the new 'construction of the subject' in the sixteenth century."[41] Alan Macfarlane has argued that England in 1300 was already a capitalist, market economy governed by rampant individualism, an England very similar in its socioeconomic structures to England in 1700.[42] Recognizing that change is seldom dramatic and seldom complete, historians usually look hard for the continuities that run across seemingly sharp divides.

Most often, however, we pay lip service to continuity and then side heavily with change. Macfarlane's argument, for example, precipitated considerable debate in the early 1980s and is now largely dismissed. It did, however, have one effect; instead of eliminating English history's great divide between medieval and early modern, it encouraged a generation of social and economic historians to push the date of that divide forward a bit, to c. 1525 instead of 1485.[43] We talk about continuity, we debate our great divides, and we even shift our dates a bit, but we cleave to the divides themselves. Why? Change, quite simply, seems to be more fun. Requiring careful tracing and analysis, its causes and effects cry out for study. In contrast, continuity can seem rather dull. As D. C. Coleman put it in his economic history of early modern England, "Change is the greater temptress; continuity appears as the bore to be avoided."[44] (Note the feminization of temptation; this is the sort of rhetoric that Bonnie Smith has critiqued so effectively in her studies of the gendering of the historical profession.)[45]

Continuity seems to be more than boring; it also calls into question the very ways that we practice history. Consider how firmly we embrace a historical consciousness founded on discontinuity between the present and the past; whether this discontinuity was a creation of the Renaissance or not matters less than its power over our ways of seeing the past.[46] Consider, too, how modern historical writing is so often driven by the power of narrative, by the telling of stories that contain crisis, adjustment, and resolution. And consider how often historians use a concern with differences between the present and the past—transformative changes that differentiate our lives from the lives of those who preceded us by twenty years or two hundred years or two thousand years—to distinguish ourselves, rightly or wrongly, as professionals. We like to imagine that it is our ability to recognize these changes and analyze them that distinguishes us not only from the general public but also from sociologists, political scientists, philosophers, and scholars in other related fields. Without clear and considerable differences between the past and the present, it seems that historical context—and with it, the work of historians—might come to mean little indeed.

For historians of women, this practice of history has particularly strong repercussions. Within the bounds of the discipline of history, feminists have had to fight against the essentialist critique, often used to undermine the viability of women's history as a field, that women's place has been unchanging and constant throughout history. In other words, feminist historians have had to legitimate women as historical subjects by showing that women's lives have history—that is, have change and transformation.[47] And for very practical reasons, historians of women have also had to try to fit the rhythms of women's history into the traditional periodizations of the profession. How else, for example, could histories of women fit into courses in European history except with distinctive Greco-Roman, medieval, early modern, and modern chronologies? Seeking not only to uncover women's history but also to teach women's history within traditional curricula, we have perhaps necessarily kept the chronology, adhered to the notion of transformative change, and marched to the pace of traditional history.

CONTINUITY AND FEMINIST PRACTICES

These two forces—the developmental context of the field of women's history, and the practice of history itself—have created a strong professional imperative to focus on history-as-transformation. This imperative has been further strengthened by the politics of modern feminism in the West, which has been more comfortable with transformation than continuity. After all, the tracing of transformations in women's status in the past implicitly promises similar transformations in the future, and it can even offer lessons about achieving positive progress. For example, we have learned from the experiences of working women in England and the United States during the two world wars of the twentieth century that expanding war-time economies can open new possibilities for women workers and that contracting postwar economies are often hostile to women's work (this is, of course, the story immortalized in the film *The Life and Times of Rosie the Riveter*). And we have been able to apply this knowledge to economic change in our own time—to try to keep women from being among the last hired and first fired in skilled occupations. Working for transformation in the present, we are often encouraged and informed by histories of transformation in the past. In contrast, continuity in women's status is a frightening prospect to many of us, for it suggests (wrongly, in my view) that women's subordination might be rooted in insurmountable obstacles. If nothing much has changed in the past, then some worry that women's plight is based so firmly in biological or social or material or psychological constraints that positive transformations in women's status in the future are simply impossible.

These are pressures enough, but they have often been further strengthened by the actual practices of feminism within the academy. Many feminisms have been influential in academia, and some have dealt more readily than others with continuities in women's past. Radical feminism—from which came some of the earliest popular formulations of women's history in the 1970s—has readily accommodated to the notion of long-term continuities in women's status. Black feminism has also developed the critical concept of a "matrix of domination" which effectively speaks about the varied forces that can work to maintain the status quo between oppressors and oppressed.[48] Moreover, since few feminist historians adopt specific ideological labels or interpretative lines, much feminist history tends to reflect eclectically the influence of several different feminist positions. These are important caveats, but I think it is nevertheless fair to say that two strands of feminism have been particularly influential in the production of academic women's history in the West: liberal feminism and socialist feminism.

In their original formulations, both these feminisms posited (albeit in different ways) transformation in women's status as a fundamental feature of women's past. For liberal feminists, women's subordination was not a fundamental feature of modern society but was instead caused by many small accretions and vestigial traditions of the past. Because female subordination was seen as an incidental rather than substantial aspect of modern life, liberal feminists tended to see women's status as improving with modernity (for example, with Europe's Renaissance or industrial revolution) and as readily subjected to change. For socialist feminists, gender inequality was linked with the development of private property and capitalism. Because women's plight was seen as arising from the triumph of capital over labor, socialist feminists expected women's status to shift with changes in economic structures, and they depicted women's status as declining with modernity (for example, with Europe's commercial and industrial revolutions). Liberal feminists and socialist feminists, therefore, certainly disagreed about the direction of change in the past, but they agreed about one crucial thing: transformation in women's status had occurred. Liberal feminism and socialist feminism have moved on from their early formulations, but it is often possible to see these foundational ideas about the status of women exercising a continuing influence on feminist history. In the history of women's work, for example, the eclectic approaches of feminist historians still usually draw on either liberal or socialist traditions.[49] Both the politics of feminism in general and the specific practices of feminism in the academy have encouraged historians of women to look for past transformations in women's status.

CONTINUITY IN OUR OWN LIVES

Finally, these professional and political forces are strengthened by a fourth force: our own personal experiences. As Carolyn Steedman has reminded us, "any scholarly use of historical material takes place not only within the academy, but also in the commonplace, everyday world of which the academy is a part."[50] In that commonplace, everyday world, modern women and men have seen many things change for women in Western societies (and mostly change for the better). Consider, for example, higher education in the United States. Forty years ago, the most elite colleges in the United States did not admit women at all; very few women were earning doctorates; and even fewer women were finding tenured employments. All this has now changed: women now graduate from colleges and universities in higher numbers than men; women go to Harvard, Yale, and Princeton; and about one-third of all doctorates and entry-level faculty positions in history are held by women. This is inspiring stuff, and it encourages us to believe that women's status can be transformed, and transformed rapidly.

Against this, however, we must place enormous continuities in the status of women in our own times, continuities that we may prefer to overlook. In the United States, women with college degrees still have the earning power of men with high school diplomas; most women in the university still work in the secretarial and clerical pink-collar ghetto; female faculty cluster in fixed-term and untenured positions; even the best careers can still be held in check by an academic "glass ceiling"; and sexual harassment, rape, and other forms of violence against women on our campuses have continued unchecked and perhaps, indeed, have increased. We must also be alert to the possibility that we ourselves are caught in a pattern often observed in women's history—a pattern of women gaining access to institutions only when those institutions are in decline. Recent attacks on higher education (especially on public funding of universities and on academic freedom) suggest that women—as both students and teachers—have been gaining access to higher education at the very time that its influence might be waning. Bill Gates, after all, is a college dropout.

We have good reasons, then, to be more comfortable with a Berkshire Conference entitled "Transformations" than with one entitled "Continuities." In part, we seek to distance ourselves from popular histories of women that once emphasized continuity along with a package of ideas—particularly essentialism, female victimization, and false universalism—from which we now wish to disassociate women's history. And in part, we see transformation in women's history because our profession expects it from us, our feminist politics seem to need it, and our own lived experiences apparently support it. These are compelling pressures indeed, but we can resist them, and if we do, we will move toward more measured ways of seeing the past. If we question apparent transformations in women's status, consider new periodizations based on women's histories, and feel comfortable thinking about long-term continuities, we can see women's history in new ways.

Brewsters

One new way of revisioning women's history is to question whether the conventional historical narrative of crisis, adjustment, and resolution is itself a gendered tale. Working with medieval saints' lives, Caroline Bynum has observed that male biographies take shape as "social dramas" involving crisis, inversion, and resolution, but that female biographies often offer "a life in which 'nothing happens' at least if we expect to find a social drama." Bynum has suggested that both social facts (that is, the limited ability of women to change their lives) and psychological differences might account for the comparative continuity of female life-stories within this medieval genre.[51] Or perhaps the difference lies less in male and female lived experiences and more in the interpretation of those experiences by biographers.[52]

In any case, there can be little doubt that a tale of transformation does not effectively explain fundamental dimensions of women's past. As Georges Duby has noted for the central Middle Ages, despite the many changes of that era, "the hierarchical distance between the sexes was not noticeably diminished."[53] As Olwen Hufton has observed about the common notion that early modern women enjoyed a more equal relationship with men, "So far the location of this *bon vieux temps* has proved remarkably elusive."[54] And as Susan Staves and Amanda Vickery have suggested for more recent times, there might be much less transformation in women's status since the eighteenth century—particularly in property law and family relations—than we once thought.[55] In my own work on medieval brewsters (that is, female brewers) in late medieval England, I found a similar gap between, on the one hand, my assumption of transformation and, on the other hand, continuities suggested by the archival and literary evidence. By looking hard at these unexpected continuities, I came to see a "patriarchal equilibrium" that sustained women's (low) status despite the enormous—indeed, transformative—expansion of the brewing trade.[56]

In the 1980s, when I began examining the history of brewsters, I anticipated a story of radical change, a story of how women were forced out of the trade as it became profitable and prestigious. Indeed, brewing seemed to provide a classic illustration of a negative transformation in women's status accompanying a major turning point in economic history. In 1300, women controlled the trade in brewed drink; by 1600, it was controlled by men. At the same time, brewing was transformed by economic changes of the sort commonly aggregated under the rubric of "commercial revolution." Capitaliza-

tion, centralization, professionalization, monopolization, even industrialization—all these describe how English brewing changed between
1300 and 1600. As I had expected, I found that this slow commercial-
ization favored men over women. When business opportunities
expanded, women had little capital to invest in new equipment, limited authority over large workforces, and few contacts for obtaining
supplies and opening new markets. When guilds began to offer brewers fresh ways to foster trade solidarity and power, wives found themselves second-rank members in fraternal organizations run by their
husbands. When beer (made with hops) began to replace unhopped
ale in the English diet, women suffered from poor access to the new
technology of beer-brewing and from an inability to respond effectively to the commercial opportunities it offered. When the production and marketing of brewed drink came under closer governmental
regulation, women's modest enterprises were deemed less reliable
than the larger enterprises run by men. And whenever local authorities worried about the drunken disorder of alehouses, they tended to
blame brewsters more than male brewers.

In short, I expected to find transformation, and I did. In 1300,
brewing was a ubiquitous trade requiring little specialized skill or
equipment, conferring minimal trade identity, and offering only
small profits. As such, it was accessible to women, and compared to
the other, even more limited economic options for women, it was a
good trade for them. By 1600, brewing in many places had been transformed into a specialized trade requiring training and investment,
conferring social prestige and guild status, and offering considerable
profits. As such, it had ceased to be a trade of women and had
become a trade of men. Brewing had prospered, and brewsters had
faded away. Or, as Alice Clark put it in her classic study of the negative
effects of industrialism and capitalism on women's status, "with the
growth of capitalism and the establishment of a monopoly for 'Common Brewers' women were virtually excluded from their old trade of
brewing."[57] Yet as I dug more deeply into the archives, I began to see
my information about brewsters in new ways. I found that this story
of dramatic loss only partly described what happened in English brewing between 1300 and 1600.

To begin with, this story too readily idealized the "old trade" of
brewsters. In 1300, brewing was low-skilled, low-profit, low-status
work—that is, work then seen as appropriate for a woman. There was,
in other words, no "golden age" when prosperous brewsters enjoyed
the fruits of a profitable and prestigious women's trade. There was,
instead, a time when brewing was among the many petty employ-

ments available to women as they tried to patch together a living—women worked by the day for wages; they sought work as servants or prostitutes; they sold eggs, cheese, and other foods; they hawked old clothes; they cared for the sick and prepared the dead for burial; they brewed and sold ale. I am sure that many women took satisfaction in these labors, put their small profits to good use, and were even proud of their abilities. But in the broader context of their villages and towns, these were modest employments that offered relatively little prestige and profit. Brewing was among the best of these modest employments, but it, like women's other options, attracted little interest from men, who could get better work.[58]

Clark's story also worked to stabilize the trade of brewing in ways that obscured its transformation between 1300 and 1600. By the seventeenth century, when women were being "virtually excluded from their old trade," their "old trade" had, in fact, virtually disappeared. Indeed, what had changed was not women's work but instead brewing itself, which had so prospered and professionalized that it was a new industry apparently no longer suitable for women. To be sure, in 1600 women still worked in the drink trade but only in lowly pursuits—they worked as unskilled servants in breweries, they carried ale on their backs from breweries to the houses of customers, they retailed ale and beer that was supplied to them by breweries. But, except in isolated areas, they rarely worked as brewsters, rarely enjoyed the high profits that male brewers took from the commercial production of ale or beer.

And, finally, Clark's tale of decline and loss tended to mingle together two discrete concepts—the *experiences* of women and women's *status*. Many things changed in the experiences of women who sought to profit from brewing between 1300 and 1600. Some women had to shift from producing ale to merely selling ale brewed by others; some became employees of brewers rather than brewsters in their own right; some had to find new sources of petty income in lace making, stocking knitting, and other new employments. These were real changes, real accommodations that women had to make as commercial brewing became a less viable option for them. Yet these changes in women's experiences did not transform women's status as workers. Brewing changed, and women's access to brewing changed, but in 1600, as had been the case in 1300, women's work was humble work. Much change in women's experiences; no transformation in women's status.

Both these histories of brewing—one emphasizing the change entailed in women ceasing to brew and the other emphasizing continuities in the low status of women's work—are useful. But it is the latter story—the story of continuities—that most enriched my understanding of brewsters in late medieval and early modern England. It emphasized for me that although some of the *forms* of women's work changed between 1300 and 1600 (for example, women worked less in brewing and more in stocking knitting), its *substance* as low-status, low-skilled, and low-profit work remained the same. By examining brewsters and their trade in this way, I saw new and productive questions that had before eluded me. History-as-transformation asked me to explain decline—to explain brewsters' descent from paradise as they lost control of a trade once their own.[59] History-as-continuity asked me to explain something quite different—to explain why brewsters were unable to accomplish an ascent to paradise, unable to take advantage of the expansion of the market for brewed drink after 1350. Why did brewsters not respond as effectively as male brewers to the late medieval growth of their market? What were the pressures for continuity—for maintaining the low work status of women—that ensured that brewsters could not retain control over the trade once it began to prosper? Built not around a history of transformation but instead around a history of missed opportunity for transformation, these questions allowed me to understand English brewsters in new ways.

The answers that I have found to these questions have eased my mind about three of the problems long associated with history-as-continuity. First, for brewsters, biology was not destiny. Indeed, traditional essentialist explanations for female disadvantage in the workplace—that women either are less strong than men or are more burdened by reproductive work—had no effect on brewsters. Quite the reverse was true. As requirements for physical strength in brewing eased, women worked less in the trade; in 1300, brewsters themselves had to haul the water, fuel, and grain used to brew ale, but by 1600, many male brewers pushed paper instead of barrels, employing workers who did the hard labor. There was a similarly inverse correlation between brewing and childbirth/child rearing: the first women to leave brewing as the trade grew more profitable were those with the *fewest* reproductive responsibilities—that is, singlewomen and widows. Despite being "distracted" by pregnancies and childcare, wives more tenaciously kept their place in the brewing trade. Essentialism—or what Karen Offen has recently called "physiological concerns particular to women"—remains a powerful thread within some feminist understandings of the perdurability of patriarchy. That it is a frayed thread in the case of brewsters speaks, again, to the importance of assuming nothing about biological constants and subjecting all such possibilities to hard study. We cannot explain women's subordination, past or present, by simple reference to childbearing and infant feeding.[60]

Second, although brewsters were, in the end, unable to take full advantage of the expanding profitability of their trade, they were not passive victims. I found no evidence that brewsters protested the obstacles they faced as women, but I found abundant evidence of their creative reactions to problems. Some left off brewing and took up the selling of drink; some associated as closely as they could with the guilds that began to regulate their trade; some operated in a brewing black market beyond the control of guilds and cities; some continued to brew even when their husbands assumed all public responsibility for the trade; and some found employment in other trades altogether. Instead of passively withdrawing from brewing, in other words, women actively sought new ways in which they could support themselves and their families; they faced changing circumstances, reacted to them, and made history. Their choices were, of course, shaped and defined by the circumstances in which they found themselves. But if a woman ceased brewing and took up, say, lace making, she accommodated to changing times without either freely choosing to leave the brewing trade (agency) or suffering direct exclusion from it (victimization).

Third, differences among brewsters were critically important in understanding how and why they left the trade. Brewsters in rural villages maintained their businesses much longer than brewsters in many towns and cities, and, as just mentioned above, married brewsters retained a place in the trade long after most widows and single-women had to seek work elsewhere. Indeed, the experiences of brewsters illustrates well how appreciation of differences among women is essential not only for nuance and clarity but also for understanding the experiences of all women, as Elsa Barkley-Brown has argued so persuasively in U.S. history.[61] The slow masculinization of the trade—a trend which eventually embraced women of different places, classes, and marital statuses—cannot be understood without reference to how, in the earliest stages, some women left off brewing earlier than others.

Thus, my work on medieval brewsters suggested to me that history-as-continuity need not necessarily lead to essentialist explanations, to a history of female passivity, or to false generalizations that obscure differences among women. This might have been true of some history-writing in the 1970s; it need not be true today. Sandra Greene has noted much the same for the history of women among the Anlo-Ewe of Ghana and for African women's history more generally. In these instances, too, an appreciation of continuity is now enabling historians "to emphasize African women's creative reactions to problems, differences among African women, and the varied character of patriarchal power."[62]

Instead of being compelled by biological imperatives, female victimization, or an eternal battle between two sexes unmarked by class, race, sexuality, or other factors, the brewsters of late medieval England faced changing circumstances and reacted to them in diverse ways. Their history is one of much change for brewsters but little transformation for women's work. This immobility was not of their own making, for at every turn, brewsters found themselves unable to respond as effectively as men to new opportunities. They encountered historical circumstances that discouraged them from brewing and encouraged men to take up the trade: household economies that required wives to assist husbands at their trades (rather than the other way around); laws that limited the contractual powers and economic autonomy of women; economic practices that inhibited women's access to capital and credit; local and national governments that sought to control brewsters through their husbands; and ideological presumptions that made it difficult for brewsters to establish themselves as reliable and trustworthy tradespeople. These factors affected some women differently from others, but they affected all women to some extent. These factors shaped the lives of men as well, but they constrained most women more than most men. And these factors grew from fundamental institutions of English life at the time, patriarchal institutions that were nevertheless much more than mechanisms for the subordination of women. I use "patriarchal institutions" advisedly, defining institutions as "any organized element of a society" and applying "patriarchal" to any such elements that reinforced male power, *in part*.[63]

The lives of English brewsters were shaped, in short, by a patriarchal equilibrium. Brewsters faced a host of institutions that worked, at least in part, to subordinate women to men. As a result, changes which undermined the force of patriarchy in one sector were subtly countered by responses in other sectors. The expanding brewing trade of late medieval England posed a real threat to the patriarchal order: women controlled a trade that was suddenly becoming very profitable. Yet this possibility of female advance in the economic sphere was met by strong responses from other patriarchal institutions. Representations of brewsters in poems, plays, and other media began to emphasize the filthiness and untrustworthiness of brewsters; civic officers started to worry about how women were a disruptive force in the trade; new regulations sought to proscribe not-married women from the brewing trade so that married men could be supported by it; and the traditional authority of husbands over their wives began to assert itself in new ways. Put more abstractly, what happened is this: an economic change that might have advantaged women was countered effectively by responses rooted in ideology, law, politics, and family.

What was—and remains—particularly confounding about this patriarchal equilibrium was that none of these institutions existed solely to keep women in their place or acted self-consciously in tandem with others to keep women in their place. Indeed, each had advantages that could appeal to women as well as men. Guilds were not formed with the explicit intention of excluding women from skilled trades; family structures were not designed solely to subordinate women to male householders; and the laws that limited the economic opportunities of women were not written just to keep women poor. For a woman, these institutions could offer good as well as bad. A guild might have solidified male privilege, but it also offered solidarity with other brewers, better bargaining with city officers, and protection for those who fell on hard times. All of these could benefit brewsters as well as male brewers, and if male privilege was part of the package, it might have seemed to some brewsters an amorphous, ancillary, or even unimportant part. In a sense, patriarchy was an effect of many institutions in late medieval England, but it was neither the sole effect nor sole intention of any one.

The circumstances of brewsters were made even more disconcerting by the different strategies that guilds and other institutions adopted to maintain male advantage and female disadvantage. *Exclusion* was a powerful weapon of patriarchy. Brewsters were excluded from the regulation of their trade, excluded from many guilds, and excluded sometimes from the trade altogether. *Segregation* also worked effectively to limit brewsters. Women belonged to the London guild in the early fifteenth century but were not full members; women brewed ale more readily than beer (ale was much less profitable than beer); women fell from brewing ale into selling ale brewed by others, but not out of the trade altogether. And the strategy of *division*—divide and conquer—might have been particularly powerful. Patriarchal adjustments to the changing profitability of brewing—regulations proscribing brewing by singlewomen, or the establishment of guilds for husbands of married brewsters, or the development of depictions of brewsters as foul and filthy workers—might have been especially effective because they harmed some brewsters more than others and thereby impeded common identification and, possibly, common action. These varied strategies meant that brewsters faced not only many adaptable patriarchal institutions but also a variety of ways whereby they were disempowered within them.

By looking at brewsters in a new way that saw continuities in the midst of change, I was able to observe some critical aspects of patriarchal power in England during these centuries: its location in multiple sites; its production as an effect of essential social institutions; its flexibility and endurability; and its powerful strategic use of exclusion, segregation, and division. The best way I have found to describe what might have happened to brewsters is with a metaphor of ballroom dancing: a dance where women and men—many different sorts of women and men—move across the room, alter their steps, movements and rhythms, even change partners or groups, but *always the men are leading.* In this patriarchal dance, there has been much change in women's lives, but little transformation in women's status in relation to men. If we are willing to see other aspects of women's past in this way, we will find more new histories to be written, histories that trace changes in women's lives without resort to narratives of transformation, histories that seek to problematize continuity, and histories that grapple with the challenge of understanding patriarchy.

Historicizing Patriarchy

As we saw in Chapter 2, historians of women have most recently dwelt on integrating women into the discourses of traditional historical fields, examining discourses of gender, and unpacking the intersection of gender with race, class, sexuality, and other differences. Just as feminism is an inherently plural noun, fueled by multiple feminist approaches, so, too, is women's history diverse, varied, and many-voiced. As we saw in Chapter 3, however, the many voices of women's history are speaking predominantly about recent historical eras, lingering with loving attention on the twentieth century and rarely venturing back before 1800. This chapter argues that that lack of historical depth profoundly hinders our ability to trace continuities in women's history. Although I have focused here on how confronting continuity can positively reshape the specific project of historicizing patriarchy, all the main approaches within women's history—integrationist histories, gender analyses, studies of difference, and others—will yield better results if we attend to the distant past and the continuities, as well as changes, that this longer perspective can suggest to us.

I do not believe that history-as-continuity excludes history-as-change, and indeed, my understanding of English brewsters has been informed by both perspectives. But I do believe that we need to hold these two "ways of seeing" in better balance, and to explore more fully than we have yet done the implications of long-term continuities in women's status. A healthy skepticism about narratives of transformation does not require us to abandon all talk of change, transformation, or even progress. Quite the contrary, for this skepticism allows us to replace loose talk about change, transformation, and progress with hard talk about the same. In other words, instead of writing from a gut-level, perhaps even panicked, assumption that we *must* find and explain change, we can ground our discussions of change in firmer, more careful analyses of what is and is not new. We thereby ensure that when we say "change" or "transformation" or "progress," we really mean it. By being more attentive to continuity, in other words, we recognize real change, too. A healthy skepticism about transformation also should not provide us with a reason, as some scholars have suggested, to retreat into studies so detailed and specific that we need not worry about continuity or change.[64] History relies on empirical study, but it is fed by broad overviews and daring generalizations. This is true of all history, but especially women's history. If women's historians are to generate historical perspectives on critical questions of feminist scholarship and activism, we must continue to think in broad—and broadly temporal—ways about continuity and change.

I have suggested here that broad swathes of the past might have been shaped by a dynamic of "patriarchal equilibrium," by patriarchal institutions that have adapted remarkably well to the conflicts, contradictions, and confusions they produce. I hope that more historians of women—not all, but more—will start their work from a consciousness of the need to study in such ways the workings of patriarchy and will return, in the end, to that same consciousness. If some of us make patriarchy (not its origins, but instead its mechanisms, its changes, its endurance) a central problem of women's history, our work will address one of the greatest general problems of all history (the problem of the nature, sustenance, and endurance of power structures), it will eschew gut-level notions of times getting "better" or "worse" for women, and it will grapple with the pressing feminist problem of overall constancy in the (low) status of women. We can also liaise more effectively with feminist colleagues in other disciplines—in anthropology, which has played a central role in exploring the origins of patriarchy; in social and political theory, where current theories of patriarchy are severely limited by lack of historical context; and in law and literature, where so much of the ideological power of patriarchy has been manifested.[65] And by analyzing the nature and causes of women's oppression in the past, we can directly contribute to feminist strategies for the present. The history of women's work, explored in the next chapter, provides one example of this feminist pay-off, for a deep-into-the-past and attentive-to-continuities view of women's work suggests to me that current strategies to achieve gender equality in the workplace—for example, the legislative enforcement of pay equity, or programs such as affirmative action and comparable worth—might prove insufficient to the task.

Chapter 5

Less Money Than a Man Would Take

Women who work in England today share an experience with female wage earners seven centuries ago: they take home only about three-quarters the wages earned by men. In the 1360s, women earned 71 percent of male wages; today, they earn about 75 percent. Of course, no parallel across six centuries can be quite this precise. The medieval figure draws on one particularly detailed list of wages paid to harvest workers in the East Riding of Yorkshire in 1363–64, whereas the contemporary wage gap is estimated from datasets for all of Great Britain in 2002.[1] Medieval wageworkers were paid in food as well as cash, although my comparison is based on cash wages alone.[2] And most important of all, the economic contexts are profoundly different. In 1363, most people took their living from the land, and relatively few worked for wages; today, agriculture has given way to manufacturing and service, almost everyone works for wages, and our economy is shaped, in ways unimaginable to medieval people, by capitalism, industrialism, and globalization. The medieval woman worker was certainly not her modern counterpart, but her wages nevertheless haunt our modern ones: 71 per cent in 1363 . . . 75 percent in 2002.

It is hard to know what to do with such a uncanny similarity because we have been taught to see the past in terms of "us" and "them," with a wide chasm separating the modern West from the world of medieval Europe. This chasm partly reflects real differences—an agrarian medieval Europe and a modern industrial one; a medieval Christendom and a modern plethora of religions; medieval monarchies and modern democracies. It also partly reflects popular assumptions about the horrors of the Middle Ages, commonly misremembered as a thousand years without a bath when humanity "lay dreaming or half awake."[3] And this great divide thrives, in part, because of our own investments in it, for those of us who teach and write about the past collaborate in a story of the making of modernity that perceives the Middle Ages as the sociocultural antithesis to modern life.[4] "Medieval" functions in this story as an inversion of modernity, as a premodern culture and society utterly foreign to the modern world that succeeded it. In such a context, the continuity suggested by wage gaps of 71 percent and 75 percent simply *has* to be nonsensical, more a matter of coincidence than substance.

Women's history has not escaped the grasp of this modernity tale, and it has swung us in two contrary directions. For some—they are sometimes called the "optimists"—women's status is seen as having steadily improved ever since Europeans shrugged off the Middle Ages, woke up, bathed, and stopped grievously oppressing women. "Pessimists" take an opposite view, for they see women's status as plunging with the advent of capitalism, industrialism, and modernity in general. Both sides posit the Middle Ages as antithetically not-modern, but the pessimistic view, influenced by both feminism and socialism and relatively untouched by modernization theory, has long reigned as almost a foundational faith of women's history.[5] For most of the twentieth century, historians of medieval women and modern women agreed, without trespassing too much into each other's periods, that women's lives changed for the worse sometime during the transition from medieval to modern (that is, between 1350 and 1700). Social historians such as Martha Howell and Merry Wiesner argued that sixteenth-century changes limited and disadvantaged women. Urban historians such as Caroline Barron and Jeremy Goldberg posited a brief "golden age" for city women that had disappeared by 1500. Intellectual historians such as Joan Kelly and Margaret King asserted that humanist ideas denigrated and marginalized women in new and nefarious ways. Literary scholars such as Linda Woodbridge, Catherine Belsey, Katharina Wilson, and Elizabeth Makowski traced in literary texts a new reduction of women's options and status. In women's history, when we sang of the advent of modernity in Europe, we sang of crisis and decline.[6]

Our chorus drew on a repetitive tune—an "earworm"—that still hums in the minds of most European historians: medieval apogee in the twelfth and thirteenth centuries; devastating famines and plagues in the fourteenth century, renaissance in the fifteenth century; reformation and exploration in the sixteenth century; capitalism, absolutism, and constitutionalism in the seventeenth century; full modernity in the eighteenth and nineteenth centuries. Between 1350 and 1700, Europe changed from medieval to modern, and as its religions, economics, politics, and social structures changed, so, too, *must* have changed the status of its women. The rhythmic repetition of this tune is explanation enough for its presence in women's history, but feminist historians have accepted it for other reasons, too: because it rested on authoritative works in the field of women's history (especially Alice Clark's study in 1919 of seventeenth-century Englishwomen's work and Joan Kelly's critical reassessment in 1977 of women in the Renaissance); because it suited our presumptions about the evils of our own society and our longings for another world (in this case, premodern) of a kinder and gentler variety; because it fit within the dominant historical tradition, neatly inverting Jacob Burckhardt's history in a feminist rereading of the past (yes, there was a Renaissance, but it was no Renaissance for women); because it accorded well with the influential trajectories of Friedrich Engels's *The Origins of Family, Private Property, and the State* (1884); and because women's history, revolutionary in its subject matter and newly institutionalized, simply could not afford to question the master narrative of modernity.[7]

But question we must, for this narrative is crumbling, and women's history, in any case, has no place for such masters. The authoritative works that once propagated the notion that modernity hurt women—the studies of Clark, Kelly, and Engels—are valued today for their breadth of vision and theory but generally acknowledged to be flawed in matters of detail and analysis. Their model of negative change has eroded under the weight of substantial evidence of continuity in women's experiences across the late medieval and early modern centuries, continuity that belies the paradigmatic assumption of a great transition. One challenge to the model is posed by the wage gap with which this chapter began, a gap that has been wider at some times and sometimes slightly narrower, too, but it has hovered between one-half and three-quarters for many, many centuries. Taking this gap as my cue, I undertake here a case study of change and continuity in one specific aspect of women's history in the transition from medieval to modern—the history of women's work in England between 1350 and 1700. I focus on the English case not only because of my own expertise but also for two further reasons: first, only close study of specific societies can yield the sort of hard-nosed evidence needed to debunk long-cherished assumptions, and second, English archives—and the studies done from them—provide an exceptionally rich field for this work.

In examining Englishwomen's work, I will focus (as have most historians) on women's productive work, setting to one side women's extensive labors in biological and social reproduction. The notion of a dramatic downturn in women's productive work, articulated early in the twentieth century by Clark, remains alluring to both medievalists and early modernists. In the early part of this century, medievalists such as Annie Abram, Marian Dale, and Eileen Power emphasized women's extensive role in the medieval economy, arguing, as Eileen Power put it, that medieval women enjoyed a "rough-and-ready equality" with men.[8] In the decades since, medievalists such as Caroline Barron, Peter Franklin, Jeremy Goldberg, Barbara Hanawalt, Simon Penn, and Kay Lacey have repeated and redrawn this positive assessment of the medieval economy, which they have even been willing, at times, to label as a "golden age" for working women.[9] Early modernists like Susan Cahn, Roberta Hamilton, Bridget Hill, Keith Snell, Michael Roberts, W. Thwaites, and Margaret George have agreed that women's options as workers declined after 1500, although some would date the decline later than others. Objections to this paradigm have been raised, to be sure, but many historians of Englishwomen's work during these centuries still concur with some version of what Susan Cahn once called "woman's descent from paradise."[10]

Marjorie McIntosh's new *Working Women in English Society 1300–1620* exemplifies the enduring presence of this story of decline. She rejects talk of "golden ages" and "paradises" but retains nevertheless a muted version of the old tune. Acknowledging continuity in many aspects of women's work, she also maintains that it became "more difficult for women to engage in profitable economic activities" across the medieval/early modern divide. This pessimistic trajectory pervades an empirically rich book that is, in fact, not structured to analyze such temporal shifts, because the bulk of McIntosh's new archival evidence is available only from very late in the period (1470).[11] Nevertheless, women's worsening work status is the book's familiar backbeat. In a backward glance that clouds her view of medieval women, McIntosh—rightly aware that early modern women were unable to compete in the new, large-scale commercial ventures that were emerging c. 1600 (brewing is one example; moneylending another)—creates medieval businesswomen "of independent authority" in trades and crafts who suffered a "real loss."[12] In a book rich with stories about working women and thick with description, the pessimistic theme provides an analytical frame that operates almost as an article of faith. Medieval women had economic clout; early modern women lost it.

Yet when viewed without the backbeat of emerging modernity, the history of Englishwomen's work between the fourteenth and seventeenth centuries provides exceptionally clear evidence to the contrary. Much changed in England and its economy between 1350 and 1700, but in important ways women's work stood still. In 1350 and again in 1700, in any village or any town, women's work was considered to be less skilled and less valuable than the work of men. ("Skill" is a tricky concept, and I rely here, and throughout, on contemporary standards. I cannot spin, nor can I weave; both strike me as skilled occupations; but to medieval people, the former was unskilled and the latter skilled.) There was no golden age or paradise from which women descended with the advent of modernity; nor was there "real loss" for women as the economy changed; there was, instead, exceptional continuity. This can be seen with particularly clarity in four crucial aspects of women's work in late medieval and early modern England: the work of women within the household economy; the types of work undertaken by women; the involvement of women in guilds; and the wages paid to female workers.

The Household Economy

In almost all histories of women's work, the preindustrial "household economy"—in which household and workplace were merged and family members worked interdependently for the common good—is assumed to have provided medieval women with a relatively egalitarian working relationship with men. Clark formulated the now-classic position in 1919. In her view, women were especially valued in precapitalist households because their work was essential to the success of the collective enterprise. When work became more individualized and removed from the household (a change Clark located in late seventeenth-century England), women's work declined in extent and value. In the time since Clark's book was published, her rosy view of the household economy has been repeated and elaborated by numerous scholars. Within a decade, Power echoed Clark's views in her evocation of a "rough-and-ready equality" in medieval households, and later in the twentieth century, Hanawalt wrote about the economic "partnership" of medieval husbands and wives, Hill described a "working partnership" in eighteenth-century households, and Louise Tilly and Joan Scott argued that women's ability to work was "strongly correlated" with the household economy.[13] Yet in England, at least, the household economy never really offered women anything close to equality with men.

First, on the basis of theory alone, we should treat the household economy with much more caution. We know that households were not natural phenomena; we know that families were not free of conflict and individual interest; we know that the notion of the "common good" is an ideological construct; we know that women's work in *social* reproduction—child rearing and domestic labor—was not biologically ordained; and we nevertheless tend to treat the household economy as the best *natural* venue for women's work.[14] Our essentialist assumptions are betrayed in the very language we use, for scholars often describe as a *family* economy what were essentially *household* economies, places of employment and production as well as reproduction. Households commonly included servants, apprentices, and lodgers, as well as persons related by blood or marriage.[15] When women mingled productive work with child rearing and domestic duties in such households, their work was shaped by marriage patterns, household structures, guild regulations, child rearing customs, household ideologies, and the sexual division of labor, not by nature. As social phenomena, households reflected also the patriarchal authority of men. This was clear to men and doubtless women, too. As Edmund Tilney put it plainly in 1568, "The office of the husband is to bring in the necessaries; of the wife, well to keep them. The office of the husband is to go abroad in matters of profit; of the wife, to tarry at home and see all be well there. The office of the husband is to provide money; of the wife, not wastefully to spend it . . . The office of the husband is to be Lord of all; of the wife, to give account of all."[16]

My second point builds from Tilney's observation: it was quite clear to contemporaries that women took second place to men in the productive functions of the medieval household economy. We should beware of assuming, as some historians have done, that women's extensive, essential work within the household economy is ipso facto evidence of women's empowerment, for we have considerable evidence that women's work—although extensive and essential—was less valued than men's work. Work within the medieval household economy was divided according to sex (as well as age and status), and women's work was generally less specialized, less skilled, and less respected than men's work. In both countryside and town, the work of the household's male head was primary, focused, and central to the household economy; the work of wife and children was secondary, diverse, and supplemental. Married men often worked at a single occupation, publicly recognized as a husbandman, artisan, or merchant. Their wives juggled many tasks at once. The late medieval "Ballad of a Tyrannical Husband," for example, told of a marital squabble over whether husband or wife worked harder. The husband spent his day plowing. The wife spent her day brewing, baking, caring for poultry and animals, making butter and cheese, working wool and flax into cloth, and also watching children, cleaning house, and preparing meals.[17] The multiple tasks of women were recognized in 1363 by legislation that restricted male artisans to one trade but permitted women to follow several.[18] Women's occupational eclecticism strikes me today as awesomely impressive, but it was not the surest route to economic empowerment. Women juggled so many tasks because none sufficed to support them and their families; thus, for example, Matilda Monioun in late fourteenth-century Exeter often brewed and sold ale, sometimes hawked eggs, butter, cheese, or fish, occasionally made woolen cloth, and sometimes profited from receiving stolen goods. As Maryanne Kowaleski has noted, based on her exhaustive study of Exeter, the activities of women like Monioun suggest "not their talents and high work profile but their general inability to secure anything more than marginal, low-paying positions within any trade."[19] Tax lists and censuses for English towns and villages regularly reveal that the labor of husbands was the recognized and defining occupation of their families, and their wives were, in the words of L. F. Salzman, "eternal amateurs."[20]

Third, the distribution of resources within the household economy was just as inequitable as its division of labor. We should beware of assuming that women controlled the value produced by their labor, for women—whether daughters, wives, or widows—clearly did not enjoy equal access to the collective resources of their families. We should also beware of assuming that women—bolstered by an ideology of common interest and common good—were content to take less from their households than did their brothers, sons, and husbands. In most English medieval villages, parents more readily and more generously transferred land to their sons than to their daughters, and when they died, remaining properties were divided according to inheritance laws that similarly favored sons over daughters. In towns, inheritance customs often dispersed goods equally to sons and daughters (at least in theory), but usually sons alone enjoyed the privileges of following their fathers' trades, gaining admittance to their fathers' guilds, and acquiring the freedom of their municipalities via patrimony.[21] The effects of these legal and customary prescriptions were very real. As Richard Smith has noted in his study of women's land tenure in seven medieval manors, daughters rarely acquired land when parents died, either through deathbed transfers (where parents displayed a "noticeable reluctance" to give land to daughters) or by inheritance claims (where daughters actually acquired land less frequently than they theoretically might have done).[22] In fourteenth-century Winchester, heiresses accounted for only about one in ten property holders.[23] In fifteenth-century Southampton, daughters inherited household goods while their brothers got stock, tools, and property; women accounted for less than 15 percent of individual property owners in 1454.[24]

Once married, a woman experienced even more sharply the economic inequalities of the household economy. Medieval women gained many advantages by marriage: a new wife partook of her husband's greater earning power, and more likely than not, his greater assets in land and goods, too; she assumed the socially approved roles of wife and, in most cases, mother; she acquired a sexual and personal companion; and she could hope for the genuine pleasures of a good marriage, a well-run household, and a happy family. But in English law and custom, a husband enjoyed extensive authority over all familial resources (including properties brought to the marriage by his wife or given explicitly by others to her). The condition of the married women, the *femme couverte* in common law, was a condition of public invisibility, especially in economic matters. As one late twelfth-century legal commentator put it, "since legally a woman is completely in the power of her husband . . . her dower and all her other property are clearly deemed to be at his disposal."[25]

There was some gray area in the law, especially as regarded lands that a wife could claim once widowed (that is, either her dower lands or lands she had inherited). In law, husbands could alienate such lands freely, but by 1300 it was becoming common, in both common law and customary law, for wives to add their consent to their husbands' sales of such lands; the end result was not greater control of resources by wives but instead greater security-of-title for those who purchased or otherwise acquired such properties.[26] The pressure on wives to consent to such sales could be immense; one case from 1289 tells us of a wife who consented "crying in court" (*lacrimentem in pleno halimoto*).[27] In most cases, a wife's assets were so absolutely her husband's that they were forfeited if *he* misbehaved. Thus, for example, when the lords of Pelham in Sussex wished to punish Henry Clifford in the 1440s for his "various offenses, trespasses, and rebellions," they confiscated sixty acres that his wife Joan had inherited from her wheelwright father.[28] As a new wife, a woman customarily brought critical resources to the household economy created by her marriage, and in the years that followed, her labor would critically support it, but the household's resources belonged, in the final analysis, to her husband alone. Any wife could find, as did Quena at Cross who went to the court of Brigstock in 1315, that she could not sell land without her husband's cooperation because, as the court put it, "a wife's sale is nothing in the absence of her husband."[29]

One legal loophole eased the couverture of wives in England, but only for a few. In London and some other towns, married women were permitted, if formally registered as *femmes soles*, to trade independently of their husbands—that is, to trade as if they were unmarried (*sole*). *Femme sole* status did not alter the household economy per se because, although it allowed wives to work independently, it so separated a wife's work from the household headed by her husband that she could not draw on its assets. A wife who traded as a *femme sole*, therefore, had some autonomy, but since her capital and assets were limited, she doubtless found it difficult to compete effectively with married men who were supported by the labor of wives and children; she also might have been disadvantaged in relation to singlewomen and widows, as they were relatively more free of family responsibilities. Moreover, the actual effects of this custom are hard to assess. It was confined to urban areas and, indeed, to only some urban areas; towns such as Shrewsbury and Salisbury apparently offered no such option to married women.[30] It was applied inconsistently and messily in courts; in London, for example, some records show wives, designated as *femmes soles*, nevertheless acting in concert with their husbands (acting, in other words, as *femmes couvertes*). It was not universally welcomed by women, for some wives clearly chose not to acquire *femme sole* status. And, finally, it seems to have been most important as a means not of freeing women from the legal coverage of marriage but instead of freeing husbands from the debts of their wives. The custom seems primarily to have benefited men.[31]

Even at the time of death, the distribution of resources within the household economy was inequitable. The situation was strikingly different for men and women. Bereaved husbands usually retained full control of all household resources, for the death of a wife usually did not precipitate dissolution of the household economy. Bereaved wives, however, faced a much more difficult situation, for the death of a husband effectively dissolved the household economy; his death, not hers, was the impetus for resources to be dispersed, at least in part, to the next generation. In a few localities, widows were able to claim full control of household resources, but most were able to retain only one-half or one-third. The customs of London were more generous than those of many towns, but even there, a new widow could claim only the following: (a) the marital house for as long as she lived or until she remarried, (b) one-third of the land and tenements of the household, and (c) one-third of the household's movable goods and chattels.[32] Worse yet, there was a difference between claiming a widow's portion and actually getting it, as heirs, creditors, and others commonly obstructed, delayed, and frustrated widows' rights. This was so common that London courts developed a special "writ of dower" whereby widows could sue to recover withheld properties. Only about half such suits were even partly successful.[33] London's customs were not everywhere emulated, but the fundamental premise—that the household economy remained intact if a wife died but dissolved with a husband's death—never wavered, and many new widows therefore faced not only bereavement but also impoverishment.[34]

Some parents, of course, generously provided for their daughters as well as their sons, some husbands went to court to give their wives joint title to household properties, and some widows acceded fully to their husbands' workshops and goods.[35] But such mitigation was not the rule, and, to paraphrase John Stuart Mill, we should judge the household economy not by the behavior of good men (who often ease the force of patriarchal institutions) but rather by the behavior of bad men (who often exploit such institutions to their fullest extent).[36] Hence, we cannot ignore the fact that medieval English laws and customs permitted husbands to deny their wives control over both their capital resources and their labor. With a good husband and a happy marriage, a woman could achieve a satisfying working life. But such personal egalitarianism—when or even if it existed—was shadowed by inequality, for the husband's power remained in reserve, not fully yielded. With an indifferent husband or an abusive marriage, a woman could find herself a sort of servant to her husband or even cast aside altogether. We can rarely glimpse such miseries in medieval sources, but ecclesiastical courts—a recourse only for women of some wealth—offer a few examples. There, such women as Matilda Trippes of the Canterbury diocese in 1373 had to seek court orders to force their husbands to provide them with the basic necessities of life.[37] In both conceptualization and practice, the household economy was the *husband's* household economy.

The household economy, then, was never a site of rough and ready equality for women; instead, it was shot through with sexual inequality—from its basis as a social foundation of a patriarchal society, to its sexual division of household labor and its inequitable distribution of material resources. Hence, although historians have repeatedly described the household economy as a "partnership" of husband and wife, this description masks practical inequality beneath a rhetoric of mutuality; we tend to interpret "partners" as equals (as in "domestic partnerships"), but only if we understand partnerships as unequal—as containing both senior and junior partners—can the word be properly applied to medieval households. Daughters worked as hard as sons, but they took much less than their brothers from their household economies; wives worked as hard as their husbands, but their tasks were ancillary and their control of family wealth was strictly abrogated; widows worked as hard as widowers, but they alone faced massive insecurity, as their household resources began to be dispersed to the next generation. Most medieval women lived and worked within some variation of a household economy, but at every point in their lives, final control over the resources of that household economy rested in the hands of men.[38] For women, the medieval household economy was not an egalitarian refuge that capitalism and industrialism somehow cruelly undermined.

Female Occupations

Nor was the broader economy a refuge for medieval women. In England, "women's work" was limited, modest, and remarkably stable across the transition from a medieval economy to a modern one. Comparisons of women's occupations across the centuries are difficult to draw: extant sources vary widely; occupational designations shifted; and of course, economic contexts also changed. Let me compare, however, two unusual "snapshots" of women's occupations, one from the late fourteenth century and another three centuries later.[39] Because the fourteenth-century data apply to singlewomen and widows only, I will focus on this subset of women in both times. My first snapshot is drawn from the 1381 poll tax for the London suburb of Southwark; my second from Peter Earle's tabulations for all of London (including Southwark) between 1695 and 1725. Table 4 matches as closely as possible the occupations of the late fourteenth century to the broad categories used by Earle for the early eighteenth century.

A comparison of this nature is fraught with difficulty. Are fourteenth-century servants fully comparable to domestic servants in 1700? Can a fourteenth-century suburb (and a poor suburb, at that) be fairly compared to a seventeenth-century metropolis? Should glovers and girdlers be regrouped with manufacturers? Yet if we pass over these conundrums and look at general patterns, some striking similarities emerge. First, note the basic stability in the occupational structure. Some occupations attracted remarkably similar proportions of single female workers—especially domestic service, but also laundering, making clothes, and victualing. Others varied, but in ways that suggest either changing economic structures in the London region (for example, the decline in textile manufacture) or problems of categorization (for example, shopkeeping, as opposed to hawking and carrying). Second, consider that most not-married women—in 1381

TABLE 4. NOT-MARRIED WOMEN'S WORK IN LONDON AND VICINITY, 1381 AND
C. 1700

Earle's occupational categories	London women, 1695–1725	Southwark women, 1381	Categorization of Southwark occupations in 1381
Domestic service	39.8%	38.0%	Servants: 62
Making/mending clothes	17.9%	12.3%	Dressmakers: 11
			Tailors: 4
			Cappers: 2
			Girdler: 1
			Lacemaker: 1
			Glover: 1
Nursing/medicine	8.4%	1.2%	Midwife: 1
			Barber: 1
Charring/laundry	7.0%	3.7%	Washerwomen: 6
Shopkeeping	7.8%	1.8%	Upholdsters: 3
Catering/victualing	5.9%	8.0%	Brewers: 3
			Cooks: 2
			Ostlers: 2
			Tapsters: 2
			Baker: 1
			Garlicmonger: 1
			Fisherman: 1
			Fruitier: 1
Hawking/carrying	4.5%	13.5%	Hucksters: 21
			Fishbearer: 1
Textile manufacture	3.6%	17.2%	Spinsters: 24
			Kempsters: 2
			Dyer: 1
			Fuller: 1
Misc. services	2.8%	0.6%	Gardener: 1
Misc. manufacture	1.7%	3.7%	Skinners: 3
			Shoemaker: 1
			Saddler: 1
			Carpenter: 1
Hard labor/day work	0.6%	0%	

Sources: The National Archives, PRO, E179 184/30, and Peter Earle, "The Female
Labor Market in London in the Late Seventeenth and Early Eighteenth Centuries,"
Economic History Review, 2nd ser., 42 (1989), 328–53.
Note: I have excluded not-married women in the 1381 poll tax whose occupations were
not specified.

as well as 1700—worked in either service or the textile and clothing trades. In both 1381 and 1700, two of every five women found employment in service and a third worked in textile or clothing man-ufacturing. Third, note the absence of certain high-status and high-income occupations in both periods. In neither 1381 nor 1700 were singlewomen and widows able to find employment in long-distance trade, professional occupations, or civil service.[40]

These data, difficult as they are to compare across the centuries, present two further interpretive challenges. First, they report on the occupations of only never-married or widowed women. What about married women? When wives sought to supplement their household economies with paid labor, they found employment in the same occu-pations as not-married women (with the important exception of domestic service, which often required residence at the place of employment). In late fourteenth-century Howdenshire, for example, poll tax assessors took the unusual step of recording the occupations of many wives, and their lists show that married women most fre-quently worked in victualing, especially brewing. In Bristol in the 1530s, the main nondomestic trade of wives was the making or mend-ing of clothes.[41] In late seventeenth-century London, Earle's figures show that wives worked most frequently in clothing manufacture, charring and laundering, victualing, and nursing.[42] With the excep-tion of domestic service, wives differed from singlewomen and widows not in the occupations they pursued as much as in the more intermit-tent nature of their work; wives, even more than women of other mar-ital statuses, were eternal amateurs.[43]

Second, these data report only on the experiences of women in London and its suburbs, atypical places in the fourteenth century as well as the seventeenth century. What about women elsewhere in England? Information from other localities—such as Oxford, Bristol, Exeter, and Howdenshire—suggests the same trends: more women worked in service than in any other sector of the economy; after ser-vice, textiles and clothing manufacturing attracted considerable num-bers of women; very few women worked in high-status trades or occupations; and most of these few were widows wrapping up their husbands' businesses.[44] In this sense, it is quite misleading to state, as one medieval historian has done, that women's occupations consti-tuted the "medieval equivalent of the Yellow Pages."[45] Most women found work in very limited sectors of the economy, and they were con-spicuously absent from a large number of high-status occupations.

Moreover, wherever women worked—whether as domestic ser-vants, seamstresses, launderers, or brewsters—their "women's work" had certain defining characteristics. It tended to be low-skilled; it usually yielded low remuneration in terms of either wages or profits; it was regarded with low esteem; it was work that combined easily with a wide variety of other tasks or remunerative work. These characteristics are numbingly echoed in studies of women's work in medieval and early modern England: in my study of early fourteenth-century Brigstock; in Maryanne Kowaleski's study of late fourteenth-century Exeter; in Diane Hutton's study of Shrewsbury in the same century; in P. J. P. Goldberg's study of fifteenth-century York; in Sue Wright's study of early modern Salisbury; in Mary Prior's study of early modern Oxford; in Jane Whittle's study of rural women's work between 1450 and 1650; in Peter Earle's study of London c. 1700.[46] No matter what the actual occupations of women, they tended to work in low-skilled, low-status, low-paid jobs, and they also tended to be intermittent workers, jumping from job to job or juggling several tasks at once. This was true in 1350; it remained true in 1700. And, although this stretches beyond my chronological scope, it was true in 1850, too.[47]

Guilds

Guilds have seemed to promise the best chance of finding medieval Englishwomen engaged in high-status, well-remunerated work. The term "guild" had wide uses in the Middle Ages and was applied to many sorts of associations, religious and political, as well as economic; I will here focus on craft and trade guilds, also known as *mysteries* or *artes* or *métiers*. Women's access to guilds and guild-supervised work has been a keystone of descriptions of a great transition between medieval times (when such access was supposedly extensive) and modern times (when access supposedly waned). Guilds wield little clout in the cities of today's European Union, but they were once central to urban life. By forming guilds, people engaged in the same trade or craft—that is, all wool merchants, all shoemakers, or all butchers—cooperated with each other to their mutual economic, social, and religious benefit. As a rule, only skilled workers organized guilds, and they were thus able to enjoy monopolistic control over their specialty, since only members could, in theory, engage in the trade or craft supervised by that guild.

Although guilds included all members of a trade or craft, they were not egalitarian. Only the *masters* of a guild could maintain workshops, hire apprentices and other workers, and participate in guild politics and decisions. Women were sometimes guild *mistresses*, but most mistresses acceded to this role as widows and never, as we will see, wielded powers equivalent to those of masters. Subject to the control of masters (and sometimes mistresses) were two tiers of workers: trained wageworkers called *journeymen* or *journeywomen*, and *apprentices* indentured to be trained by a master (or mistress) for a set period of years. The main purpose of merchant or craft guilds was economic (they provided training for apprentices, regulated wages, set prices, and stipulated trade practices and quality), but they also took on social functions (such as sponsoring annual feasts), pursued pious activities (burying the dead and participating in religious festivities), distributed charity (especially by caring for the families of dead members), and accrued political clout (guild membership was often a prerequisite to civic enfranchisement). Guilds wielded all these powers in many European cities for centuries; merchant guilds were organized first, usually in the twelfth and thirteenth centuries, and craft guilds followed, usually within a few generations. In English cities and towns, guilds flourished from the thirteenth through the seventeenth centuries and in some cases survive even today, mainly as social institutions.[48]

In a movement so widespread, diversity was the rule—among guilds, between cities and regions, and, of course, over time. This diversity makes it difficult to generalize about the complex and varied story of women's relationships to this important form of urban association.[49] Yet it is fair to say that two contrary pressures shaped women's place in guilds. On the one hand, the exigencies of the household economy required some accommodation of women within guilds. Most crafts and trades in medieval English towns operated out of household workshops in which materials were processed, goods were produced, and commodities were sold. Because women's work was a critical part of these household workshops, guilds often had to recognize women in some way. On the other hand, guilds fostered companionship and protected privilege, creating what Sheilagh Ogilvie has recently characterized as a form of "social capital."[50] This companionship and privilege was largely a male prerogative, for it was mostly men who feasted and drank together, wore common guild livery at public functions, benefited from guild charity, controlled guild governance, received training under guild aegis, and profited from guild monopolies. Balancing these two pressures, guilds from their earliest days both accommodated women and restricted them.

This balancing act was continuous and delicate, but it has been flattened in many histories of women's work into a single tilt of the scales across the centuries—that is, into an argument that women once enjoyed a good access to guilds that slowly declined after 1500.

As Bridget Hill put it in 1993, "From the late fifteenth century urban guilds began systematically to attack women as workers either by marginalizing their participation in guilds or by totally excluding them, by carefully defining the restricted area of work in which women were allowed, and by barring women from entry to certain trades."[51] Other historians have described "gradual exclusion," "mounting restrictions," "the ouster of women," and even an "onslaught."[52] Claims such as these are supported by five buttresses—ordinances that excluded women, evidence about female apprenticeships, mentions of the "sisters" of guilds, the presence of widowed mistresses within guilds, and the existence of some exclusively female guilds. All have crumbling foundations.

It is an easy matter to cite ordinances that excluded women from guild-supervised work, but the newness and effectiveness of such ordinances is more a matter of opinion than hard proof. Since, for example, the weavers guild of Bristol in 1461 ordered its members not to employ their wives, daughters, or female servants in weaving, then, as the thinking goes, those wives, daughters, and female servants *must* have been doing such work before 1461 and were *not* doing it thereafter.[53] Yet guild ordinances of this sort provide iffy evidence of decline. First, proclamations restricting women's work in guilds can be found in every century between 1300 and 1700 (and beyond), so they might indicate more an ongoing antipathy toward women's continuing work than any new development. Second, like all ordinances, these reflect more intent than effect; indeed, one reason why ordinances repeat over many centuries might be that they so inadequately regulated women's informal work in guild-supervised trades. Third, these ordinances especially seem to proliferate in later centuries simply because more records are extant for later periods; in other words, their greater numbers after 1500 are, at least in part, an archival artifact. And fourth, as several historians have noted, at least some of these ordinances seem to address short-term responses to economic crises and cannot, therefore, be placed within any story of long-term decline in female work.[54]

It is also often claimed that female apprenticeships—and hence, the ability of young women to pursue a professional life under guild aegis—declined with modernity. The argument rests largely on numbers. Caroline Barron has suggested that in medieval London "there were quite large numbers of unmarried girl apprentices" and that these numbers are a stark contrast to the late sixteenth century when "among 8000 apprentice enrollments not one was a woman."[55] But, in fact, we know about relatively few female apprentices in late medieval London and relatively more later. Indeed, if we relied on numbers alone (which we should not), we would see expansion rather than contraction: Stephanie Hovland has the best figures for the later Middle Ages; working with the mayor's court of London, she found five female apprentices between 1300 and 1350, sixteen between 1351 and 1400, and twenty-three from 1401 to 1450. Compare these figures to what Nancy Adamson found in the apprentice lists of the twelve great companies for Elizabethan London: seventy-three female apprentices.[56]

The significance of numbers like these lies not in any trends they might show but instead in the impossibility of arguing from them. In this instance, as in so many others, the incomparability of records is a problem that plagues numerical comparisons across the medieval-modern divide: numbers derived from the mayor's court simply tell a different story from numbers derived from guild records. Another problem arises from different or incomplete sampling. In contrast to Adamson, Vivien Brodsky Elliott found no female apprentices in the records of fifteen London companies between 1570 and 1640, and her negative finding is often cited, by Barron and others.[57] Either Elliott's companies must not have encompassed the twelve examined by Adamson or she missed what Adamson found, especially in the records of the Haberdashers.[58] A third problem is simply one of scale: documented female apprenticeships in London are so few and far between—five here, nineteen there—that statistically significant conclusions cannot be derived from them. And a fourth problem rests in substantive changes that numbers can obscure. In some times and places, "apprenticeship" for girls was a system of fostering poor female orphans, not a system of craft training; as a result, rises and falls in numbers of female apprentices can sometimes tell us more about orphans and poor relief than about women in guilds. As Derek Keene has noted, even as early as the fourteenth century "it is possible that with women apprenticeship served more as a means of retaining cheap and relatively unskilled labour than as a way of passing on skill."[59]

The numbers do tell us one thing, however: in both medieval and early modern London, girls were *occasionally* apprenticed, but boys were *regularly* apprenticed. Moreover, what we know of the experiences of those relatively few female apprentices before 1500 does not encourage optimistic interpretations. Hovland has recently shown that female apprenticeship in late medieval London followed similar legal forms but was otherwise distinctive from male apprenticeship: many fewer girls were apprenticed (perhaps one girl for every ten boys); girls were apprenticed mostly in textile crafts in which "the end-product was not necessarily managed by the producer"; and no female apprentice is known to have taken up the City's freedom at the end of her term, although this was common for males.[60] What Hovland found in London is generally true elsewhere in England and, indeed, on the Continent. Unmarried girls were sometimes apprenticed under guild aegis, but their numbers were exceedingly modest compared with those of men; they tended to predominate in textile trades; and the end of their apprenticeships did not lead to guild or civic enfranchisement. Apprenticeship—whether in medieval or early modern towns—seldom entailed for women what it offered for men; it was rarely a route to recognized status as a skilled artisan.

Guild references to "brothers and sisters" have also led historians to assume that the structures of guilds were sexually egalitarian. As Lucy Toulmin Smith put it in the introduction to her edition of guild records, "Scarcely five out of five hundred were not formed equally of men and of women."[61] References to "brothers and sisters" are not quite as common as this, and they especially proliferate in parish guilds, organizations that were devoted to piety, not trade or craft.[62] In distinct and perhaps telling contrast to parish guilds, the records of craft guilds refer more often to brothers only. Moreover, the presence of sisters in a guild's records is not an automatic sign of sexual egalitarianism. I have examined the relative roles of women and men in one such medieval guild, the Brewers' guild of London, during the three decades (1418–38) when a clerk kept exceptionally detailed records about the guild's personnel and business.[63] At the time, most London guilds tolerated no sisters at all; this was true of the Grocers in 1383, the Coopers in 1439–40, and the Weavers in 1456.[64] The Brewers seem to have forthrightly welcomed women, who constituted one-third of the guild's membership from 1418 to 1425. Many women—both brewsters who produced ale and hucksters who sold it—opted not to belong to the guild, but significant numbers of sisters paid twelve pence annually, just as did brothers.

Nevertheless, the sisters of the Brewers' guild were not like its brothers. Most sisters joined the guild because they were married to guildsmen; they attended guild feasts and other communal occasions in reduced numbers; few wore the livery of the guild, the hoods or gowns worn by nearly all male members at funerals, guild functions, and civic events; and none at all participated in the governance of the guild. All told, the sisters of the Brewers' guild were in the guild but not fully part of it; they might best be described as *working* members rather than *corporate* members. Participating in reduced numbers in some aspects of guild life and fully excluded from others, these Brewers' sisters represent a best-case scenario for women in late medieval guilds; after all, their guild was one of the few in London to accommodate sisters at all. In this relatively open circumstance, women associated with the guild to the extent necessary to follow their trade, but they did not fully partake of the rituals and customs through which the guild defined and asserted its collective identity. This best-case scenario reveals, then, the practical limits of what it could mean to be a guild sister.[65]

What, then, about widows, who enjoyed the most extensive guild privileges of all women? In the interest of maintaining the workshop of a deceased guildsman, guilds often allowed widows to supervise workshops, employ apprentices and other workers, and participate in selected religious and social activities. In many guilds, in fact, the *only* female members—the only "sisters"—were widows. But even widows were restricted members of guilds. As Keene's study of tanners' widows in London before 1350 clearly shows, widows rarely maintained their husbands' businesses for long, and they were primarily viewed as "vessels for the transmission of resources from one generation of male practitioners of the craft to the next."[66] This was the intent of their dying husbands, as expressed in their wills, and it was guild policy, too. Widows were not enfranchised within guilds; they customarily did not participate fully in guild society and ceremony; they could sometimes lose their privileges on remarriage; and their numbers within guilds were always small.[67]

The resolute maleness of guilds was ameliorated by a few guilds for women alone. Most women's work was considered either too low-skilled or too low-status to merit a guild, so the majority of urban women—who worked as domestic servants, petty retailers, spinsters, prostitutes, and the like—were never recognized as skilled, much less organized into guilds.[68] Of the few women's occupations that were then considered to be skilled, most failed to organize into guilds. Medieval midwives apparently never tried to organize themselves or even develop a licensing system; eventually, civic authorities imposed organization on them.[69] The female silkworkers of medieval London were both skilled and numerous, but they, too, never formally organized; by the time a guild finally took shape in the seventeenth century, the craft was controlled by men.[70] But a few exceptional female guilds existed in Rouen, Paris, Cologne, and Nördlingen. All these female guilds supervised textile work, such as silk spinning, ribbon making, embroidering, and fashioning women's clothes. In these guilds, women exercised considerable economic competence: they maintained craft secrets, trained apprentices, determined prices and quality, hired journeywomen, and guarded their monopolistic privileges. To some extent, their "powers over their craft were real."[71] Yet almost all these female guilds were subjected to exceptional external supervision, usually by men who served as governors. In any case, these female guilds were exceptional, indeed rare; none have been found, for example, in medieval England.[72] And since some female-only guilds flourished well into the eighteenth century, their presence manifestly cannot support a thesis of decline after c. 1500.[73]

Ogilvie has recently commented that "most historians of women's work have in recent years come to a clear-sighted recognition that there was no 'pre-capitalist' golden age within the guild framework." She might be broadly correct, but historians of women nevertheless persist, as Ogilvie's own examples show, in telling a story of "constraints placed on females by early modern guilds."[74] We have, in other words, kept the storyline but made it more subtle: medieval guilds were not golden, but they were still more hospitable to women than guilds after 1500 or so. We need, in my view, to question this narrative more thoroughly. Our evidence suggests neither a massive nor a subtle tilt of the scales against women; it suggests instead that, for guilds, women's labor within the household workshop was in constant tension with the male community at the heart of every guild.

Wages

There is a different sort of tension in my final index of women's work: women's wages across the medieval and modern divide. Although only a minority of women worked for wages during these centuries, the sums they earned provide unusually precise measures of the perceived and real value of women's work. Our very earliest records of remunerated work show clearly that women's work was already poorly valued. In the twelfth and thirteenth centuries, the *famuli* employed on manorial estates were mostly males, and the few tasks designated for females were unskilled and poorly paid. These patterns continued into the fourteenth century and beyond.[75] Medieval England was no promised land for wage-earning women.

But historians have long believed that it was just that, at least in the late fourteenth century when workers were few and wages high, in the wake of the 1348–49 plague which killed at least one-third and possibly as much as one-half of England's population. As long ago as the 1880s, James Thorold Rogers asserted that women's unskilled work "was equally well paid with that of men" during the subsequent golden age of laborers when even unskilled workers could negotiate good wages. In the 1950s, William Beveridge just as confidently pronounced that the "principle of equal pay as between men and women for the same work was . . . accepted and put into practice more than 600 years [ago]." And in the 1980s, Simon Penn concluded from his study of harvesters in the late fourteenth century that "it is clear that whatever the actual task involved, the women were being paid at the same rate as men."[76]

Not so. This appearance of wage equity—from records that show, for example, both women and men receiving 4d. a day for reaping—obscures how wages were differentiated by age and ability as well as sex. Relying less on anecdotal evidence and more on careful quantitative analysis, Sandy Bardsley has recently established that there was, indeed, some sexual parity in late fourteenth-century wages, for "the highest-paid female wage-earners . . . might have sometimes earned as much as the lowest-paid male workers."[77] But she has also shown that a female paid as much as a male was, more often than not, a healthy full-grown woman paid as much as a young boy or a disabled man. Moreover, Bardsley's analysis of an usually detailed wage list for 1363–64 demonstrated that female harvesters earned on average 71 percent of the wages paid to male harvesters. She also found that the labor shortages that followed the devastation of plague in 1348–49, probably did not narrow the wage gap, for women in the 1330s were earning about the same. Nor did the easing of labor shortages by the fifteenth century much alter the wage gap: Mavis Mate and L. R. Poos have found similar ratios in their analyses of data from fifteenth-century Sussex and Essex, respectively.[78] All told, a "convincing case" has now been made that women's wages in late medieval England were about three-quarters the wages paid to men.[79]

Clearly, then, women's wages do not support a tale of medieval "good times" followed by modern "bad times," especially in light of statistics showing a wage gap of 75 percent in 2002. But it would be wrong to think that the wage gap has barely budged between 1400 and 2000. Women's wages have sometimes responded, in limited ways, to market forces. Thus, for example, Penelope Lane's recent figures for the eighteenth century suggest that women were often then paid only one-half the wages of men, although some women received wages in the 75 percent range.[80] It is fair to say, however, that ever since a wage-earning sector emerged in the Middle Ages, the wage gap has fluctuated within a fairly stable range, with women paid about one-half to three-quarters the wages of men: this was true of female laborers in the early fourteenth century; of female harvesters in the early fifteenth century; of female reapers and other workers in the eighteenth century; of female agricultural workers in the nineteenth century; and of women working in the modern wage market.[81] There is little that the economy of a fourteenth-century Westminster manor shares with a Westminster business today, but in both, women's wages fell significantly short of the wages earned by men. Medieval employers were apparently as keen as modern employers to exploit this fact to cut costs. The author of a thirteenth-century treatise on estate management advised hiring a woman for certain tasks because she could be relied on to work "for much less money than a man would take."[82]

This historic wage inequity cannot be rationalized out of existence. Some historians, relying on neoclassical economic theory, are now asserting that women's lower wages reasonably reflected their lower productivity. Joyce Burnette has explained women's lower productivity more in social terms (less education, less skill, poorer nutrition) and John Hatcher more in biological terms (less strength, more family distractions), but both agree that women's lower wages reflect not unfair sex discrimination but simply sex differentiation.[83] In their view, women have rightly earned less because their work has been less valuable to employers. But as Lane has meticulously shown in her recent study, such arguments inadequately account for the wage gap. Lane has analyzed all the arguments that seek to justify the wage gap—that stronger men are more productive than weaker women, that men spend more hours at work than women distracted by domestic duties, that wages paid in kind quite properly give more food to men than to women, and that women are less skilled than men—and she has found each lacking in explanatory power. Lane has thereby demonstrated that women's wages were not market-rate wages but were instead based on an expectation that a woman should earn one-half to three-quarters of a man's wage for the same work. She concludes—and I agree—that women's wages certainly fluctuated in response to labor shortages, occupational alternatives, and other economic forces, but that women were usually paid a wage that relied more on custom than on the market.[84] In women's wages, gender ideologies trump economic forces. As a result, the wage gap, which seems to have a history as old as wage work itself, long antedates modernity.

Qualifications and Implications

In the history of English women's work between 1350 and 1700, then, we may fairly conclude that there was no great divide between a pre-capitalist medieval golden age and a capitalist modern age of growing inactivity and exploitation. This does not mean that the history of women's work in medieval England is a story of "unalloyed gloom and repression."[85] Yes, medieval Englishwomen faced considerable economic obstacles, but most managed to support themselves and their families, many were likely satisfied by helpmeet roles and the social approval they received as "goodwives," and some, fortunate in situation, family, or personality, were even able to prosper. But these circumstances—many obstacles, much coping and satisfaction, some prosperity—seem to have been not much different in 1350 than in 1700. Changes occurred during these centuries, to be sure: the household economy lost its effectiveness in some economic sectors; women left some occupations and took up others; guilds became gen-erally more exclusive; female wage earners competed more or less effectively for good wages; capitalized businesses began to emerge in, for example, brewing and moneylending, and these businesses were run almost exclusively by men. Yet, using the terms I outlined in the preceding chapter, these were, for women, *changes*, not *transforma-tions*.

Many of the changes that occurred were of quite short duration. For example, economic theory, backed by some evidence, suggests that the labor shortages of the decades that followed the Black Death improved the lot of wage-earning women. During the underpopu-lated late fourteenth century, wage differentials between unskilled and skilled laborers narrowed considerably, and since women's work was generally unskilled work, women's wages—together with wages paid unskilled men—gained ground on skilled wages. The wage gap per se did not narrow much or at all, but because unskilled wagework-ers had better bargaining power, women benefited along with men. For another example, many guild ordinances against women's work seem to have been prompted by hard times and to have been enforced, if at all, only briefly. Hence, such ordinances were common in Lon-don during the difficult years of the 1540s; they are rare before and rare thereafter.[86] Changes such as these are important, for, among other things, they indicate both the vulnerability of female workers and the economic usefulness of their occupational adaptability. We need to study shifts such as these in more detail, but we also need to remember that they proved to be ephemeral.

Moreover, even the most positive shifts affected only a small minority of women. Most of our evidence for an improvement in the working opportunities of women after the 1348–49 plague, for example, involves *wage-earning* women or women in *urban* locales. Yet relatively few people (and even fewer women than men) worked for wages in the later Middle Ages, and relatively few people lived in towns and cities.[87] And even in the best of circumstances, only a few women were able to take advantage of the new opportunities that were potentially theirs. For example, Goldberg has argued that women found in early fifteenth-century York an expanding and favorable economy, partly basing his argument on a rise in female admissions to the freedom of the city; he found cause for optimism in the fact that almost half (45 percent) of the women admitted to York's freedom in the later Middle Ages were admitted in the three decades from 1414 to 1444. Fair enough, but few women actually acquired civic enfranchisement between 1414 and 1444: fifty-two women, to be precise, in a population of well over 10,000, and in a city in which literally thousands of men gained the freedom during the same decades and thousands of women still worked in lower-paid female jobs.[88] Even genuine changes sometimes had very limited effect.

Finally, these ephemeral and limited changes must also be placed within a context of enduring continuities in the experiences of women workers. Most women—in 1350 as well as 1700—sought to support themselves and their families through a variety of low-skilled, low-status, and low-paid occupations. In the world of pre-industrial England, all people, men as well as women, worked hard, long, and in difficult circumstances, but the working status of women was consistently lower than that of their brothers and husbands: they received less training, they worked at less desirable tasks, they enjoyed less occupational stability, they had weaker work identities, and they received lower wages.[89] This was as true in the best of times as in the worst of times. We need to collect more information about how women's work and wages shifted within this framework of economic subordination, but the framework remained: there was no transformation.

In one sense, my argument with those who posit a great transition in women's work is a perceptual one. Some scholars look at the "glass" of women's economic activity in late medieval England and see it as half full; I see the same "glass" but it looks half empty to me. Our disagreement is, however, more substantial than this. Scholars who work within a paradigm of great transformation see women's work within an entirely different framework, a framework that best accommodates not small and temporary changes but instead dramatic transformation. This framework makes most historians comfortable, for it fits well with our standard story of a modern Europe that arises, utterly transformed, from the ashes of the Middle Ages. It also suits liberal feminism well, for it implies that a golden age for women—part of the relatively recent past of the West—can be easily recovered in the future without major structural changes. And it suits socialist feminism just as well, for it also suggests that capitalism is the main villain in women's subordination. Within this ever-adaptable framework, the Middle Ages—a time when household economies firmly subordinated women under the authority of their husbands, when women's work was characteristically low-status, low-skilled, and low-paid, when guilds poorly accommodated women workers, and when women worked for wages far below those paid to men—is *mis*remembered as a "golden age," a "paradise," or even just a time of "independent authority" which early modern women "lost."

Medieval women's work was no paradise, nor, for that matter, an inferno; it was instead, in some broad respects, remarkably similar to women's work today. This continuity is one of history's challenges for feminist theorists and activists. In the United States today, the wage gap is about the same as in Britain—that is, women earn about three-quarters the wages of men, although precise ratios vary, especially by region, race, and education level. The main feminist group working on this issue, the National Committee on Pay Equity, begins its historical understanding of the wage gap in a predictably truncated fashion, going no further back than 1932.[90] As a result, NCPE feminists see steady progress, citing on their website an improvement from 59 cents on the dollar earned by men in 1963 to about 76 cents today. If they would look further down the "long cool corridors of the past," NCPE feminists would see their short-term data in a different light.[91] It seems quite possible that U.S. women's wages have improved in recent decades only within the range of fluctuation—a wage gap of one-half to three-fourths—that has long been characteristic of the *longue durée* of European history. Placed inside the frame of a Western patriarchal equilibrium, this looks more like movement within a firm but flexible range than substantive breakthrough.[92] If so, what are the best feminist tactics for narrowing the gap even further so that women's wages move closer to parity? After all, the history I have reviewed here suggests that the wage gap is more a matter of ideology than economics or law. A wage gap that has flourished in manors, guilds, factories, and offices, in monarchies as well as democracies, and in both economic booms and economic busts seems unlikely to yield much ground to the new union policies, new employer guidelines, or new national laws.

Continuity challenges feminist historians as much as it challenges feminist activists. We have seen here how history's seductive tale of the advent of modernity obscures strong and sure continuities in women's work across the centuries. If we look critically at other aspects of women's history—family relations, patterns of marriage and fertility, political participation, religious life, and so on—we will discern similar ties that bind medieval and modern women. The tale of a great divide between that medieval age and this modern world is beguiling, but it is more fiction than fact. As the next chapter shows, unpacking that fiction in women's history does more than yield continuities, for looking into the deep past can help us to see modern times in new ways, too. It will show how the particular challenges of studying lesbians in the Middle Ages has yielded a concept—lesbian-like—that can help explode the heteronormativity of women's history, modern as well as medieval.

Chapter 6

The L-Word in Women's History

In the early 1990s when I first began talking about the L-word in women's history, some people expected me to be speaking about "liberal." With the 2004 debut in the United States of the lesbian soap opera *The L Word*, what was once obscure is now likely much clearer. By "L-word," I mean to evoke the lesbians and lesbianisms that are so often effaced in the writing of women's history. This effacement is a long-standing part of Western culture, which, in the words of Judith Brown, has adopted an "almost active willingness to *dis*believe" in female same-sex love.[1] It is also, alas, a part of feminist scholarship and feminist history. In an article first published in 1977 and much reprinted since, Adrienne Rich urged feminist scholars to cease reading, writing, and teaching from what she later called "a perspective of unexamined heterocentricity."[2] Yet more than a quarter century later, women's history still skips lightly over the presence of lesbians and the possibilities of lesbian experience. The problem is not lesbian history; it is doing just fine, thank you, with conference sessions, articles, and books galore exploring aspects of same-sex love among women in the past. The problem is women's history, within which lesbianism remains a tricky subject and sometimes an unspeakable one. Simply put, women's history has a lesbian problem.

In making this charge, I do not mean to efface the advances of the last few decades. The recent renaissance of lesbian history is an outgrowth, in part, of the safe haven women's history has provided by opening its journals and conferences to work on women's same-sex relations in past times. In 2001–4, the three main English-language women's history journals published a dozen or so articles on lesbians or lesbian-related topics, and at the 2005 meeting of the Berkshire Conference more than two dozen papers did the same; whether this is "enough" or not, I do not know, but it is certainly something.[3] Lesbians *as lesbians*—separated out, segregated, different—have become an accepted and integral part of women's history, readily included, especially when they were in-your-face, well-documented, self-naming lesbians. But—and this is the crux of the problem addressed in this chapter—women's historians regularly overlook lesbian possibilities that are more subtle, obscure, or awkward. Most of us still see the past in heteronormative terms, closeting our thinking by failing to consider that the dead women we study might have been other than heterosexuals, other than wives, mothers, and lovers of men.

This problem—I could, in a spirit of playfulness, call it a lack of "gaydar"—pervades all fields of women's history, including my own. One feminist historian has characterized the lives of medieval nuns as "distorted and unhappy," because she saw them as forced to choose between the joys of heterosexual intercourse and motherhood, on the one hand, and a life of learning and contemplation, on the other. For Gerda Lerner, nuns were to be pitied for giving up the self-evident joys of heterosexual sex and motherhood.[4] Another feminist historian has produced an impassioned history of female monasticism, a history that elides the evidence—as discussed by Ann Matter and others—of intense emotional and homoerotic relations between medieval nuns. For Jo Ann McNamara, the celibacy of medieval nuns seems to have been threatened only by men.[5] And a third feminist historian has written about peasant women in the Middle Ages as if they were all heterosexual maidens, wives, or widows. For myself, when I studied peasant women, the marriage-defined roles of not-yet-wed daughter, married wife, and bereaved widow loomed deceptively large.[6]

These are examples enough, for I wish in this chapter to explore not the problem but instead a solution to it: the concept of "lesbian-like."[7] I came to this solution in a circuitous way, while contemplating the curious fact that gay and lesbian studies, particularly of periods before 1800, abound with insightful analyses of texts produced by the powerful and privileged, but are relatively poor in scholarship about the ordinary lives of average people. Gratified by the rich insights yielded by intellectual, cultural, and literary studies of same-sex love, I aspired to complement these with more complete understandings of the same-sex relations of people who were more real than imagined and more ordinary than extraordinary.[8] For example, I was delighted to read about how medieval theologians conceptualized (or failed to conceptualize) same-sex relations between women; about how medieval nuns might have expressed same-sex desire in their kissing of images of Christ's wound; about how a lesbian character might have lurked in a thirteenth-century romance with a cross-dressed heroine; and about how a fourteenth-century Parisian play explored the meanings of accidental marriage between two women.[9] But I wanted more. I wanted to know about the actual practices and lives of ordinary women—the more than 90 percent of medieval women—who never met a theologian, contemplated Christ's wound, heard a romance, or saw a Parisian play.

I knew from the beginning that my desire for a social history of lesbians, especially medieval ones, was perverse. Before the twentieth century, sexual minorities are hard to find, and they can be traced most often in records of legal or religious persecution, records whose terse, sad entries compete poorly with the rich and illuminating writings of philosophers, monks, diarists, and novelists. Lesbian histories are, of course, even more challenging to construct than the histories of male homosexuals, for even fewer documents tell of past lesbians among either privileged or ordinary folk. Women wrote less; their writings survived less well (Sappho's works are the classic example); and they were less likely than men to come to the attention of civic or religious authorities. For more recent times, it is certainly easier to locate lesbians of ordinary circumstances—think, for example, of the love shared by Addie Brown and Rebecca Primus in late nineteenth-century Hartford (Connecticut) or the culture of lesbian bars in the mid-twentieth-century U.S. cities of Buffalo and San Francisco.[10] But even recent lesbian history abounds with women who were wealthier, better educated, more powerful, and more articulate than most: Anne Lister, Radclyffe Hall, Gertrude Stein, M. Carey Thomas, Eleanor Roosevelt, Rita Mae Brown.

As to medieval lesbians, they are almost impossible to find. We have information about lesbian practices in the writings of theologians and canonists, in some suggestive literary texts, and even in a few artistic representations, but if we want to write about actual women whom extant sources explicitly associate with same-sex genital contact, we have fifteen women for the entire medieval millennium: all but one from the fifteenth century, and all of them either imprisoned, banished, or executed for their activities.[11] This is material for only a *very* modest social history.

I sought to solve this problem by broadening my perspective to include women whose experiences were what I have chosen to call "lesbian-like": women whose lives might have particularly offered opportunities for same-sex love; women who resisted norms of feminine behavior based on heterosexual marriage; women who lived in circumstances that allowed them to nurture and support other women (to paraphrase Blanche Wiesen Cook's famous formulation).[12] I first coined the term "lesbian-like" in a paper presented in 1990; Martha Vicinus adopted it to good effect in an article published in 1994; and it is now being used by such other historians as Alison

Oram and Laura Gowing.[13] Thus far, however, the term has been deployed mostly within lesbian history, and I believe its greatest potential lies within women's history, where it can purge our historical vision of heternormativity and challenge us to acknowledge some past behaviors that are related to modern lesbianism. Today, many historians of women pause at the L-word threshold. We agonize "Was she or wasn't she?" We fret about applying our contemporary term "lesbian" to women long dead. We pause over the difference between sexual identities and sexual acts. "Lesbian-like" can get us over the threshold, out of the master's house, and into possible worlds that we have heretofore seldom been able to see.

Searching for Lesbians

It is no accident that "lesbian-like" has emerged from a quest for *medieval* lesbians, a quest that epitomizes the queer turn in gay and lesbian studies.[14] Responding to the sparse evidence for actual lesbian practices, medievalists have mostly adopted intellectual or cultural approaches, not social history. The intellectual approach has focused on why lesbianism was so underplayed—compared to male homosexuality—in the literatures of the Middle Ages. Most medieval physicians discussed male homosexuality much more fully than lesbianism; most authors of penitentials (handbooks designed to guide priests in assigning penance during confession) either ignored lesbianism or rated it a lesser sin than male homosexuality; and most theologians similarly either overlooked or trivialized same-sex relations between women. To John Boswell, lesbian practice was so relatively untroubling because it left bloodlines undisturbed; since same-sex intimacy between women neither produced bastards nor introduced false heirs into lineages, it was relatively unproblematic.[15] To Jacqueline Murray, the phallocentric sexuality of the Middle Ages best explains its obfuscation of lesbian activity; as long as women-loving women did not use dildoes or other devices that seemingly mimicked penises, their same-sex relations were not seen by many medieval writers as being fully sexual.[16] To Harry Kuster and Raymond Cormier, sperm loom larger than phalluses; Kuster and Cormier suggest that in the "spermatic economy" of medieval understandings of sex, little harm was done in same-sex relations between women, since no sperm was spilled.[17] To Joan Cadden, lesbian invisibility is part of the subordinate place of all women in the Middle Ages; seen as lesser, more passive, and secondary players in reproduction, women were easily overlooked by most physicians and natural philosophers.[18]

These explanations are plausible, intriguing, and not mutually exclusive. But they too often construe a small number of writers as representing broad medieval realities, reconstructing medieval attitudes about same-sex love between women mostly from the ideas of clerics—that is, the most male and most sexually anxious segment of medieval society. The observations and speculations of this clerical minority are certainly impressive, but their worldview too often becomes, in modern interpretations, *the* medieval worldview.[19] I am delighted to know what medieval theologians, canonists, and physicians thought about lesbianism, but their thoughts represent their sex, their education, their class privilege, and their professional contexts, as well as their time. In this sense, I am sympathetic with Catharine MacKinnon's comment that in most histories of sexuality "the silence of the silenced is filled by the speech of those who have it and the fact of the silence is forgotten."[20]

Still, in comparing how medieval theologians, physicians, canonists, and other authors treated male homosexuality and lesbianism, this intellectual approach has usefully delineated differences between elite perceptions of male same-sex relations, on the one hand, and female same-sex relations, on the other. To these medieval writers, same-sex love between women seemed less sexual than male homosexuality; it more often prompted explanations based on purported physical deformities; it was doubly perverse for positing love not only of the *same* sex but also of the *lesser* sex; and if it resulted in marriage resistance, it could be profoundly disruptive.[21] Among these authors, same-sex relations between women and between men in the Middle Ages were not entirely unrelated, but they were certainly distinct. These elite understandings usefully remind us that when a medieval woman had sex with another woman she did so within physical, social, familial, sexual, and gendered contexts quite different from those of a medieval man who had sex with another man.[22]

Literary and cultural scholars have also responded in creative ways to the virtual absence of actual women from the sources of medieval lesbianisms.[23] In their provocative readings of medieval texts, these critics have found homoerotic possibilities not only in the medieval media mentioned earlier but also in the music of the twelfth-century polymath Hildegarde of Bingen; in the piety of the mystic Hadwijch of Brabant; in the admonitions of the anonymous author of *Holy Maidenhead*, a treatise for the guidance of holy virgins; in the ravings of the would-be mystic Margery Kempe; and even in the cross-dressing of Joan of Arc.[24] Although these analyses offer insightful commentaries on how we might better imagine the sexual mentalities of the Middle Ages, even the best of them can give me pause. As literary criticism, these readings reach plausible conclusions, but as guides to social history, they are considerably less convincing.

To begin with, many of these readings draw on mystical texts, texts that were profoundly obscure at the time of their composition and are profoundly hard to interpret today. As Ulrike Wiethaus has suggested, the obscurity of these texts *might* have allowed female mystics to express and still mask same-sex desires.[25] But the obscurity of these texts *might* also encourage modern scholars to read desires into them that would have been foreign to their authors: fascinating readings, in other words, rather than historically plausible ones. Caroline Bynum, whose opinions have considerable authority in studies of mysticism, female spirituality, and conceptions of the body, has resisted lesbian readings of such texts, arguing that we too readily sexualize medieval somatic experiences and expressions. Others, such as Karma Lochrie, vehemently disagree, arguing that Bynum resolutely sees maternity where same-sex affections might, in fact, have been at play.[26] The debate on this issue has only just begun, but in the meantime, those who are, like myself, interested in actual people and plausible behaviors might best respond with caution to literary readings of same-sex expressions in mystical texts.

In other cases, I have been more impressed by the cleverness of modern critics than I am by the historicity of their arguments. It is great fun, for example, to read Lochrie's impressive exploration of the artistic, literary, and linguistic ties between Christ's wound and female genitalia, and to speculate, therefore, that the kissing of images of Christ's wound by medieval nuns somehow paralleled lesbian oral sex. Even Lochrie, however, does not claim that any medieval nun who contemplated Christ's wound ever, in fact, was really thinking about the last night's tumble in bed with a sister nun.[27] Within the traditions of literary scholarship, readings such as Lochrie's can stand on their own, properly appreciated for their careful and insightful explication of interpretive possibilities. These readings also have a power of their own, helping us to explode medieval taxonomies that might have obscured or overlooked relationships between women.[28] Yet they speak less directly about the historical issues that concern me—about the possibilities of same-sex love between actual women in the Middle Ages.

"Lesbian-like" seeks to move beyond elite understandings of lesbian relations and intriguing but not fully historicized readings that interrupt, redirect, or even queer canonical texts. In complementing these intellectual and cultural approaches with social historical study, it also replaces paucity—the brief notices of the fifteen women who found themselves in legal trouble for same-sex relations in the Middle Ages—with plentitude. What lesbian-like does for medieval women's history, it can do for women's history more broadly, too. There might always be only a few women in past eras for whom we can be reasonably confident about same-sex genital contact, but these need not be the only women whose stories are relevant to lesbian history, and relevant, as well, to a women's history that is more open to lesbian possibilities.

Lesbian-Like

It may seem crazy to create yet another piece of jargon and to link to it a troubled term like "lesbian." After all, no one today is really sure what "lesbian" means. Are lesbians born or made? Do lesbians delight in sex with women only or can the term encompass those who enjoy sex with men as well as women? What defines lesbian sex— genital contact, "bosom sex," or an even more amorphous "erotic in female terms"?[29] And, indeed, might sexual practice be less determinative of lesbianism than *desire* for women, *primary love* for women (as in "woman-identified woman"), or even *political* commitment to women (especially as manifested in resistance to "compulsory heterosexuality")? Lesbian theorists offer us debate on these questions, not firm agreement, and this definitional fluidity has been a source of both anxiety and flexibility.

Nevertheless, the ever-changing contemporary meanings of "lesbian" have often been belied by a persistent assumption of a core lesbian identity, especially when used in such expressions as "she came out as a lesbian." This invocation of identity is both affirming and embarrassing. To me, it still speaks powerfully about the revelation of self I felt when I first had sex with another woman in 1973, but it also now seems unduly naive, simple, and maybe even silly. Still worse, it can work to obfuscate critical differences. Do various sorts of women who love women—femmes and butches, lesbian feminists and lipstick lesbians, vanilla lesbians and sexual radicals, American lesbians and Jamaican lesbians, rich lesbians and poor ones, fifteen-year-old lesbians and fifty-five-year-old lesbians, African American lesbians and Asian American lesbians, and perhaps most challenging of all, transgender lesbians—really share enough to fit comfortably under the rubric "lesbian"?

These are troubles enough, but, for historians, "lesbian" is also troubled by its apparent contemporaneity. To many scholars, the use of "lesbian" to describe women before the late nineteenth century reeks of ahistoricism, and especially of the naive search for past heroines plucked out of historical context and reclaimed for contemporary uses. For some (mostly premodernists), it is important to preserve the past from present concerns. For others (mostly modernists), it is important to preserve the distinctiveness of modernity, especially as represented by a pseudo-Foucauldian paradigm that restricts sexual identities and, indeed, sexuality itself to the modern era.[30] Strange bedfellows—traditional premodernists and lesbian/gay/queer theorists—and their coalition is powerful enough to encourage many scholars to abandon "lesbian" in favor of terms less laden with contemporary identities, such as "homoerotic" or "same-sex relations." Indeed, the refusal to apply the term "lesbian" to historical subjects often serves to affirm an author's historical professionalism, offering a strategic seal-of-approval that is especially important for scholars working on marginalized topics.[31] This concession is both unnecessary and counterproductive.

To begin with, "lesbian" has considerable antiquity, and its use by historians accords well with long-accepted professional practices. More than a thousand years ago, the Byzantine commentator Arethas associated "lesbian" with same-sex relations between women. By equating *Lesbiai* with *tribades* and *hetairistriai*, Arethas indicated that, to at least one person in the tenth century, the term "lesbian" roughly signified what it roughly signifies today.[32] It might have meant much the same to the poet Louise Labé who, in mid-sixteenth-century France, wrote about "l'amour Lesbienne."[33] In English, the first uses of "lesbian" to denote same-sex relations between women date as early as the 1730s.[34] Unlike "gay" or "queer," then, "lesbian" has deep historical roots. Yet even without these roots, "lesbian" can, with due care, apply just as well to the past as do many other terms that have recent origins or meanings. In historical writing, it is common practice to use modern words to investigate past times; for example, "feudalism" and "courtly love," both inventions of the nineteenth century, are firmly enshrined within the discourses of medieval studies.[35] And it is not uncommon to find that Jakob Fugger was a "capitalist" (long before Adam Smith and Karl Marx), that Thomas Aquinas was "Catholic" (although he lived several centuries before Catholicism took on its post-Reformation meaning), or that the Black Prince prepared for "kingship" (even though it was kingship of a different sort from that anticipated today by Charles Windsor). Historians well know that part of our task is to assess the changing meanings of words over time and to weigh differences as well as similarities in their uses.

We should try to allow the same historical range, with the same comparative cautions, for "lesbian."

Indeed, to do otherwise does more harm than good. First, the refusal to use "lesbian" defers to homophobia and thereby promotes heteronormative misconceptions of the past. To some people, "lesbian" is a more upsetting word than "capitalist," "Catholic," or "king," and it can seem rude or slanderous to suggest that women such as Margery Kempe or Hildegarde of Bingen had feelings or experiences that we might associate with modern lesbianisms. This homophobic anxiety works on many levels, some articulated and others unacknowledged. Its main effect is bad history, history driven by heteronormative imperatives. For example, our modern sexual regime of dividing women according to sex of lovers—and thereby labeling them as lesbian, heterosexual, bisexual, queer, or whatever—does not seem to work well for the European Middle Ages. Penitentials suggest that medieval theologians thought in terms of a wide range of sexual activities, among which choosing a lover of the same sex was only one of many possible sexual sins. Romances suggest that aristocratic husbands worried most that their wives might produce illegitimate heirs and less that their wives might love others or, indeed, might sexually play with lovers in nonreproductive ways. And a wide variety of sources indicate that medieval people identified themselves less by any sexual practice and more by other criteria—willful or repentant sinner; householder or dependent; serf, free, or well-born; Christian or Jew. Insofar as there *were* sexual identities in the Middle Ages, the best articulated might have been those of the celibate and the virginal.[36] These are important and profound differences that separate the world of medieval Europe from our world today, but they disappear in history-writing that eschews lesbian possibilities and seeks out heterosexuality as pervasive, natural, and ideal.[37]

Second, a refusal to apply "lesbian" to the distant past stabilizes things that are better kept in a state of productive instability.[38] Is there such a stable entity as a modern lesbian? Clearly not. Was there such a stable meaning to "lesbian" in any past time? Probably not. We should play with these instabilities and learn from them, not reify one in order to deny relationship with the other. For example, medieval sexual regimes look very different from our own, but our information is, as yet, preliminary and even contradictory. Some scholars are finding that medieval people operated on a one-sex system;[39] others that medieval people embraced a two-sex binary that rigidly separated male and female;[40] and still others that medieval people played readily with ideas about intermediate genders or third sexes.[41] The meaning of this variety—whether an artifact of sources or historians, or an accurate reflection of medieval ideologies—is not yet clear. We need more reading, more research, and more speculation before we can sort out even the most basic aspects of medieval sexual practices. In these circumstances, it would be counterproductive to create a tidy discrimination between the abundance of modern lesbianisms and what we still have to learn about medieval sexualities.

In short, one of our first steps toward understanding the antecedents of modern sexual identities must be to examine how well and how poorly our modern ideas of "lesbians" and "heterosexual women" and "bisexuals" and "queers" work for the past. If we avoid these terms altogether, we will only create a pure, inviolable, and irrelevant past: a fetish instead of a history. In her recent study of early modern lesbianism, Valerie Traub opted to italicize "lesbian" and "lesbianism" for almost five hundred pages in order to remind her readers of "their epistemological inadequacy, psychological coarseness, and historical contingency."[42] I appreciate her hesitations, but ultimately any noun is similarly inadequate, coarse, and contingent. "Housewife" is, like "lesbian," a modern identity whose meanings cannot be readily transposed from the twenty-first century to the fifteenth. But we trust historians of housewifery and domesticity to manage the differences. Since no word has transparent meaning, now or in the past, surely we need not single out "lesbian" as a word that must be proscribed or even merely italicized.

In any case, I am suggesting not the use of "lesbian," but instead the use of "lesbian-like," a hyphenated construction that both names "lesbian" and destabilizes it.[43] The "lesbian" in "lesbian-like" articulates the often-unnamed, forcing historians who might prefer otherwise to deal with their own heteronormative assumptions and with the possibilities of lesbian expressions in the past. Yet at the same time as the term forthrightly names the unnamed, the "like" in "lesbian-like" decenters "lesbian," introducing into historical research a productive uncertainty born of likeness and resemblance, not identity. It allows us to expand lesbian possibilities beyond a narrow and quite unworkable focus on women who engaged in certifiable same-sex genital contact (a certification hard to achieve even for many contemporary women), and to incorporate women who, regardless of their sexual pleasures, lived in ways that offer affinities with modern lesbians—such as sexual rebels, gender rebels, marriage-resisters, cross-dressers, singlewomen, and women who found special sustenance in female worlds of love and ritual.[44]

"Lesbian-like" allows a social historian like myself to explore affinities that are broadly sociological—affinities related to social conduct, marital status, living arrangements, and other behaviors that might be traced in the archives of past societies. I would therefore like to play with the implications of naming as lesbian-like a range of practices that impinge on our own modern—and very variable—ideas about lesbianism. If women had genital sex with other women, regardless of their marital or religious status, let us consider that their behavior was lesbian-like. If women's primary emotions were directed toward other women, regardless of their own sexual practices, perhaps their affection was lesbian-like. If women lived in single-sex communities, their life circumstances might be usefully conceptualized as lesbian-like. If women resisted marriage or, indeed, just did not marry, whatever the reason, their singleness can be seen as lesbian-like. If women dressed as men, whether in response to saintly voices, in order to study, in pursuit of certain careers, or to travel with male lovers, their cross-dressing was arguably lesbian-like. And if women worked as prostitutes or otherwise flouted norms of sexual propriety, we might see their deviance as lesbian-like.

Unlike Adrienne Rich, I do not want to label all woman-identified experience—from maternal nurturance and lesbian sadomasochism to the esprit de corps of an abortion rights march—on a lesbian continuum. The essence of Rich's continuum is "primary intensity between and among women," an intensity that involves both "sharing of a rich inner life" and "bonding against male tyranny."[45] Some behaviors that I would identify as lesbian-like—such as singleness—were not necessarily based in the female bonding at the center of Rich's analysis. To my mind, a singlewoman in a sixteenth-century European town, regardless of her emotional life, lived in ways relevant to lesbian history: she tended to be poor, in part because her household was not supported by the better earning power of men; she was viewed by her neighbors with some suspicion and concern; she could expect to be tolerated, *if* she was well-behaved in other respects. This singlewoman might have shared neither an emotional life nor any political commitment with other women, but her life circumstances were, in some respects, lesbian-like.

Yet I also do not want to privilege sexual behaviors in defining lesbians past or present; I agree with Martha Vicinus that much lesbian history—and women's history, too—is "excessively concerned with knowing-for-sure" about *sexual* contact between women.[46] Many lesbian-like behaviors—such as the deep attachments formed between some medieval nuns—were not necessarily sexual in expression. I do not want to wash sexuality out of lesbian-like, but same-sex relations

are not a sine qua non of lesbianism (as the debates of lesbian theorists make clear), and if we treat lesbianism as rooted in sexuality, we
create very limited social histories, as I have rehearsed above for the
Middle Ages. In thinking about both "lesbian" and "lesbian-like,"
sexual behavior is certainly important, but it need not be defining.

I am hesitant to restrict the purview of "lesbian-like," for, as Greta
Christina has argued so well, patrolling the borders of any loaded
term is a divisive and elitist business.[47] But I am also cognizant of the
risk of "lesbian-*lite*," and I hope we might use "lesbian-like" playfully
and wisely. Obviously, "lesbian-like" can be extended to ridiculous
dimensions, by arguing, for example, that since some modern lesbians wear sandals, all sandal-wearers in past times were lesbian-like.[48]
Let us stick to essentials that will allow us, first, to construct histories
that have meaning for sexual minorities today, and second, to avoid
heteronormativity in our writing of women's history. I will not define
those essentials, for to do so would be as pointless as trying to secure
the meaning of "lesbian" or "sexual minorities" or even, indeed,
"history with meaning." We stand on shifting sands, but we need not
lose our balance. Obviously, "lesbian-like" also will overlook some lesbians in past times, particularly those who conformed to social norms.
And obviously, "lesbian-like" speaks more about circumstance than
choice; some singlewomen in early Europe willfully determined to
avoid marriage, but most found themselves unmarried thanks to poor
luck, family circumstances, religious imperatives, or plain poverty. Let
us appreciate the sociological uses of "lesbian-like" without endow-
ing it with motivational meanings.

To my mind, "lesbian-like" offers not an endless set of possibilities
but a set that is multidimensional, allowing any one of several criteria
to call forth "lesbian-like" as an analytical tool. In playing with the
possibilities of "lesbian-like," I am more comfortable applying it to
practices than to *persons*, for most women whom I might label "lesbian-
like" seem to have engaged in some lesbian-like behaviors (such as
living in single-sex communities) but not others (such as indulging in
sexual relations with other women). But perhaps we will eventually
come to decide that we *can* call some of these women "lesbian-like"—
maybe, for example, those whose behaviors evoked several criteria at
once. Certainly, I would think that a woman who never married and
shared an emotionally rich life with another woman might safely be
considered "lesbian-like" *as a person*. But, then again, if I consider
the case of Sarah and Elizabeth Delany—two never-married African
American sisters well known in the United States not only for a mem-
oir of their life together but also for the play and movie produced

from it—they strike me as lesbian-like in their *behavior*, not their *persons*.[49] Again, the sands shift; again, wise play is necessary.

Possibilities

In the earliest years of the fifteenth century, a young woman—we do not know her name—disguised herself as a man and studied at the University of Krakow. Although her story has many literary antecedents, Michael Shank has argued effectively for its plausible historicity. This student maintained her male identity for two years, and when discovered, she was more marveled at than punished. Like most other discovered female cross-dressers in the Middle Ages, she was admired and rewarded for improving herself through a male persona: she became the abbess of a nearby monastery.[50] We have only two words reputedly spoken by this young cross-dresser, and they explain her decision to take on a male persona in clear and nonsexual terms. When asked why she had deceived everyone, she replied, "amore Studii" ("for love of learning").[51]

This young woman never, as far as we know, had sex with another woman, but her lesbian-like cross-dressing deserves consideration in women's history.[52] After all, she lived as a man for two years in one of the least private of all-male environments. The account of her deception notes that she did not frequent the baths (where male students would have gone in search of prostitutes as well as cleanliness), but it tells us that she lived in a student hostel, that she attended lectures regularly, and that she got on well with her fellow students. In other words, she likely shared beds with men, disrobed in the presence of men, urinated in their company, and somehow managed, through all this, to conceal her breasts, her menstrual blood, her genitalia. To be sure, the Krakow student had some important assistance in her deception: she moved to Krakow from northwest Poland, thereby ensuring that she was unknown to anyone in the city; her parents had died, thereby freeing her from familial supervision; and she had a small inheritance, thereby giving her some financial independence. Still, if she could pass as a man in what was one of the most male and most sociable of medieval surroundings, other medieval women—motivated by love of women rather than love of learning—might have managed to do the same. The medieval world was much less private than our own, but there were many more private surroundings than a student hostel. The story of the Krakow student can, in other words, help historians of medieval women think outside the heteronormative box. After all, her story describes a society that tolerated female cross-dressers who "improved" themselves by becoming men; it reminds us that some medieval women found themselves—through migration to cities, parental death, or both—relatively free of familial control; and it even encourages us to consider the possibility that medieval households could readily accommodate—in their much more private circumstances than those provided by student hostels—married couples in which the one partner was a cross-dressed woman.

At about the same time that this unnamed Krakow student was first donning men's clothing, Laurence, the sixteen-year-old wife of Colin Poitevin, sought from her prison cell a pardon from the French crown. She told a story of how, some two years earlier in her small town of Bleury (near Chartres), she had been seduced by Jehanne, wife of Perrin Goula. The two had walked out to the fields together one August morning, and Jehanne had promised to Laurence that "if you will be my sweetheart, I will do you much good." As Laurence tells it, she suspected nothing evil, acquiesced, and suddenly found herself thrown onto a haystack and mounted "as a man does a woman." Orgasm followed, certainly for Jehanne, but perhaps also for Laurence, who enjoyed herself enough to desire further encounters. In subsequent days and weeks, Laurence and Jehanne had sex together in Laurence's home, in the vineyards outside their village, and even near the communal fountain. But eventually, the affair ended—and violently so, when Laurence's efforts to terminate the relationship caused Jehanne to attack her. (Perhaps this attack, not the sexual relationship per se, first brought the matter before the authorities; many women prosecuted for same-sex relations were guilty of other antisocial offenses, suggesting that we would not know of their *sexual* behaviors but for their *social* misconduct.)[53] Jehanne's fate is unknown; Laurence ended up in prison from whence came the document that tells her version of their encounters.[54] To us today, the behavior of both women is readily labeled lesbian-like, for this explicit story of sexual relations can make them seem much more resolutely "lesbian" than, for example, the cross-dressing of the serious—and seemingly celibate—student of Krakow. Yet even such clear-cut cases of same-sex relations are not transparent. Laurence cast her plea for clemency in terms as familiar as they were successful; she was a good woman, regretful of her sin, and a victim of an unnatural aggressor. Allowed to return home, reputation secured, after six months in prison, Laurence had indulged in a behavior with affinities to modern lesbianisms, but it would be crude to identify her as a "lesbian" or even as a lesbian-like *person*; she had clearly, however, engaged in lesbian-like *behaviors*.

A few decades before Laurence and Jehanne first dallied in the fields outside Bleury, the city of Montpellier merged its two convents of ex-prostitutes, probably because, in the wake of the bubonic plague of 1347–49, both houses had fewer inmates than before. The regulations of one of these communities suggest that it served, as Leah Otis has put it, "a social more than a religious purpose." The sisters were not cloistered; they performed modest religious duties; and they could, for all practical purposes, leave whenever they wished. Their house was directed by city officers who sought to encourage orderly behavior among some of the more disorderly inhabitants of Montpellier, but it also served the purposes of the women themselves, charitably sustaining some prostitutes in old age, sheltering others who were truly repentant, and providing a transition for still others as they moved from work as prostitutes to work as wives.[55] The prostitutes and ex-prostitutes of Montpellier were lesbian-like not only in their transgressive sexual practices but also in their joint living, whether in a city-sponsored brothel or a city-sponsored convent. The "historical sisterhood" between prostitution and lesbianism has been explored for modern times, particularly in a wide-ranging essay by Joan Nestle, but it seems to have escaped the recognition of historians of premodern Europe.[56] Bernadette Brooten has let pass with little comment the semantic association of *hetaira* (Greek for "courtesan") with *hetairistria* (a word used by Plato and others for same-sex female love).[57] John Boswell has dismissed as a "convenient derogation" a twelfth-century monk's description of same-sex female relations as an *innaturalem prostitutionem.*[58] And in their excellent books on medieval prostitution, neither Leah Otis nor Ruth Karras has been able to explore the relationship between female sex work and female same-sex relations.[59]

At the same time that the ex-prostitutes of Montpellier were settling into their newly merged houses, a widow in Ferrara amalgamated her dowry funds with contributions from other women and purchased a substantial property. Bernardina Sedazzari's intention, she claimed, was to establish a female monastery that would fall, as required by the ecclesiastical hierarchy, under the supervision of a male order. But, in fact, it is likely that Sedazzari never intended to submit her community to ecclesiastical control. As Mary McLaughlin has put it, Sedazzari preferred "autonomy to authority," cagily preserving the independence of her foundation for nearly two decades and governing about a dozen companions in a regular regime of religious devotions, good works, and common living. When Sedazzari died, she named one of those companions, Lucia Mascheroni, as her "universal heir," having extracted from her a sworn promise to maintain the community as it then existed. For more than two decades, Mascheroni observed this promise with "obsessive fidelity."[60] Sedazzari was a strong-willed woman, a pious woman, a woman experienced in both monastic life and marriage, and a woman who in midlife made a lesbian-like decision to avoid the governance of men—either that of the ecclesiastical hierarchy or that of a second husband. Sedazzari expressed her hopes for her community in pious terms, and we have no reason to doubt the sincerity of her words. But in an age that celebrated female chastity, piety might also have been the medium through which resistance to marriage could be most acceptably—and most effectively—expressed. The distinction between piety-as-motivation and piety-as-explanation might have often blurred in the minds of women who avoided marriage, but as Sedazzari's story suggests, it merits further study, not least because so many women—10 percent and more in some areas—opted for religious life. For Sedazzari and many others, piety provided not only a way to avoid remarriage but also a method of sidestepping ecclesiastical control (that is, male control) of her holy household.

The Europe of Krakow's crossed-dressed student, Laurence and Jehanne, the prostitutes of Montpellier, and Bernardina Sedazzari also accommodated many adult laywomen—several millions of them—who never married men. Unlike nuns and other women religious, these laywomen lived in the secular world, seeking work, shelter, and companionship as "singlewomen," the English term by which they were known from the fourteenth century. In England in 1377, almost one-third of all adult laywomen were single; in Florence fifty years later, singlewomen accounted for about one-fifth of women; and in Zurich fifty years after that, nearly half of all women had never taken a husband.[61] Many of these women eventually married, for especially in northern and western parts of Europe, traditions of late marriage left many women single well into their twenties. Some singlewomen, however, never married, and in late medieval England and perhaps elsewhere, these lifelong singlewomen accounted for about 10 percent of the adult female population. Whatever their sexual or affective practices, these singlewomen—both those who never married and those who eventually did; both those who chose to avoid marriage and those who sought it without success—were lesbian-like in their never-married state.[62] Singlewomen lived without the social approbation attached to wifehood; most lived without the support offered by the greater earning power of a male; and some lived independently, an anomalous state among people who sometimes thought, "When a woman thinks alone, she thinks evil."[63]

The Past and the Present

As these five examples show, "lesbian-like" replaces a mere handful of women prosecuted for same-sex contact with a plenitude of new possibilities for medieval women's history. It offers this same plenitude to women's history more generally. I read modern women's history because it helps me to think in new ways about medieval women's history, and as I argued in Chapter 3, I think that modern historians can similarly profit by reading more widely about ancient, medieval, and early modern women. "Lesbian-like" is an example; the idea arose from the peculiar challenges of medieval scholarship, but it has much wider uses.

"Lesbian-like" is not a perfect term: it adds new jargon to our field; it is as impossible as "lesbian" to define precisely; it highlights deviance more than conformity; it stresses circumstances over motivations; and if overused, it might even create a lesbian history that lacks lesbians (however defined). Yet "lesbian-like" offers two critical advantages. First, it adds nuance to behaviors that we might too readily identify as lesbian, for the experiences of women like Laurence and Jehanne are surely more lesbian-like than lesbian. Second, it adds many sorts of behaviors to the historical study of lesbianisms: cross-dressing; pious autonomy from male control; singleness; monastic same-sex community; prostitution; un-remarried widowhood. Each of these practices shares affinities with contemporary lesbianisms, and insofar as lesbian history, like all history, plays with the interplay between past and present, these lesbian-like behaviors are arguably as important as sexual practices. The sexual pleasures and legal difficulties of Laurence and Jehanne are notable parts of lesbian history, but so, too, might be the appropriation of male prerogatives by the Krakow student; so, too, the sexual disorder of Montpellier's prostitutes; so, too, Bernardina Sedazzari's resistance to male authority in either marriage or monasticism; so, too, the social and economic marginality of medieval singlewomen. These possibilities matter in both lesbian history and women's history.

If we strategically appropriate all these sorts of behaviors under the rubric of "lesbian-like," lesbian history looks very different. Again, the Middle Ages are a good example. The approaches of intellectual historians and cultural critics have suggested that the Middle Ages were either indifferent toward lesbian practice or hostile to it. A social

history that includes not only Laurence and Jehanne but also the Krakow student, the Montpellier prostitutes, the community founded by
Bernardini Sedazzari, and the never-married women of medieval
Europe draws a different picture. Social approval of manly women;
tolerated regulation of prostitutes; religious practices that accommodated considerable female autonomy and female community; a world
that abounded with singlewomen, young as well as old. All these suggest that, although medieval elites were coldly dismissive of lesbian
practices, medieval society might have been, in fact, filled with possibilities for lesbian expression.

More importantly, whether we end up with histories of lesbianisms
that stress hostility or possibility, "lesbian-like" facilitates the development of histories that modern lesbians, gays, bisexuals, and queers
rightly seek from the past. This search has parallels in the social histories of other minorities; it is rooted deeply within the feminism at
the heart of women's history; and it reflects the emancipatory possibilities of all history. "Lesbian-like" speaks to this modern need for a
usable past, for what Margaret Hunt has called the "cautious kinship"
that can link our many lives with the histories of those long dead.[64]
This cautious kinship is most emphatically not identity, for even the
most lesbian-like women in the past are unlike most modern lesbians.
Consider, for example, how Valerie Traub has differentiated early
modern tribades—assumed to be highly sexed and possessed of large,
capable-of-penetration clitorises—from modern lesbians:

> How is the tribade *not* like a contemporary *lesbian?* . . . *Lesbians* today are
> not assumed to be marked by anatomical deviation. (Such marking, rather,
> is reserved for a discourse of intersexuality.) Their erotic practices are not
> assumed primarily to take the form of vaginal penetration. (Quite the con-
> trary; oral sex is widely assumed to be "what *lesbians* do.") Nor are *lesbians*
> believed to be more lustful than heterosexual women. (Even within the *les-
> bian* community, jokes about "lesbian bed death" abound.) Most impor-
> tantly, according to the logic of modern homophobia, *lesbians* hate (or fear)
> men; in contrast, according to the Renaissance psychomorphology of the cli-
> toris, the tribade enacted that sincerest form of flattery: emulation.[65]

Rather than seeking identity, lesbian-like allows us to imagine in plausible ways the opportunities for same-sex love that actual women once
encountered, and to do so without asserting a crude correlation
between our varied experiences today and the varied lives of those
long dead. It moves beyond what Traub has called the "melancholy
of lesbian identification" with the past, allowing recognition without
identification, difference without obfuscation, and mourning without
melancholy.[66] In the process, of course, we become able to under-

stand ourselves better, for it is through exploring likeness, resemblance, and difference with past times that we can better understand the fraught interplay of identity and nonidentity in lesbian, queer, and even, indeed, heteronormative communities today.

For women's history, the stakes are different. History is not just, of course, about understanding the present through the past; it is also about understanding those who lived before us—and understanding them in respectful ways that take full account of past historical circumstances. Do we understand the Krakow cross-dresser (who loved learning, not women), or medieval prostitutes (whose sexual disorder might have often sprung from poverty, not desire), or medieval nuns (often celibate and solitary), or never-married servingwomen (most of whom might have eagerly sought marriage) if we think of some of their behaviors as lesbian-like? Certainly, many of these women would not have recognized themselves as lesbian-like in any way.[67] Certainly, their lives included intellectual, religious, social, and economic concerns that cannot be reduced to a matter of sexual object choice.[68] And just as certainly, women's history can benefit from pondering the lesbian-like possibilities of their histories.

Consider, for just one example, the singlewomen whose never-married state has prompted me to incorporate them under the rubric of lesbian-like. No doubt, many singlewomen never had sex with other women, but "lesbian-like" can nevertheless help us understand their lives more fully. Singlewomen have usually been seen through a heteronormative lens—and therefore seen as pathetic, sex-less, and lonely failures in a game of heterosexual courtship and marriage. If we use lesbian-like to put aside this distorting lens, we can discover that, although singlewomen might have often been economically deprived, their lives were not devoid of either sexual possibility or emotional richness. Many singlewomen were sexually active, and since procreative sex was problematic for the not-married, singlewomen might have particularly engaged in forms of sexual pleasure that easily accommodated partners of either sex. Similarly, although singlewomen lived without husbands and (often) children, their emotional lives could be quite full—and woman-identified. Some lived together in what demographers have dubbed "spinster clusters"; many others congregated in neighborhoods in which not-married women predominated; most worked in occupations—as servants, spinsters, lacemakers, laborers, or hucksters—that brought them into daily contact with more women than men; and many had close female relatives and friends with whom they shared life's sorrows and joys.[69] If we do not use "lesbian-like" to see singlewomen in new ways—if we do not do thereby startle ourselves out of our own heterosexist assumptions—we might continue to interpret their lives as "distorted and unhappy."[70] In this sense, "lesbian-like" is shock therapy for practices in women's history—modern as well as medieval—that not only have long overlooked lesbian possibilities but also have resolutely, albeit often subtly, defined "women" as "heterosexual women."[71]

"Lesbian-like" will not yield real-life lesbians in past times; it will not help us identify every past instance of same-sex relations; it will not address motivation as much as situation; it will not resolve the definitional dilemmas that both plague and enrich the term "lesbian"; and if used as a blunt instrument, it will produce blunt results. But if used in playful, wise, and careful ways, "lesbian-like" can address difficult problems that now confront lesbian historians, on the one hand, and women's historians, on the other. In helping us imagine possibilities and plausibilities that have hitherto been closed off from lesbian history, "lesbian-like" can expand the purview and evidence of lesbian history. And in encouraging us to see past societies in more complex ways, "lesbian-like" can promote the writing of feminist histories that are less hindered by heteronormative blinders, sexist ideologies, or modernist assumptions. As a new way of thinking about the past, "lesbian-like" can both enrich lesbian history and reform women's history.

Chapter 7

The Master and the Mistress

When women's history began to take root in the 1970s, history departments in the United States and Europe were places where men communed with one another about the histories of other men, most of them well-born, Christian, and of European descent. These stag affairs are blessedly rare these days. More women and more people of diverse races, faiths, and social origins now populate history departments, and in at least some contexts, the practices of history now broadly consider women as well as men, poor as well as rich, and the full diversity of the human past. But the practices of history today are unavoidably tainted, even in the best of circumstances, by the masculinist foundations of our craft. When professional history began to emerge in nineteenth-century Europe, it took shape as a discipline of empirically minded men who defined themselves in opposition to an older, more popular history often authored by women. Some hundred and fifty years later, what constitutes "history" still draws on the nationalist and imperialist visions of the nineteenth-century European elite, as well as on the assumption that history-writing is properly the work of men. As Bonnie Smith and others have traced this legacy, the ideal of the male historian who transcends his own history-writing remains so compelling that "while we see powerful historians as men, we also see only truth, pure intelligence, and compelling explanation." In other words, some voices in history are heard more readily than others. Although feminist historians might think that we "need only work harder for the truth to appear," it is difficult for our voices to prevail in a historical discourse still tuned to "the fascinating self of the male historian, as *the* authority on the past."[1]

History as a sign of masculinity troubles the project of feminist history on many fronts, but this chapter focuses on two especially important hurdles: first, the challenge of mainstreaming women's history into our discipline's master narratives, those teleological tales born of Victorian enthusiasm for change, progress, politics, high culture, and the deeds of great men; and second, the challenge of teaching a femi-

nist history that boldly considers continuity as well as change, patriarchy as well as agency, and the distant past as well as more recent times.
Both of these tasks speak to the pedagogical work of feminist historians, taking us into the college classrooms where we teach students to
think more deeply about past times, history-writing, and feminism.
Both also speak to the critical role of feminist historians in bridging
the generational gaps that trouble—and have long troubled—the
feminist project. As Gerda Lerner has traced so well, feminist thought
in Europe before the nineteenth century was afflicted by repeated
failures of generational transmission, so that each woman's critiques
of patriarchal power "sank soundlessly into the sea" and each subsequent woman "had to argue as though no woman before her had
ever thought or written."[2] Generational fissures have likewise
plagued feminist activism during the last century. In the 1920s, after
the achievement of women's suffrage in many parts of the West,
younger women spurned first-wave, older feminists as "old, unattrac-
tive, manless" malcontents whose views were "unmodern and unap-
pealing."[3] In the United States and Europe today something similar
is happening, with many young women eschewing second-wave feminism as uncool and anti-youth; as the singer Bjork, daughter of a feminist and product of a hippie commune, recently conceded, "I might
become a feminist in my old age."[4] Other young women, variously
identified as "third-wave" feminists or "postfeminists," embrace a
feminism of assertive femininity, personal empowerment, and aggres-
sive contemporaneity.[5] Generational challenge is, of course, inevita-
ble and productive, but feminist paralysis in the face of such
challenge is neither. In feminist classrooms, students and teachers
can speak more effectively across the generations—the dead and the
living, the older and the younger—to better facilitate the transmission, criticism, understanding, and respect that will sustain feminist
struggle into future generations.

Mainstreaming without Apology

Master narratives are the common stock of history, the stories we all
know. As a historian of late medieval women, for example, I might
share precious little intellectual community with someone who
researches the dynastic struggles of the seventh-century Merovingians
or someone else whose scholarly beat is the Christianization of Scan-
dinavia at the turn of the first millennium, but all three of us share a
common story about the decline of the Roman Empire in the West,

the establishment of Carolingian hegemony, the rise of papal monar-
chy, the "renaissance" of the twelfth century, and a host of other
waymarks in the master narrative of medieval history. This *grand récit*
gives medieval historians a common ground in which we root our specific research projects and across which we take our students every
semester. A master narrative is, in short, what everyone *must* know
about a specific historical period, whether medieval history, U.S. history, Chinese history, or the history of European imperialism. And
what everyone must know is very predictable, because master narratives usually build their stories around politics, high culture, and elite
men, telling a tale of steady progress, even if a few breakdowns and
detours have to be accommodated.

From the earliest days of second-wave feminism, historians of
women have tussled with the vexed relationship between these dominating master narratives and the new findings of feminist history.
"Tussled" is too kind a word; in fact, feminist historians have repeatedly *assaulted* history's master narratives, demanding that they be
transformed in the light of feminist scholarship, and quickly so. In
1975, Lerner called for a new type of "universal history," which she
described as "a history of the dialectic, the tensions between the two
cultures, male and female."[6] A year later, Joan Kelly had no doubt
that women's history had "shaken the conceptual foundations of historical study," and in the next year, she rattled those foundations
even more when she suggested, in her essay on women in the European Renaissance, that women's history might invert the male-
focused master narrative.[7] By the 1990s, we were assaulting not just
the content of master narratives but also its very genre. Elsa Barkley
Brown argued that the narrative style of history-writing—reminiscent
of the recurring and dominating theme of a classical music score—
had to be replaced by a new style that would evoke the polyrhythms
of jazz, allowing diversity and difference without domination.[8] And
Gianna Pomata, worried by the "temptation of universality, so insidi-
ously lurking in the textbook format," argued against any synthesiz-
ing narratives at all and in favor of what she called "particular"
history.[9]

The master narratives that have so attracted feminist critique haunt
all forms of historical writing, but textbooks are their natural genre.
We can all be thankful, of course, that textbooks are not the sum total
of history. I came to love history through novels, not textbooks, and
it was research, not textbook reading, that turned my fascination into
a career. I cannot today read a textbook (even my own) without fight-
ing sleep, and I sympathize with Catherine Morland's bemusement,

in *Northanger Abbey*, that historians would go to "so much trouble in filling great volumes only for the torment of little boys and girls."[10] But textbooks are a necessary evil in history teaching, particularly for introductory courses (in which students need to learn the "basic story," or master narrative) and perhaps particularly in public universities in the United States, where large class sizes and heavy teaching loads virtually compel assignment of a textbook. Year after year, teachers shake their heads in frustration, students groan in boredom, and textbooks are still assigned. Hate them we might, but we also have to concede their power, especially their power over how women are remembered in history. We can lecture on women, we can add supplementary readings on women, and we can encourage special projects on women, but if the textbook ignores women, all these efforts are swimming upstream. As students obediently slog through their textbooks, they take heart from one self-evident truth: "if it's not in the textbook, it's not important."[11]

Yet, despite concerted feminist critique over the last three decades, textbooks—and the master narratives they convey—remain remarkably unchanged. Perhaps this is because feminists have asked too much, too quickly. I was entirely sympathetic with Pomata's suggestion that we abandon textbooks altogether, until I remembered my first chilling lessons in Latin, at the hands of a teacher who thought grammar books were oppressive and students should learn Latin as Roman toddlers once did—by using the language. After an utterly demoralizing year of Latinate babbling, I was probably the happiest student ever to encounter Frederic Wheelock's masterly and rule-bound *Latin* textbook. Pomata's approach has some intellectual justification and considerable political appeal, but it is simply impractical. Perhaps, too, some responsibility for the endurance of old master narratives within new textbooks rests with the economics of textbook production in which publishers, seeking a return on investment, ask authors to produce standard narratives against which teachers can then weave their own interpretations. "Standard" is the operative word here. As scholars, we tend to like quirky, cutting-edge, and provocative history, but as teachers, we often prefer textbooks that offer more conventional wisdoms than new hypotheses. We know we can teach the new hypotheses and tell the quirky stories ourselves; we want the textbook to deliver the broad outline that even we find too tedious to lecture through. And perhaps some of the endurance of master narratives in the face of feminist critique must be attributed to sheer resistance and antifeminism. Many textbooks now aspire to expanded coverage on women and gender, but some explicitly eschew such emendation. Thus, Denys Hay reported in his revised textbook on late medieval Europe that he had rejected pressure from his publisher to include more material on women, proudly noting, "I am sure that Longman would have been happy if I had contrived a chapter on feminine developments (other than the female religious with whom I occasionally spend a few lines) in the later middle ages. But I have a feeling that this historical mode is passing."[12]

Whatever the causes, the lack of progress is clear. Textbooks in medieval history are one good example. Between 2002 and 2004, five major textbooks were published in North America for use in college classrooms, three entirely new creations and two revised editions, including one of which I am the co-author.[13] All but one promise—on the cover, in the preface, or in both locations—to offer updated coverage on women and gender in the Middle Ages. But they promise more than they deliver. First, at the core of each of these textbooks rests a master narrative: teachers and students begin with "Western Europe before the Barbarian Invasions," then consider "The German Invasions and the Break-Up of the Roman Empire," then move on to the "Rise of the Papacy," "The Conflict between Gregory VII and Henry IV," "The Development of France," and "England in the Middle Ages" until everything gets neatly wrapped up with "The Italian Cities States and the Renaissance." These drearily familiar categories could be titles from any just-published textbook, but they are, in fact, chapter titles from James Harvey Robinson's textbook of 1903, the Ur-textbook of the master narrative of medieval history, as it was and is taught in North America. The story has changed in bits and pieces since 1903—all textbooks now, for example, include sections on Byzantium and Islam—but Robinson's master narrative of the slow development of the institutions of Church and state has endured for more than a century with remarkably little change.[14]

Second, although feminists have long derided inadequate "compensatory" revisions that merely add a few women worthies to a male-driven narrative, these twenty-first-century textbooks have not even managed to compensate very much—that is, they contain remarkably few women worthies. Only five medieval women are mentioned in all five of these textbooks: Dhuoda (c. 810–50), Joan of Arc (c. 1412–31), Catherine of Siena (1347–80), Christine de Pizan (1364–1430), and the Virgin Mary. Three decades of feminist critique, and we still have just five women firmly placed in the master narrative of Europe's medieval millennium, at least as it is told in North America. One woman was more iconic than historical, and not one wielded power in the classic political mode beloved of master narratives. Two were

The Master and the Mistress   133

authors (Dhuoda and Christine de Pizan), and the other three were divinely empowered and are remembered, interestingly enough, largely because of their influence over more powerful males: Joan of Arc and Charles VII; Catherine of Siena and the popes Gregory XI and Urban VI; the Virgin Mary and God. In theory, the master narrative's love of high politics should have created space for at least some of the many medieval women who ruled by virtue of birth or position—the Empress Irene (c. 750–803), Matilda of Tuscany (1046–1115), Eleanor of Aquitaine (c. 1122–1204), Margaret of Denmark (1353–1412), Isabella of Castile (1451–1504), to name a few. These empresses, duchesses, and queens are mentioned in some of the textbooks, but not all five—that is, none has yet achieved the "must-mention" status of the hundreds of men mentioned in all these textbooks. To judge by this "must-mention" measure, Jean de Meun (d. 1305), author of the most misogynist parts of the thirteenth-century *Romance of the Rose* and featured in all five textbooks, is a more important figure in medieval history than Hildegard of Bingen (1098–1179), abbess, prophet, advisor of popes and kings, composer, and author of dozens of theological, mystical, homiletic, scientific, and hagiographic manuscripts, who is mentioned in only four.

Third, many other incorporations of women in these textbooks constitute what Carol Berkin has aptly called "dangerous courtesies."[15] They acknowledge women's presence but in ways that leave the master narrative uncontaminated by substantive female presence. Thus, for example, in most of these medieval textbooks, students learn about early monasticism as a male phenomenon, with the experiences of women tacked on as an afterthought. This presentation dutifully replicates the profound maleness of the early medieval Church as depicted in the original master narrative, but it does not reflect what we now know about the deep involvement of women in monasticism from its earliest days. The documentary record tells us of female hermits, of monastic rules for female houses, of schools and *scriptoria* (or writing centers) in female monasteries, even of missionary nuns, such as Leoba, who in the eighth century answered St. Boniface's call to Saxony. In most aspects of medieval monasticism, it is no stretch at all for authors to write about "monks and nuns," but most textbooks, even in the twenty-first century, still tell students about "monks" and then dutifully add "there were also women . . ."[16]

A master narrative of male action, precious few women worthies, many dangerous courtesies. All told, we can safely say that when the master takes a mistress in medieval history textbooks, he chooses very carefully, he prefers women who empower, inspire, or amuse him, and he keeps his mistress on the side, safely tucked away from the manly business of real life. These enduring problems are not peculiar to the master narrative of medieval history. In the 1990s, *National History Standards* for the teaching of world history and U.S. history were published, revised, and republished in the United States. Some thirty professional organizations, thousands of history teachers, and dozens of professional historians—including such historians of women as Deborah Gray White, Evelyn Brooks Higginbotham, and Joan Scott—participated in the project, which represents, according to its own literature, "the best historical research and the finest teaching practice in history education that this country has to offer."[17] This best and finest includes shockingly little material on women, even in the world history component, a relatively new area of historical writing whose master narrative is not only young but also less inflected by nationalism. By Barbara Moss's estimate, women and women's history account for about 5 percent of the recommended teaching program in world history (nearly 6 percent in the original 1994 recommendations but less than that in their 1996 revisions).[18] Women of European descent predominate in this tiny group, and although references to women vary with chronological units, women are most before students' eyes in the earliest era (before 4000 B.C.E.) and least present in the twentieth century. World history is a young master narrative, and it has come of age in the late twentieth-century United States, where many historians are comfortably familiar with both feminist scholarship and women's history. But this master, too, prefers a submissive and quiet mistress.

    If our previous critiques have failed so grievously to effect real change, what new feminist tactics might work better? Lisa Bitel has confronted the master narrative of medieval history and counseled its wholesale rejection. In her view, the chronological nonsynchronization of women's history with the master narrative precludes any hope of egalitarian union.[19] Joan Scott has confronted the master narrative of the *National Standards* and advised historians of women to work harder. In her view, feminists hitherto have insufficiently rethought, reconceptualized, and rewritten the general narratives of history.[20] I have a different idea. No matter how politically appealing, purist stances such as these—reject master narratives or transform them—have proven ineffective in the last thirty-odd years. Feminists might, indeed, be able to reject or transform master narratives in the long term, but in the meantime, generations of students are getting their women's history in tiny portions, on the side. For the medium term, therefore, let us approach the problem in strategic and pragmatic ways: let us accept the power of the master narrative but give him a new sort of mistress.

I recently had occasion to do just this when I revised the late C. Warren Hollister's textbook *Medieval Europe: A Short History* for a new edition.[21] The publisher did not want me to replace Hollister's text—a widely used, much loved, and traditional retelling of medieval history—with a demastered version. My charge was merely to update the book by adding more social history and more women's history. In other words, I agreed to undertake an approach regularly ridiculed in feminist critiques of the master narrative's reaction to women's history: I agreed to add women and stir. To my delight (and relief), I found that "add and stir" produced more than a cosmetic touch-up; it changed what had been a relentlessly masculine story into a tale of two sexes.[22]

For example, thanks in large part to feminist research during the last three decades, it is no longer a stretch to add individual women to master narratives. Numerous "women worthies" can now be substantively placed at many steps in the mad march from Rome to the Renaissance. How could women be included in the investiture controversy that pitted male popes against male emperors? Matilda of Tuscany (1056–1115) does just fine. It was at her castle at Canossa that emperor Henry IV (r. 1056–1106) and pope Gregory VII (r. 1073–85) met, and it was her disputed legacy after 1115 that further soured relations between papacy and empire. How about the Norman conquest of England in 1066? Emma of Normandy (c. 985–1052)—daughter of a Norman duke, wife of two English kings, and mother of two more—is the central fulcrum that explains how a Norman duke could claim an English crown. What about the expansion and Christianization of Europe? What Jane Schulenburg has dubbed "domestic proselytization"—that is, the marriages of Christian women to pagan kings who subsequently converted—provides a broad theme well suited to master narratives: the fifth-century marriage of Clothilde and Clovis (conversion of the Franks), the union of Bertha and Ethelbert in the sixth century (conversion of the English), the tenth-century marriage of Anna and Vladimir (conversion of the Rus), the fourteenth-century marriage of Jadwiga and Jagiello (conversion of the Lithuanians), and many others.[23] In all these cases and many others, adding women and stirring has the ironic effect of actually *improving* the master narrative, according to its own terms. Thus, for example, Emma of Normandy is not just a woman added to salve my feminist conscience; she is the explanatory pivot of the messy story of the English royal succession in the mid-eleventh century, a story that has simply made less sense without her.

Feminist principles of gender neutrality in language and style also make it exceedingly easy to humanize the masculine bent of textbooks. This is partly a simple matter of remembering the presence of women within master narratives—nameless women who were simply *there*, part of the story from beginning to end. Thus, as we have just seen, women can be seamlessly included in the history of monasticism by the straightforward—and historically accurate—device of replacing "monks" with "monks and nuns." Similarly, women can also be reintegrated into the history of medieval manors and villages by using language that makes it clear that there were ladies of manors, as well as lords, and that peasants were female as well as male.

Master narratives can also be easily washed of their pervasive masculinity—that is, the assumption that all authors, readers, and subjects are men. In the nineteenth century, Leopold von Ranke and his colleagues so thoroughly understood history as a male enterprise that they even saw an archive, as Ranke once put it, as "an absolute virgin. I long for the moment I shall have access to her . . . whether she is pretty or not."[24] Modern textbooks often do much the same, creating a common cause—one perhaps designed to ease the pain of textbook reading—of male author, male audience, and male subject. My favorite instance of this male solidarity involves both ahistoricism and acrobatics: a textbook description of medieval advice on birth control as "all one must do to prevent a woman from conceiving is to bind her head with a red ribbon during intercourse."[25] This would, of course, have required considerable agility on the part of a male lover, but more to the point, the "one" is gendered male whereas the proper actor, as in most matters related to birth control, was, of course, a woman; it was a woman who needed to bind her head with a red ribbon. In such simple but subtle ways, textbooks can now be easily rewritten to humanize what was once a resolutely male alliance of author, audience, and historical actors.

It is harder, but not impossible, to incorporate into master narratives the topics and findings of women's history per se. We will need more rethinking and reconceptualizing before we can, as Scott has advised, rewrite master narratives to incorporate studies of changing patriarchal regimes, or changes and continuities in gender rules, or more attention to the play of differences among all people, including women. But other subjects of feminist inquiry can be easily woven into master narratives. I found, for example, that the attention of students was easily drawn to the particular prominence of women in medieval slavery, or to the different wages paid to women and men, or to the effect of educational expansion in the central Middle Ages on women, or to the particular importance of women as patrons of vernacular literatures.

Changes such as these are practical, effective, *and* limited. They recognize the power of master narratives but infuse them with more coverage of women. They leave the master narrative intact, unchallenged, and, indeed, even strengthened, but they also wash out its masculinity and enhance women's place. Given the current state of our textbooks—a grand total of five must-mention women in the narrative of medieval history, and a whopping 5 percent devoted to women in the U.S. *National Standards* for world history—these practical compromises are our best bet for getting better textbooks (and, indeed, better lectures) into our classrooms quickly. I suggest that we strategically ask master narratives to work with a "mistress" more common in premodern than modern uses of the term—that is, a woman married to the master, busy with productive work and household management, important, appreciated, and even authoritative in some contexts, but usually working to support the more primary occupation of her husband. Some historians look at such medieval households and see "partnerships"; to me, they seem at best *unequal* partnerships. Yet many medieval women seem to have considered this junior partnership a good option, a patriarchal bargain that offered them economic security, productive work, social approbation, authority over children, servants, and apprentices, and perhaps even love— all these, in return for a helpmeet's role. Given the enduring power of master narratives, which seem able, like so many other forms of patriarchal power, to shift a bit, adjust here and there, and endure untransformed, I have come to think that an equivalent bargain in history textbooks—a sort of artisanal marriage between women's history and master narratives—is not a bad deal either. It is certainly the best deal we can get, for now.[26]

History without Apology

"We don't much remember."[27] If master narratives present one challenge to feminist historians, an equally awesome challenge is the offhand rejection of history by postfeminists. As we saw in Chapter 3, this rejection has academic as well as popular roots; in women's studies classrooms today, history has little place, and historians, especially historians of the distant past, are characterized as self-indulgent, whimsical, unproductive, and even nonfeminist.[28] What possible relevance can the distant past offer to teachers and students in today's feminist classrooms? Quite a lot. By looking back with their students into the distant past, teachers can find rich examples of history-writing and historical debate; unusual opportunities for exploring the meanings of difference, past as well as present; fertile ground for illuminating ideologies of gender; and a plethora of subjects that will enliven classrooms and enlighten students. I will take as my example the hard case of the European Middle Ages, which students often imagine (wrongly) as a time when one faith reigned supreme, all people knew their place, and nothing ever changed. Students generally fall into one of two camps on the subject of medieval women—imagining them as hopelessly oppressed or wonderfully free—but in either case, they generally agree that the lives of medieval women are utterly foreign to the feminist challenges of our own day.

This was not always so. When feminists first began to organize in late nineteenth-century Europe, they looked to the Middle Ages for information about pressing contemporary issues: women's work; women's education; women's status under the law; women's participation in political life. Turning toward the Middle Ages at precisely the moment when history was establishing itself as a professional discipline, these medievalists produced many of the earliest works of feminist history. In reconstructing the early development of women's history, we often look no further than the 1970s and the early work of such scholars as Gerda Lerner and Joan Kelly, or we adventurously trek as far back as Mary Beard's *Woman as Force in History* (1946).[29] But feminist historians—many of them medievalists—were active, articulate, and appreciated from the 1890s on. In that decade, Florence Buckstaff peppered her exposition of the legal rights of married women in Anglo-Saxon England with the arch observation that "the sexes are not equal" in her contemporary America, Mary Bateson suggested that St. Columban was "a woman-hater" in her study of medieval monasticism, and Elizabeth Dixon attacked the "modern view that good industrial training and anything above a bare subsistence wage are unnecessary . . . and superfluous for working women" in her study of craftswomen in thirteenth-century Paris.[30] For early feminists, the study of the Middle Ages provided a highly relevant past, a platform for feminist advocacy, *and* a relatively accessible profession.[31]

Through much of the twentieth century women were coldly received in most academic disciplines, but women repeatedly proved their historical professionalism at the hot forge of medieval history. Some succeeded within the highest level of academia, as did Eileen

Power, who took a professorship at the London School of Economics in 1931; Helen Cam, who did the same at Harvard in 1948 (Harvard's first female professor); and Nellie Neilson, who became the first female president of the American Historical Association in 1943. Many others relied on sex-segregated training and employment, especially at Bryn Mawr College and Mount Holyoke College, where generations of young women were inspired to take up careers in medieval studies. As Linda Kerber noted in a recent retrospective on graduate training in the 1960s, her courses in United States history lacked any attention to women, a deplorable situation that "would have been less true had we been medievalists."[32] No wonder, then, that even at the end of the twentieth century, women were more active in medieval scholarship than in most other branches of academia.[33] Feminist medievalists remain just as numerous and active today, boasting an association, a journal, and several bibliographic and research collaborations.[34]

Feminist teachers and students must not forget this past—both the distant past of medieval women's history and the more recent past of feminist scholarship on the Middle Ages. Expensively trained in long-dead languages, feminist medievalists study a region with an exceptionally troubled history of racism and colonialism, and they even tend to focus, within Europe, on a tiny minority of rich, literate, and powerful people. They are also peculiarly handicapped, for feminist medievalistss must approach a distant past through incomplete and intransigent sources that were, with few exceptions, created and preserved by men. Yet despite these obstacles and partly because of them, investigations of the Middle Ages are critical to feminist scholarship—and especially, as I hope to show here, to feminist teaching.

TEACHING FEMINIST HISTORIOGRAPHY

Simply because of its longevity, the feminist study of the Middle Ages offers unique opportunities to teach students the history of feminist history-writing. For more than a hundred years, feminist medievalists have brought their own generation's concerns to the study of medieval women. It is no accident, for example, that Annie Abram published an article on medieval women's work when many of her fellow Englishwomen were entering the workforce during World War I. Nor is it an accident that she then reached the encouraging conclusion that medieval women were "persons of strong character and undeniable business activity."[35] Her article is just one example of how the relatively long historiography of medieval women's history can provide students with short, clear, and unforgettable lessons about the historical positioning of feminist historians themselves.

Medieval women's history also exemplifies for students the enduring power of foundational visions within feminist history—and, indeed, within all history. In 1926, Eileen Power crafted what has become a master (mistress?) narrative for medieval women's history in a short article that offered a compelling, albeit flawed, conceptualization of the history of medieval women. Power focused her essay on the relative position of women vis-à-vis men, raising a question—how might we best assess the status of medieval women?—that teachers and students ponder even today. In her answer, Power stressed three points that still arise in today's classrooms. First, she balanced theory against practice, arguing not only that medieval ideas about women were distinct from the everyday experiences of women but also that these ideas were so confusingly self-contradictory that they must have had little real effect on everyday life. Second, Power favorably judged the overall status of medieval women. She recognized that medieval women faced some serious problems—a culture rife with misogyny, a legal system based on assumptions of female inferiority, and a social structure that invested men with considerable power over women's lives. But arguing that the true position of medieval women "was one neither of inferiority nor of superiority, but of a certain rough-and-ready equality," Power positively assessed medieval gender roles, constructing an image of the Middle Ages as a time that, if not golden for women, was nevertheless very good indeed. Third, Power focused on class as *the* critical marker of differences among medieval women. Ignoring matters of religious difference and devoting only a few paragraphs to singlewomen, widows, and nuns, Power's essay implicitly equated "medieval women" with "Christian wives." The bulk of her essay was devoted to studying these Christian wives within three discrete social classes: feudal ladies, bourgeoises, and peasants.[36]

Today, teachers and students can read almost any textbook on medieval women and find therein the enduring force of Power's historical imagination. Most modern descriptions of medieval women begin, as her essay did, with medieval theories about woman and female nature. Whether called "the heritage of ideas," "the mold for women," or "the origins of medieval attitudes," these introductions seek, as Power did long ago, to understand both the internal ambiguities of medieval gender ideologies and their social meanings. Similarly, most studies of medieval women echo Power's upbeat assessment of women's lot in the Middle Ages. As Margaret Wade Labarge put it, medieval women might have been viewed "as subordinate and inferior by medieval men . . . but they were neither invisible, inaudible, nor unimportant."[37] And most textbooks categorize the subject of medieval women, as Power did, primarily according to class and, to a lesser degree, marital status or religious faith: feudal ladies compared to townswomen and peasant wives; all these compared to those who took holy vows; and perhaps some brief comparisons with Jewish and, more rarely, Islamic women. In the textbooks and classrooms in which medieval women are studied today, they can still be seen, as Power saw them in 1926, as living in a Christian world that was fraught with ideological ambivalence about the female sex, filled with practical opportunity for female action, and fractured by profound divisions of class. Women's history has its *grands récits*, too.

As a relatively mature field of women's history, the study of medieval women is also rich with historiographical debates that can enliven feminist classrooms. My students are especially taken with arguments about whether, when, and how the status of women changed during the medieval millennium. This is a ticklish and difficult topic for any era, much less one as remote as the European Middle Ages. Yet despite the uncertainties of assessing "status" and the ideological freight of the process, the desire to trace advances and declines in the status of women over time persists among both students and teachers. The Middle Ages—far distant, much studied, and long in duration—provides an excellent case study for confronting this pedagogical challenge head-on.

"Change for the worse" is so common a theme in medieval women's history that a teacher can stand at almost any historical marker and find a negative trend. The centralizing reforms of Charlemagne, c. 800: bad for women. The Norman invasion of 1066: bad for women. The new monastic orders of the twelfth century: bad for women. The growth of humanism in the fourteenth century: bad for women. The rapid development of capitalism in the fifteenth century: bad for women. Although "change for the worse" has been found in almost every century in the medieval millennium, it has been most fully elaborated for the central Middle Ages (1000–1300). As developed particularly in studies by Jo Ann McNamara and Susan Mosher Stuard, the eleventh and twelfth centuries have been figured as a time of "gender crisis" when an old ideology of gender *similarity* was usurped by a new ideology of gender *difference*.[38] Other historians, building on the pioneering work of David Herlihy, have pointed to various ways in which the shifting boundaries of public and private during the central Middle Ages also worked to the disadvantage of women. For example, early feudalism, with its reliance on private power and household-based administration, offered considerable scope to elite women who could participate, in their capacity as wives, in the day-to-day affairs of feudal governance. But in the central Middle Ages, as monarchs began to assert control over localities, as bureaucrats began to replace ad hoc administrators, and as formal institutions began to supplant the informal arrangements of the household, the informal household-based power of feudal women waned.[39]

These histories of "change for the worse" work well in the classroom. On the one hand, they conform to expectations, providing the sort of chronological change students expect from history and offering useful examples of how shifting boundaries of "public" and "private" can shape the experiences of women. On the other hand, they upset expectations in pedagogically useful ways, suggesting that the history of women is not a history of steady improvement, that a good period for men can be a bad period for women (the twelfth century is conventionally seen, after all, as the apogee of medieval civilization, the so-called "high" Middle Ages), and that some medieval women were not as utterly subject to men as most students seem to assume. Most usefully of all, these histories provide examples of historians-in-debate, for despite the pedagogical usefulness of the "change-for-the-worse" perspective, it is a highly contested interpretation; it does not jive well, for example, with my own hypothesis of patriarchal equilibrium. The Norman conquest provides students with perhaps the best example of how historians have differently interpreted the fate of women in a time of historical trauma and transition: women's lot falling under the burden of the Norman yoke; or women taking on newly powerful roles as intermediaries between conquered Anglo-Saxons and triumphant Normans; or perhaps, as Pauline Stafford has cautioned, women's power, always limited, merely waning in some areas as it waxed in others.[40]

TEACHING DIFFERENCE

Because of its distance from our own time, the medieval millennium offers students unique opportunities for exploring the critical matter of differences among women. The feminist trinity of "race, class, and gender" is now often expanded to accommodate such other differences as sexuality, religion, and world region; medieval history expands our understandings of difference even more. In part, it does so simply by its distance, for chronology creates difference, too—not utter alterity, but subtle differences. Students rightly recognize parts of themselves in medieval people, but they also find that the medieval past is profound, compelling, and rich with meaning for feminist understandings of what "difference" really means (especially since the difference-of-time has relatively less resonance in modern life than such differences as race, class, and gender). Students also profit from interrogating the distinctive fissures that created many different sorts of "medieval women." *Marital status* critically shaped the lives of women in the Middle Ages. A surprisingly high proportion of women in some parts of late medieval Europe passed their entire lives as never-married singlewomen; others married so young they spent all their adult years as wives; still others lost their husbands so early that their lives were mostly shaped by widowhood; and, of course, some women passed slowly through all three stages. Each stage presented women with sharply different opportunities and restrictions, so much so that students can profitably debate whether singlewomen, wives, and widows might be best conceptualized as different genders. *Religious status* created another essential difference, and it cut along many lines: Christian, Muslim, or Jew, to be sure; but also laywomen, professed nuns, or pious mystics; and orthodox Christians as opposed to heretics. *Legal status* similarly carved deep divides among women, especially differentiating free, serf, and slave. *Ethnicity* mattered as well, for the various peoples who settled Europe brought with them varied customs and laws. *Sexual status* also carried weight, so much so that medieval municipalities sought to segregate prostitutes from other women by prescribing special dress, special accommodations, and special behaviors. And *region* shaped women's lives, especially since the frequency and age of female marriage differed dramatically in southern and northern Europe, by the fourteenth century, if not before.[41] None of these categories is specific to the Middle Ages, but it is medieval scholarship—and the teaching of its findings in feminist classrooms—that can especially help students to explode the conventional catalog of "race, class, and gender" and to engage more fully with the many fractures that run across the category "woman."

Medieval history also illustrates for students how the study of difference can be haunted, as discussed in Chapter 4, by assumptions that combine "difference" with "women's status" to assess civilizations. From the nineteenth century, medieval historians have often sought, almost as a matter of course, to identify some women as better off than others and, hence, to value some medieval civilizations over others. So, for example, the status of women on the peripheries of Europe was long the subject of mythic valorization, although recent scholarship has now effectively demolished Irish and Norse claims to medieval pasts of gender equality.[42] And so, for another example, the study of medieval heresies was long dominated by the Protestant-affirming assumption that women flocked to such sects because they were more woman-friendly than the misogynous medieval church. Yet, as historians have now shown for the heresies of Catharism and Lollardy, these rosy assessments have no historical basis. Women were no more numerous among heretics than among the general population; heretical practices tended, not surprisingly, to reproduce mainstream gender hierarchies; and heretical theologies did not offer women liberation from traditional Christian teachings.[43] In the classroom, these medieval examples of the subtle allure of difference-as-ranking provide fertile ground for forthright discussions. Once students recognize—in the safe arena of the distant past—the pernicious values that can be attached to such analyses, they are better prepared to criticize this practice in others and avoid it themselves.

Medieval history also offers students a safe distance from which to explore the complex ways in which ideologies about women and gender mark boundaries between peoples. In the central Middle Ages, Christian communities began to expand their territorial influence (as for example, in the so-called "Reconquest" of Iberia), and they also began to harass some who lived among them, especially Jews, prostitutes, male homosexuals, heretics, and lepers.[44] In these early days of colonization and persecution, gender shaped constructions of "otherness" in ways that strongly resonate with modern students. In medieval Iberia, for example, boundaries between Christians, Jews, and Muslims were partly maintained by prohibitions against intergroup sexual relations. Similar in some respects to U.S. laws against miscegenation, medieval prohibitions nevertheless operated on a different register from modern anxieties: all medieval groups—Jewish and Muslim minorities as well as the Christian majority—agreed on the importance of preventing intergroup sexual contact; medieval prohibitions exhibited few anxieties about any "racial impurity" that might result from children born of such unions; and intergroup sexual unions accomplished through prostitution were a particular focus of concern.[45] In medieval French epic, for another example, Muslim princesses were regularly depicted as falling in love with Christian knights and converting to Christianity in tales that evoke modern parallels with Western exoticization and commodification of non-Western women. But they, too, have special medieval twists: most epics "whiten" Saracen women, depicting them as epitomes of Frankish standards of beauty, not as women made desirable by their physical otherness; they create Saracen heroines who threaten established norms of female behavior by rejecting their families, mocking men, and committing adultery; and most importantly, these stories use women to legitimate the profits of military victory.[46] A third example—the feminization of slavery in medieval Europe—can strike modern students with particular force. Compared to both ancient and modern Europeans, medieval people relied relatively little on slavery, yet as Susan Mosher Stuard has shown, this "medieval traffic in slaves was overwhelmingly a traffic in women." On the frontiers of Europe, female slaves were easily obtained from ethnic or religious groups different from those of slave-owners, supplying Dalmatian women to labor in Italian households, Celtic women for the Norse who settled Iceland, and Muslim women for the Christians of Iberia. Medieval records leave no doubt about a matter often elided in modern accounts of slavery—that is, that these women were valued not only for their productive labor but also as sexual and reproductive workers.[47]

Differences among "medieval women" cut many ways: Christian, Jewish, or Muslim; feudal, bourgeois, or peasant; free, serf, or slave; orthodox Christians or heretics; nuns or laywomen; singlewomen, wives, or widows; Celts, Norse, Franks, Saxons, or Latins; northern European or southern European; young, middle-aged, or old. These divisions were real and important to medieval women, but they also illustrate for students how differences can be overvalued, especially if women's lives are divided along one axis alone. After all, a peasant woman was not just a peasant—she was also young or old; married or not; orthodox Christian, Christian heretic, or Jew; northern or southern European. Medieval history also suggests that women's common experiences might have sometimes smoothed over differences that mattered more to men. A feudal lord could not guide a plow and a plowman could not fight from horseback, but feudal ladies, urban goodwives, and poor countrywomen could all spin, wield a needle, care for children, and prepare a meal. Peasant women spun from need and noble ladies for leisure, but each regarded the distaff and spindle with a familiarity that would have eluded a knight confronted with a plow or a plowman with a warhorse. Thus, medieval women's history can help students to appreciate not only the extent of the differences that fractured the category "woman" but also the limits of their meanings.

TEACHING IDEOLOGIES OF GENDER

Because medieval Europe is so far removed from our own time, it can also offer an effective example—both clear and unthreatening in its distance—of the profound powers and troubling inconsistencies of gender ideologies. To begin with, medieval history itself exemplifies the powerful ways in which gender is implicated in how we imagine the past. My students tend to assume that the Middle Ages epitomize woman hating: jealous husbands who clasped chastity belts on their wives before heading off on crusade; brutal knights who, like the lord in the movie *Braveheart*, claimed the virginity of young brides on their estates; and young women who were driven, like Pope Joan, to cross-dress in order to attend school. No medieval chastity belts survive, and those found in European museums are modern creations attributed to an imagined medieval past. The myth of the "right of the first night" is a similar concoction of heated postmedieval imaginations. And the story of Pope Joan, who supposedly ruled in the ninth century, arose as an antifeminist legend in the thirteenth century.[48] It might be disappointing to students that these are myths rather than history, but, *as fabrications*, these stories show the importance of gender in modern constructions of the medieval past. For many modern people, nothing better illustrates the barbarity of medieval society than its supposedly brutal treatment of women.

Medieval thought about women was shot through with ambivalence and contradiction, but medieval people were not, of course, unique in this regard. Many medieval ideas about gender grew from ancient traditions, and the core ambivalence of medieval gender ideology still flourishes in modern times.[49] But medieval gender rules do provide exceptionally good examples of the deeply fraught nature of Western ideas about women. Defamed and defended, attacked and praised, caricatured as Eve and venerated as the Virgin, medieval women were both fully human and profoundly other.[50] In classroom teaching, medieval ideologies of gender can be useful precisely because it is so difficult for modern students to unpack their own contemporary gender rules. What students sometimes have difficulty seeing in our own culture, they can more readily perceive in the distant past.

The Virgin Mary—a fascinating topic for many students—provides an excellent example of slippery gender ideologies. Medieval Christians saw Mary simultaneously as the bride of Christ *and* his mother; as a young mother with child *and* the grieving mother of a crucified son; as the embodied throne for a child Christ held in her lap *and* his regal consort.[51] This multivalent model presented real women with deeply ambivalent possibilities. Mary's virginity provided holy women with the Middle Age's most fully articulated sexual identity, but holy virgins were both washed of their gender and derided because of it. Insofar as virginity made a woman admirable, it also made her not-woman, a virago who had triumphed over the base sexual urges characteristic of her sex. Yet this triumphant virginity never entirely degendered a woman, for many priests and monks regarded even the most devout nuns as burdensome threats to male chastity. As Saint Francis himself put it when he opposed the affiliation of nuns to his Franciscan order, "God has taken our wives from us, and now Satan has given us sisters." Nuns might have been pure in their virginity and masculine in their self-restraint, but they were not thereby freed—as the Virgin was—from their tempting, feminine sexuality.[52]

For ordinary wives and mothers, Mary's intercessory role was just as challenging to emulate as her virginity. Cast as a petitioner to her son on behalf of the needy, the sinful, and the damned, the Virgin simultaneously held power and lacked it. Although intercession was the Virgin's special forte, it was also attributed to other female saints and expected of ordinary women. Poets praised wives who wisely counseled their husbands, priests urged wives to use their "persuasive voices" to guide their husbands toward piety, and everyone expected queens to translate their wifely influence into practical power. For medieval women, this ideal of gentle persuasion was difficult to achieve in practice, for it required a deft balance of humility, shrewdness, and sagacity; no wonder that some women were maligned for overweening influence and others as malcontented shrews. Yet, no matter how challenging the role, medieval women—Virgin Mother, queen, or humble wife—were expected to exercise power through the circuitous and challenging route of influencing men.[53]

The ambivalence of medieval gender ideologies extended to the misogyny for which medieval Europe is rightly famous. Students react with justified horror to medieval misogynous texts, and it is easy to channel this horror into discussions about the meanings of medieval misogyny and its modern analogs. Nurtured by clerical celibates and strengthened by the ancient ideal of an ascetic philosophical life, medieval misogyny attacked marriage (misogamy) almost as often as it maligned women.[54] Thus cloaked in deep ambivalence toward marriage and family, medieval misogyny was also strongly inflected by humor, genre, and tradition. It drew on a remarkably small number of texts and authors, and it followed quite predictable forms, usually listing examples of evil women, relying on satirical caricatures, polemicizing against marriage, or spouting first-person complaints. In its antipathy toward marriage, its humor, and its repetitive forms, medieval misogyny is not that far removed, as students quickly grasp, from some forms of modern misogyny, particularly jokes of the "ball and chain" variety.

Students also benefit from reviewing scholarly debates about the meanings of medieval misogyny. To some medievalists, the rich literary traditions of misogyny suggest that it should be understood as a literary game, a forum in which authors could "show off their literary paces." In this view, misogyny was "a way of speaking about women as distinct from doing something to women."[55] Yet other medievalists have objected to this interpretation, pointing out that women actually suffered as a result of these misogynous ideas. Because women were perceived as naturally greedy, oversexed, and untrustworthy, medieval people preferred to buy their ale and beer from male brewers rather than female brewsters. And because medieval people believed that all women used sex in order to gain money, position, and advantage, the prostitute was seen, as Ruth Karras has put it, as "simply the market-oriented version of a more general phenomenon."[56] "Sticks and stones can break my bones but words can never hurt me." If students bring this assumption to feminist complaints about contemporary advertising and entertainment, debates about medieval misogyny will help them to think again.

TEACHING THE DISTANT PAST

Even before some postfeminists decided that they did not want to remember the past, students were arriving in history classes with more dread than enthusiasm. As historians and as feminists, we cannot surrender to this history-hating, no matter how entrenched it seems among twenty-first-century students and no matter how many of our colleagues in women's studies also embrace a persistent presentism. It is our particular responsibility to keep the past—not just the recent past but also more distant times—alive in feminist classrooms and in dialogue with the present. This task is not as difficult as it might seem. After all, as publishers and toy manufacturers know well, modern children spend many happy hours imagining medieval worlds of brave ladies, bold knights, saintly maids, and wily monks. To judge from the themes of recent movies—*Robin Hood: Prince of Thieves* (1991), *Braveheart* (1995), *The Messenger: The Story of Joan of Arc* (1999), not to mention the *Lord of the Rings* trilogy (2001–3)—medieval fantasies thrive well beyond childhood. As children grow older, however, they too often discard these youthful pleasures in a deluded notion that the distant past is a childish preoccupation. If we fight effectively against this wrong-headed idea, the rich historical imaginations of children can mature into study, discussion, and learning.

One part of this task is transforming how students approach the past. In nurseries, medieval worlds are places of fantasy and day-dream, strange worlds far removed from children's own lives. History and fantasy—Richard the Lionhearted and Buzz Lightyear—are much the same in playrooms, because both are, to a child, not now and not me. In schools, students develop a relationship to history that emphasizes their lineal connectedness to past lives, a connectedness that fosters patriotism, civic pride, and a sense of national genealogy. Thus, students in U.S. high schools customarily study the histories of both nation and state, thereby learning to understand themselves as the descendants of founding fathers (and sometimes mothers). Neither of these relationships to history—history-as-fantasy and history-as-descent—work productively in feminist classrooms; we must instead ask our students to approach history as a desk-bound sort of time travel. The history of medieval women is not a wondrous daydream, nor is it a foundational history from which all modern women descend; instead, it is a history that offers students new perspectives, new ways of seeing, new understandings, and new comparisons to their own lives. A U.S. student who travels to China acquires these things; so, too, do U.S. and Chinese students who study the history of medieval women. By studying past worlds, these students see their own worlds in new ways.

Another part of our task is to startle students with the revelations of this time travel, offering them a history that is as fascinating as it is productive. This is now easily done, thanks to the perspicacious questions and hard research of feminist medievalists into topics of immediate relevance to today's students. Students can now examine the culture of rape among the feudal aristocracy;[57] the somatic piety of female mystics, especially as manifested by such extreme fasting that some historians compare it to modern anorexia;[58] the ways in which medieval women might have sought to practice birth control and induce abortions;[59] the working lives of women in both town and country;[60] the rule of early medieval abbesses over monasteries that contained monks as well as nuns; the veneration of virginity in the Middle Ages;[61] the proscriptions, perceptions, and practices of lesbian sexuality;[62] the nature of motherhood in a world where many children died young and many others left home at young ages;[63] the construction of masculinity in medieval cultures;[64] the accepted place of prostitution in medieval towns and canon law;[65] and the gender transgressions of women who cross-dressed as men and men who cross-dressed as women.[66]

Some might see these as trendy topics; I see them as histories that speak directly to students, offering new ways of thinking about issues with which they struggle daily. For example, matters of religion and spirituality pervade modern campuses and so, too, do eating disorders; both can be revealingly brought into classrooms through the study of female spirituality in medieval Christianity. As Caroline Walker Bynum has explored so carefully, Christian women in late medieval centuries often expressed their faith through extreme acts of bodily self-denial, especially fasting. In Bynum's view, these acts, horrifying as they are to modern readers, speak to the creative and positive ways in which female Christian mystics then approached their God. Yet other historians take a less sanguine view, arguing that the extreme self-abnegation of these women illustrates the active misogyny of the medieval Church or even mental illness. My students are fascinated by the stories of these women and eager to debate whether their asceticism should be seen as positive expressions of female piety, sad proof of female oppression, or merely evidence of individual pathology (especially anorexia nervosa). As part of this debate, they think historically (interpreting the writings of medieval mystics), comparatively (placing this specific case against broader histories of women in established religions), and contemporarily (reconsidering their own ideas about faith and food).[67]

We also must not forget to share in our classrooms the pleasures that first drew us toward history. For me, those pleasures began with fiction but moved quickly to biography, and if the history sections of bookstores are any guide, biography remains today the most popular of historical genres. I have expressed concerns in Chapter 2 about how our current turn toward biography can favor privileged, articulate women, but there is no denying that biographies are a terrific teaching tool. Medieval Europe, for example, produced numerous extraordinary women whose well-documented lives allow students to explore the down-to-earth realities behind abstract historical generalizations: women such as Heloise of the Paraclete, lover of Peter Abelard and revered abbess;[68] Eleanor of Aquitaine, duchess in her own right, wife of two kings, and mother of two more;[69] Christine de Pizan, the first woman in Europe to support herself by writing and—as students can debate—perhaps Europe's first feminist;[70] Hildegard of Bingen, abbess, polymath, and visionary;[71] Joan of Arc, peasant girl, mystic, and warrior;[72] Christina of St. Trond (c. 1150–1224), known as "*mirabilis*" in the Middle Ages and just as astonishing to students today;[73] Margery Kempe (c. 1373–1438), author of the first autobiography in English.[74] These biographical forays also critically encourage students to understand medieval women on their own terms, even if those terms initially seem foreign, abstract, and even downright odd.

In a process of simultaneous identification and differentiation, students learn that what might seem peculiar to us was practical, possible, or perhaps even pleasurable to medieval women. In other words, they more fully grasp, through biography, the *differences* that distinguish medieval women from ourselves.

I have focused here on the European Middle Ages, but it is just one example of how the teaching of the history of women before 1800 can effectively draw students away from contemporary self-absorption and toward tough intellectual issues. The history of women in the distant past teaches students about the sources, traditions, and controversies of feminist history-writing; it raises hard questions—about relations between women and men, about differences among people, and about the possibility of human equality—that are of pressing interest to all feminists; and it asks students to think critically about the complex workings of ideology, culture, and religion, both in the past and today. In feminist classrooms, the distant past encourages students to critique modern assumptions, to see feminist issues in a longer view, and to acknowledge the powerful differences between ourselves and those long dead.

"What does history disclose but marks of inferiority, and how few women have emancipated themselves from the galling yoke of sovereign man?" Thus complained Mary Wollstonecraft in 1792.[75] So, too, complain some students today, easily tired by histories that seemingly harp on women's victimization and men's offense. Their tiredness divides feminist generations: older women who argue, as did Jane Fonda in a recent interview, "patriarchy is very much alive and well, and we have to do something about it," and younger women (in this case Fonda's interviewer, Emma Brockes) who counter that "the word patriarchy is an anachronism—that, while no one would deny inequality exists, lots of women would bridle at the suggestion they are victims of a patriarchal system."[76] The women's history advocated in this book—attentive to the deep past and alive to continuities and patriarchal equilibriums—can reinvigorate the feminist politics of our field. But it can also exasperate some—especially younger women and especially students—to whom it seems both debilitating and depressing.

Feminist teachers must turn this exasperation into conversation. Students do not respond well to being lectured about patriarchy, but they do jump at opportunities to tackle patriarchy as an as-yet-developing concept and a still-to-be-solved historical problem. If asked to define patriarchy and study its history, they teach themselves that

patriarchy is not the blunt instrument they had assumed, not a committee of white-haired men, not a set system, and not a war of men
against women. They also come to see that the things that most trouble them about the term—that "patriarchy" seems to imply that men
are to blame and that women are universal victims—are not inherent
to the concept. In these ways, they reclaim "patriarchy" as a usable
concept instead of a discarded bugbear. Much the same is true of the
"marks of inferiority" that can so predominate in women's history. It
would be nice, I suppose, to teach a women's history filled with
woman-affirming heroines, and it can be difficult, I well know, to
teach a history that dwells on constraint, disappointment, and frustration. But a light touch helps considerably, as does a steady focus on
many ways in which women maneuvered within patriarchy, benefited
from patriarchy, and critiqued patriarchy. In these ways, students can
grasp the full challenge of feminist struggles, as well the personal
challenges which they, both women and men, will inevitably confront
in the world beyond campuses and classrooms. Like all historians, I
seek to equip my students with new information and better skills, and
like all feminists, I seek to empower my students as well. I hope my
former students will recall, when they face disappointments and troubles later in life, that their problems have histories and are not, therefore, personal failings. I also hope they will always think more deeply
about feminist issues, and in this regard, I can do no better than
quote the classicist Amy Richlin, reflecting on parallels in masculinist
rhetoric, Roman and modern: "So what do we do with the idea that
such narratives have been operating to silence women for over two
thousand years? I always tell my students that you have to know what
you're facing before you can fix it . . . I think it is important to keep
faith with history—and then keep on working."[77]

Chapter 8

Conclusion: For Whom Are We Doing Feminist History?

Like most historians, I feel more comfortable thinking about the past than speculating on the future. This book began with recollections of my first encounters with women's history in the 1970s, and it has built its argument around both history per se (especially medieval history) and the history of feminist history-writing in the last thirty years. I know how to do the past; doing the future is much harder. But if you have come this far with me, you know that this book is not about nostalgia or melancholy; it is about assessing what we have done right, where we have gone off track, and how we might do better. I have been inspired throughout by Barbara Christian's question, posed in the late 1980s to feminist literary critics and evoked here in the title of this conclusion.[1]

The *feminism* of feminist history

Universities are feminist battlegrounds that understandably divert historians of women and gender away from such in-the-street feminist issues as economic equity, reproductive rights, and domestic violence and toward more internal, academic issues. Thus, we seek to integrate women's experiences into mainstream history, to hire more women faculty, to ensure that our campuses are safer, to create curricula that speak to the interests of *all* students, and to improve the status of women on our campuses. These are important, indeed crucial, issues that rightly absorb our energies. But they are not sufficient. As feminist historians, we are obliged to juggle two agendas: first, to eradicate the misogynistic traditions of academia in their many, entrenched forms, and second, to explain to feminists more generally—from our privileged position as researchers and teachers—how history can help us understand women's oppression and work toward its final eradication.

We historians will better serve our feminist allies if we frame our studies around feminist questions, write essays and books in clear prose, and, perhaps most important of all, dare to see our specific historical work within larger frames. The epistemological crises of the late twentieth century have made us timid about claims to knowledge, but we can still suggest and think without naively claiming to know for certain. Similarly, although we should certainly eschew universal statements that suppress difference, we can still seek patterns and elucidate comparisons through the more supple frameworks of generalization. I have disagreed above with Joan Scott's comment that "simply comparing data about women did not get us very far,"[2] and I also disagree with Sara Evans's declaration that "clearly we all understand that generalizations about women are going to be very hard to come by in the future and probably are not worth the effort."[3] In my view, feminist history will not be worth the effort if we do not compare and generalize. If we retreat into detailed histories valued for their specificity alone we might find a safe harbor in terms of knowledge claims and attention to difference, but we will have rendered women's and gender history innocuous within the discipline and irrelevant to the political imperatives of feminism. As I look to the future, I hope more of us will take the risk of setting our work within larger intellectual and political contexts.

Feminism is an inherently plural noun, for feminist approaches are always diverse and multiple. Diverse and multiple, too, are feminist approaches to the history of women and gender. But it is time for historians of women and gender to regain our feminist indignation and to reorient our history around the straightforward feminist conviction that women should share human opportunities equally with men. That conviction rightly carries us in many directions—especially into the many other inequalities that limit human lives, male as well as female—but awareness of women's illegitimate subordination to men rests at feminism's core. In the last few decades, women's and gender history has too often settled comfortably into approaches that are professionally safe and unduly timid about the sexual inequities at the heart of feminist critique. To my mind, our history should be less safe and more offensive.

The *history* of feminist history

We live in presentist times, and feminist history is especially harmed by it. My data have suggested that feminist historians collectively suffer from an acutely bad case of temporal truncation, and this is an affliction that feminism can ill afford, given the tenacity of the historical problems it poses. Even more than most other historical fields, feminist history needs the distant past. I believe as firmly today as I did in the 1970s that history has unique and critical contributions to offer to the feminist struggle, but those contributions cannot derive solely from a history of women and gender since 1800. We must look further back, attend to continuity as well as change, and take better advantage of the perspectives that only temporal distance (and difference) can offer. I hope we will also take as our brief the challenge of leading our feminist colleagues in other disciplines away from the intellectual abyss of relentless contemporaneity. We need to remind those who might prefer not to remember.

Patriarchy

In the 1970s, feminist historians spoke easily and readily about patriarchy; today, we do not. We have been encouraged to mute our voices by two contrary but powerful forces: on the one hand, the practices of a historical discipline in which, as we have already seen, study of women's oppression is characterized as "minor, amateurish, overemotional, and uncritical," and on the other hand, the aversion of postfeminists to any hint of complaint about systematic sexual inequalities.[4] These are powerful disincentives, but we must not give way before them. Patriarchy talk might be unfashionable in some circles, but it is essential to the future of feminism, essential to historical research on women and gender, and essential in our teaching. We still have many things to learn about patriarchal power in the past as well as the present, but one thing is certain: sexual equality will not be advanced by wishing away patriarchy, trivializing its effects, or ignoring it in feminist classrooms.

Notes

Chapter 1

1. Feminist history is most firmly entrenched in the United States and the Netherlands, but it is recognized elsewhere, too. For an overview of the national and institutional contexts of the development of the field as of 1990, see *Writing Women's History: International Perspectives*, ed. Karen Offen, Ruth Roach Pierson, and Jane Rendall (Basingstoke: Macmillan, 1991), esp. xxii–xxvii.

2. As cited in Anne Clark Bartlett, "Defining the Terms: Postfeminism as an Ideology of Cool," *Medieval Feminist Forum* 34 (Fall 2002): 25–29, at 28.

3. In 1970s Toronto, I learned not only about feminism and history but also about constructive criticism that facilitates change and growth. I hope that *History Matters: Patriarchy and the Challenge of Feminism* falls within that positive tradition, and if so, much credit is due to the constructive critiques of colleagues and friends. I will not repeat here my gratitude to those whose comments enriched the original articles that inform some parts of what follows, but I would like to acknowledge my debt to Sandy Bardsley, Laura Gowing, Cynthia Herrup, Nancy Hewitt, Ruth Karras, Patricia Skinner, and Martha Vicinus, who critically read this new book-length formulation; the final book is much better for their generous advice, although they do not, of course, bear any responsibility for the arguments herein. I also thank the research assistants who have made my work so much easier: Dana Brinson, Bethany Keenan, Kristina Lorusso, Jennifer Walcoff, and Janelle Werner.

4. For permission to draw on my past writings, I thank Indiana University Press, for "Confronting Continuity," *Journal of Women's History* 9:3 (1997): 73–94; the American Historical Association for *Medieval Women in Modern Perspective* (Washington, D.C.: AHA, 2000); and the University of Texas Press, for "'Lesbian-Like' and the Social History of Lesbianisms," *Journal of the History of Sexuality* 9:1/2 (2000): 1–24. My other relevant essays are "Women's History: A Study in Change and Continuity," *Women's History Review* 2 (1993): 173–84; "Medievalism and Feminism," *Speculum: A Journal of Medieval Studies* 68 (1993): 309–31; "Medieval Women, Modern Women: Across the Great Divide," in *Culture and History, 1350–1600: Essays on English Communities, Identities, and Writing,* ed. David Aers (London: Harvester Wheatsheaf, 1992), 147–75, with a revised version in *Feminists Revision History*, ed. Ann-Louise Shapiro (New Brunswick, N.J.: Rutgers University Press, 1994), 47–72; "Feminism and History," *Gender and History* 1 (1989): 251–72.

5. I borrow this phrase from Carolyn Dinshaw, *Getting Medieval: Sexualities and Communities, Pre- and Postmodern* (Durham, N.C.: Duke University Press, 1999), who herself took it from a comment in the 1994 movie *Pulp Fiction*.

6. Iris Marion Young, "Gender as Seriality: Thinking about Women as a Social Collective," *Signs: A Journal of Women in Culture and Society* 19:3 (1994): 713–39.

7. These characteristics of British, Chinese, and U.S. women's history have been often remarked on. For Brazil, see Maria Beatriz Nizza da Silva, "Women's History in Brazil: Production and Perspectives," in *Writing Women's History*, 369–380. For Japan, see Hiroko Nagano, "The Unique Relationship between Women's History and Gender History in Japan: In Search of Direction for the Future," a paper given at the International Federation for Research in Women's History subconference at the 20th International Congress of Historical Studies in Sydney, Australia, in July 2005 and available online at the IFRWH website at http://www.ifrwh.com/. See also Noriyo Hayakawa, "The Development of Women's History in Japan," in *Writing Women's History*, 171–79.

8. Lest my self-reflection contribute further to an often caricatured moment in feminism and feminist history, see Alice Echols, *Daring to Be Bad: Radical Feminism in America, 1967–1975* (Minneapolis: University of Minnesota Press, 1989), and Lise Vogel, "Telling Tales: Historians of Our Own Lives," *Journal of Women's History* 2:3 (1991): 89–101.

9. For medieval data, see Sandy Bardsley, "Women's Work Reconsidered: Gender and Wage Differentiation in Late Medieval England," *Past and Present* 165 (1999): 3–29. For contemporary British data, see Wendy Olsen and Sylvia Walby, "Modelling Gender Pay Gaps," Equal Opportunities Commission Working Paper Series 17 (2004): esp. 8–11 (available online at www.eoc.org.uk). Recent figures for the United States suggest that women earn 76 cents for every dollar earned by men; see data released in April 2004 by the American Association of University Women (www.aauw.org). For worldwide figures, see the reports of United Nations Development Fund for Women (www.unifem.org).

Chapter 2

1. Christine de Pizan, *The Book of the City of Ladies*, trans. Earl Jeffrey Richards (New York: Persea Books, 1982), 256.

2. Christine de Pizan was not, of course, a feminist in contemporary terms; see Beatrice Gottlieb, "The Problem of Feminism in the Fifteenth Century," in *Women of the Medieval World*, ed. Julius Kirshner and Suzanne F. Wemple (Oxford: Blackwell, 1985), 337–64.

3. Barbara Ehrenreich and Deirdre English, *Witches, Midwives, and Nurses: A History of Women Healers* (Old Westbury, N.Y.: Feminist Press, 1973). As Monica Green has recently noted, this empirically weak book nevertheless "succinctly captured a narrative of female empowerment that had potent political uses in the climate of second-wave feminism." Monica H. Green, "Bodies, Gender, Health, Disease: Recent Work on Medieval Women's Medicine," *Studies in Medieval and Renaissance History*, 3rd ser., 2 (2005): 1–46, at 17.

4. Sheila Rowbotham, *Women, Resistance and Revolution: A History of Women and Revolution in the Modern World* (New York: Pantheon Books, 1972); Linda Gordon, *Woman's Body, Woman's Right: A Social History of Birth Control in*

America (New York: Grossman, 1976); Joan Scott and Louise Tilly, *Women, Work, and Family* (New York: Holt, Rinehart, and Winston, 1978).

5. Krista Cowman and Louise A Jackson, "Time," in *A Concise Companion to Feminist Theory*, ed. Mary Eagleton (Oxford: Blackwell, 2003), 32–52, at 36. For Evans's comment, see Anne Firor Scott et al., "Women's History in the New Millennium: A Conversation across Three 'Generations': Part 2," *Journal of Women's History* 11:2 (1999): 199–220, at 213.

6. For international overviews of the field, see Teresa A. Meade and Merry E. Wiesner-Hanks, eds., *A Companion to Gender History* (Oxford: Blackwell, 2004); Karen Offen, Ruth Roach Pierson, and Jane Rendall, eds., *Writing Women's History: International Perspectives* (Basingstoke: Macmillan, 1991); Jay Kleinberg, eds., *Retrieving Women's History: Changing Perceptions of the Role of Women in Politics and Society* (Oxford: Berg, 1988). The figure of seventy U.S. graduate programs was given by Gerda Lerner in her "Women among the Professors of History: The Story of a Process of Transformation," in *Voices of Women Historians: The Personal, the Political, the Professional*, ed. Eileen Boris and Nupur Chaudhuri (Bloomington: Indiana University Press, 1999), 1–10, at 7. The International Federation for Research in Women's History was founded in 1987; their website is at http://www.ifrwh.com. The three journals are *Gender and History*, published by an Anglo-American editorial team; *The Journal of Women's History*, based entirely in the United States; and the *Women's History Review*, based in the UK.

7. Women's history also is especially well institutionalized in the Netherlands, from whence is produced, among other things, the Virtual Library in Women's History (http://www.iisg.nl/w3vlwomenshistory) and the *European Journal of Women's Studies*. See Maria Grever, " 'Pivoting the Center': Women's History as a Compulsory Examination Subject in all Dutch Secondary Schools in 1990 and 1991," *Gender and History* 3:1 (1991): 65–80, and Marjan Schwegman and Mineke Bosch, "The Future of Women's History: The Dutch Perspective," *Gender and History* 3:2 (1991): 129–36. I must confess that I am often struck by the relative *absence* of women's history courses in many non-U.S. universities; look, for example at the intercollegiate offerings at the University of London (http://www.history.ac.uk/syllabus/intercol.html). But a great deal of progress seems to have been made beneath the public surface of curricula. As has been recently noted for Britain, "It is now virtually impossible to undertake a history degree without encountering material on women's history (although in the great majority of institutions the subject still remains discreetly contained within options)." Cowman and Jackson, "Time," 34.

8. See, however, Susan Mosher Stuard, "American Feminism and the Annales School," *Signs: A Journal of Women in Culture and Society* 6 (1981): 135–43.

9. Offen et al., eds., *Writing Women's History*.

10. In her *No Turning Back: The History of Feminism and the Future of Women* (New York: Ballantine, 2002), 7, Estelle Freedman defines feminism as "a belief that women and men are inherently of equal worth. Because most societies privilege men as a group, social movements are necessary to achieve equality between women and men, with the understanding that gender always intersects with other social hierarchies."

11. Denise Riley, *Am I That Name? Feminism and the Category of "Women" in*

History (Minneapolis: University of Minnesota Press, 1988); Judith Butler, *Gender Trouble: Feminism and the Subversion of Identity* (New York: Routledge, 1990); Audre Lorde, "An Open Letter to Mary Daly," in *This Bridge Called My Back: Writings by Radical Women of Color*, ed. Cherríe Moraga and Gloria Anzaldúa (New York: Kitchen Table Press, 1983), 94–97; Elizabeth V. Spelman, *Inessential Woman: Problems of Exclusion in Feminist Thought* (Boston: Beacon Press, 1988); Chandra Talpade Mohanty, "Under Western Eyes: Feminist Scholarship and Colonial Discourses," in *Third World Women and the Politics of Feminism*, ed. Chandra Talpade Mohanty, Ann Russo, and Lourdes Torres (Bloomington: Indiana University Press, 1991), 51–80.

12. Jee Yeun Lee, "Beyond Bean Counting," in *Listen Up: Voices from the Next Feminist Generation*, ed. Barbara Findlen (Seattle: Seal Press, 2001), 67–73, at 72.

13. Toril Moi, "What Is a Woman? Sex, Gender, and the Body in Feminist Theory," in her *What Is a Woman? And Other Essays* (New York: Oxford University Press, 1999), 3–120, at 10.

14. Riley, *Am I That Name*, 112.

15. Mary Maynard, "Beyond the 'Big Three': The Development of Feminist Theory in the 1990s," *Women's History Review* 4:3 (1995): 259–81, at 274–75. See also the wise advice of Jane Roland Martin, "Methodological Essentialism, False Difference, and Other Dangerous Traps," *Signs: A Journal of Women in Culture and Society* 19:3 (1994): 630–57.

16. See especially Iris Marion Young, "Gender as Seriality: Thinking about Women as a Social Collective," *Signs: A Journal of Women in Culture and Society* 19:3 (1994): 713–39; and Deirdre Keenan, "Race, Gender, and other Differences in Feminist Theory," in *A Companion to Gender History*, ed. Teresa A. Meade and Merry E. Wiesner-Hanks (Oxford: Blackwell, 2004), 110–28.

17. Dorothea Oschinsky, ed., *Walter of Henley and Other Treatises on Estate Management and Accounting* (Oxford: Clarendon Press, 1971), 427.

18. Barbara Ehrenreich and Arlie Russell Hochschild, eds., *Global Woman: Nannies, Maids, and Sex Workers in the New Economy* (New York: Metropolitan Books, 2003).

19. Gisela Bock, "Women's History and Gender History: Aspects of an International Debate," *Gender and History* 1:1 (1989): 7–30, at 21.

20. Sally Alexander and Barbara Taylor, "In Defence of Patriarchy," 1979, reprinted in *People's History and Socialist Theory*, ed. Raphael Samuel (London: Routledge and Kegan Paul, 1981), 370–73, at 372.

21. Michael Roper, *Masculinity and the British Organization Man since 1945* (Oxford: Oxford University Press, 1994). See also Michael Roper and John Tosh, "Historians and the Politics of Masculinity," in *Manful Assertions: Masculinities in Britain since 1800*, ed. Michael Roper and John Tosh (London: Routledge, 1991), 1–24.

22. Alice Walker, *In Search of Our Mothers' Gardens: Womanist Prose* (San Diego: Harcourt Brace Jovanovich, 1983).

23. Antoinette Burton, "'History' Is Now: Feminist Theory and the Production of Historical Feminisms," *Women's History Review* 1:1 (1992): 25–39. Burton provides cites to many relevant studies. Those published since include Aparnu Basu, "Feminism and Nationalism in India, 1917–1947," *Journal of Women's History* 7:4 (1995): 95–107; Noriyo Hayakawa, "Feminism and Nationalism in Japan, 1868–1946," *Journal of Women's History* 7:4 (1995):

108–19; Yung-Hee Kim, "Under the Mandate of Nationalism: Development of Feminist Enterprises in Modern Korea, 1860–1910," *Journal of Women's History* 7:4 (1995): 120–45; Sanjam Abluwalia, "Rethinking Boundaries: Feminism and (Inter)Nationalism in Early-Twentieth-Century India," *Journal of Women's History* 14:4 (2003): 187–94; Donna J. Guy, "The Politics of Pan-American Cooperation: Maternalist Feminism and the Child Rights Movement, 1913–1960," *Gender and History* 10:3 (1998): 449–69.

24. For RAWA, see their website at http://www.rawa.org/. For Africa, see Gwendolyn Mikell, "African Feminism: Toward a New Politics of Representation," *Feminist Studies* 21:2 (1995): 405–425. The website for MADRE is at http://www.madre.org/. For a list of feminist organizations worldwide, go to http://www.distel.ca/womlist/womlist.html or, if the URL changes, search Global List of Women's Organizations.

25. See, for example, Joan W. Scott, "Deconstructing Equality vs. Difference, Or, the Uses of Poststructuralist Theory for Feminism," *Feminist Studies* 14:1 (1988): 32–50.

26. Barbara Smith, "Racism and Women's Studies," in her *The Truth That Never Hurts: Writings on Race, Gender, and Freedom* (New Brunswick, N.J.: Rutgers University Press, 1998), 96.

27. Scott, "Introduction," to *Feminism and History*, 13.

28. Charlotte Bunch, "Not by Degrees: Feminist Theory and Education," in *Learning Our Way: Essays in Feminist Education*, ed. Charlotte Bunch and Sandra Pollack (Trumansburg, N.Y.: Crossing Press, 1983), 248–60, at 250.

29. William L. O'Neill, *Everyone Was Brave: The Rise and Fall of Feminism in America* (Chicago: Quadrangle Books, 1969), viii.

30. Brian Harrison and James McMillan, "Some Feminist Betrayals of Women's History," *Historical Journal* 26:2 (1983): 375–89, at 387.

31. Helen M. Jewell, *Women in Medieval England* (Manchester: Manchester University Press, 1996), 7.

32. Joan Wallach Scott, *Gender and the Politics of History* (New York: Columbia University Press, 1988), 32–33.

33. Bernard Capp, responding to Laura Gowing's review of his *When Gossips Meet: Women, Family and Neighbourhood in Early Modern England* (Oxford: Oxford University Press, 2003) in *Reviews in History* 365 (January 2004): available online at http://www.history.ac.uk/reviews/.

34. C. H. McIlwain, "Medieval Institutions in the Modern World," *Speculum* 16 (1941): 275–83, at 277. I quote McIlwain for his succinct phrasing, but this concern is not confined to the 1940s. For example, Geoffrey Elton attacked Marxist and feminist historians in 1991 for using "previously constructed schemes which guide research ostensibly designed to test them." G. R. Elton, *Return to Essentials: Some Reflections on the Present State of Historical Study* (Cambridge: Cambridge University Press, 1991), 23–25.

35. On the quest for an apolitical, god's-eye-view history in America, see Peter Novick, *That Noble Dream: The "Objectivity Question" and the American Historical Profession* (Cambridge: Cambridge University Press, 1988). Novick discusses the misunderstood but nevertheless powerful "*wie es eigentlich gewesen*" associated with Leopold von Ranke on 26–31.

36. Lawrence Stone, "Only Women," *New York Review of Books* 32:6 (1985): available online at http://www.nybooks.com/articles/. I have quoted Stone

from the mid-1980s because he wrote with unusual frankness on this subject.

37. Ruth Roach Pierson, "Experience, Difference, Dominance, and Voice in the Writing of Canadian Women's History," in *Writing Women's History*, ed. Offen et al., 79–106.

38. Tacitus, *Annals* 3.65. See, more recently, Gordon Wright's presidential address to the American Historical Association on "History as a Moral Science." Wright concluded with the hope that history can become one of the "moral arts," by grappling successfully with the challenge of an approach to the past that is "quite consciously suffused by a commitment to some deeply held humane values." Printed in the *American Historical Review* 81:1 (February 1976) and available online at http://www.historians.org/info/AHA_History/gwright.htm.

39. Adrienne Rich, "Resisting Amnesia: History and Personal Life," in *Blood, Bread, and Poetry: Selected Prose, 1979–1985* (New York: Norton, 1986), 136–55, at 149.

40. Sharon Sievers, "Dialogue: Six (or More) Feminists in Search of a Historian," *Journal of Women's History* 1:2 (1989): 134–46.

41. An interview with Justice Ginsburg, as quoted in Mary Anne C. Case, "Disaggregating Gender from Sex and Sexual Orientation: The Effeminate Man in the Law and Feminist Jurisprudence," *Yale Law Journal* 105:1 (1995): 1–105, as cited in Moi, "What Is a Woman?" 86.

42. Judith M. Bennett "Gender, Family and Community: A Comparative Study of the English Peasantry" (Ph.D. diss., University of Toronto, 1981). I was a bit braver in the book that emerged from this dissertation, *Women in the Medieval English Countryside: Gender and Household in Brigstock before the Plague* (New York: Oxford University Press, 1987).

43. Joan Scott as cited by Teresa A. Meade and Merry E. Wiesner, "Introduction," in *A Companion to Gender History*, ed. Meade and Wiesner-Hanks, 1–11, at 3.

44. See Section 1 of "Letter to the Bishops of the Catholic Church on the Collaboration of Men and Women in the Church and in the World," online at http://www.vatican.va/roman_curia/congregations/cfaith/documents/rc_con_cfaith_doc_20040731_collaboration_en.html.

45. Thomas Laqueur, *Making Sex: Body and Gender from the Greeks to Freud* (Cambridge, MA: Harvard University Press, 1990). For medieval thought on the subject (scarcely and inaccurately treated by Laqueur), see Joan Cadden, *Meanings of Sex Difference in the Middle Ages* (Cambridge: Cambridge University Press, 1993). For a revision of Laqueur's treatment of ancient authorities, see Helen King, "The Mathematics of Sex: One to Two or Two to One," *Studies in Medieval and Renaissance History*, 3rd ser., 2 (2005): 47–58. See also Gisela Bock's trenchant comments on the dangers of relying on biology in her "Women's History and Gender History."

46. See, especially, Butler, *Gender Trouble*. For an example of the revived uninflected use of both terms, see Joan W. Scott, "Feminism's History," *Journal of Women's History* 16:2 (2004): 10–29, at 21.

47. On translation difficulties, see Bock, "Women's History," 10; Gisela Bock, "Challenging Dichotomies: Perspectives on Women's History," in *Writing Women's History*, ed. Offen et al., 1–23; and Moi, "What is a Woman?" 5–6

(Moi also discusses the ways in which our contemporary sex/gender distinction can cause us to misread "sex" in the writings of earlier feminists).

48. I am grateful to Ruth Karras for this critical point.

49. "Why Gender and History?" *Gender and History* 1:1 (1989): 1–6, at 1. I should disclose that I was on the editorial collective that developed this statement.

50. Joan Wallach Scott, "Gender: A Useful Category of Historical Analysis," first published in the *American Historical Review* 91:5 (1986) and subsequently revised for her *Gender and the Politics of History* (New York: Columbia University Press, 1988, rev. ed. in 1999), 28–52, quote at 44. I cite pages from the 1988 version.

51. Riley, *Am I That Name?*; Joan Wallach Scott, "The Evidence of Experience," *Critical Inquiry* 17 (1991): 773–97.

52. In his review of Mary Beard's *Woman as a Force in History* in the *New York Times*, 17 March 1946: 5, as cited in Johanna Alberti, *Gender and the Historian* (London: Longman, 2002), 8.

53. Scott's formulation also generated intense debate. One good starting point in the debate is Martin Bunzl, "The Construction of History," *Journal of Women's History* 9:3 (1997): 119–31, and Judith P. Zinsser, " 'Much More is at Stake Here . . .': A Response to 'The Construction of History,' " *Journal of Women's History* 9:3 (1997): 132–39. To get a sense of the passionate feelings on both sides, see Joan Hoff, "Gender as a Postmodern Category of Paralysis," *Women's History Review* 3:2 (1994): 149–68, and debate thereafter in *Women's History Review* 5:1 (1996): 9–30. I agree with Ellen DuBois's sentiment: "As far as I am concerned, the woman versus gender debate among historians is done, it is old news, it is not worth worrying about, it has happened, and it is over. Women's history was not washed away by the rise of gender history. So I accept women's history and gender history as compatible." Nancy Cott et al., "Considering the State of U.S. Women's History," *Journal of Women's History* 15:1 (2003): 145–63, at 151.

54. Nan Enstad, *Ladies of Labor, Girls of Adventure: Working Women, Popular Culture, and Labor Politics at the Turn of the Twentieth Century* (New York: Columbia University Press, 1999), 5.

55. For Japan, see Hiroko Nagano, "The Unique Relationship between Women's History and Gender History in Japan: In Search of Direction for the Future," a paper given at the International Federation for Research in Women's History subconference at the 20th International Congress of Historical Studies in Sydney, Australia, in July 2005 and available online at the IFRWH website at http://www.ifrwh.com.

56. This was, for example, the view expressed by Kathleen Canning in the discussion that followed her talk "The Practice of Gender History: Meanings, Methods, and Metanarratives," at Duke University, March 4, 2004.

57. The full list is available at http://www.ifrwh.com/national_committees.htm.

58. For the United States, this story is told in Hilda A. Smith et al., *A History of the Coordinating Council for Women in the Historical Profession-Conference Group on Women's History* (Brooklyn, N.Y.: CCWHP-CGWH, 1994).

59. Although I look back here only to the "early days" of the 1970s, the professional development of women's history extends back into the nineteenth century. See Julie Des Jardins, *Women and the Historical Enterprise in*

America (Chapel Hill: University of North Carolina Press, 2003), and Jane Chance, ed., *Women Medievalists and the Academy* (Madison: University of Wisconsin Press, 2005).

60. Nancy Hewitt, "The Glass Tower: Half Full or Half Empty?" in *Taking Back the Academy! History of Activism, History as Activism,* ed. Jim Downs and Jennifer Manion (New York: Routledge, 2004), 93–102.

61. At the University of North Carolina at Chapel Hill, for example, faculty have spent countless hours in recent years defending History and Women's Studies from spurious but well-publicized attacks by the John William Pope Center for Higher Education Policy. See also the story of an orchestrated right-wing attack on Glenda Gilmore after she wrote an op-ed in the Yale campus paper opposing the U.S. invasion of Iraq: Glenda Gilmore, "The Most Craven Abdication of Democratic Principles: On the U.S. Attack in Iraq," in *Taking Back the Academy,* ed. Downs and Manion, 113–24.

62. "The Challenge of Women's History," lecture delivered in August 1977 and printed in Gerda Lerner, *The Majority Finds Its Past: Placing Women in History* (Oxford University Press, New York, 1979), 171.

63. Gerda Lerner, *The Creation of Patriarchy* (New York: Oxford University Press, 1986), 233–35. To my mind, the use of "oppression" applies an intellectual discipline that forces us to confront matters we might otherwise set aside. First, "oppression" expresses our consciousness that historical relations between the sexes were harmful to women, no matter what the consciousness of the women themselves might have been. Second, "oppression" creates more conceptual space for the analysis of subjects that we might prefer to ignore—evil intent on the part of men, suffering on the part of women, hatred between the sexes, and the like.

64. I included 295 substantive articles, but I excluded some forums, archival reports, book reviews, and similar miscellanea. I looked at all titles and abstracts, and I scanned or read specific articles, as necessary. About a dozen of the articles counted in the survey did not provide abstracts.

65. Joanne H. Wright, "Going against the Grain: Hobbes' Case for Original Maternal Dominion," *Journal of Women's History* 14:1 (2002): 123–48 at 123; Laura Gowing, "The Haunting of Susan Lay: Servants and Mistresses in Seventeenth-Century England," *Gender and History* 14:2 (2002): 183–201, abstract at iv.

66. Amy Richlin, "The Ethnographer's Dilemma and the Dream of a Lost Golden Age," in *Feminist Theory and the Classics,* ed. Nancy Sorkin Rabinowitz and Amy Richlin (New York: Routledge, 1993), 272–303, and "How Putting the Man in Roman Put the Roman in Romance," in *Talking Gender: Public Images, Personal Journeys, and Political Critiques,* ed. Nancy Hewitt, Jean O'Barr, and Nancy Rosebaugh (Chapel Hill: University of North Carolina Press, 1996), 14–35; Ruth Mazo Karras, *From Boys to Men: Formations of Masculinity in Late Medieval Europe* (Philadelphia: University of Pennsylvania Press, 2003); Julie Hardwick, *The Practice of Patriarchy: Gender and the Politics of Household Authority in Early Modern France* (University Park, Pa.: Pennsylvania State University Press, 1998); Dorothy Sue Cobble *The Other Women's Movement: Workplace Justice and Social Rights in Modern America* (Princeton, N.J.: Princeton University Press, 2004).

67. Catherine Hall, "Politics, Post-Structuralism and Feminist History," *Gender and History* 3:2 (1991): 204–10; Kathleen Canning, "Feminist History

after the Linguistic Turn: Historicizing Discourse and Experience," *Signs: A Journal of Women in Culture and Society* 19:2 (1994): 368–404; Judith Newton, "A Feminist Scholarship You Can Bring Home to Dad?" *Journal of Women's History* 2:3 (1991): 102–08.

68. Hall, "Politics," 209. Similarly, Mary Maynard has noted of Liz Stanley and Sue Wise, *Breaking Out: Feminist Consciousness and Feminist Research* (London: Routledge and Kegan Paul, 1983), "Long before post-structuralism and post-modernism appeared on the feminist scene, they were suggesting that terms such as 'women's experience', 'feminist research' and 'feminist analysis' were constructed rather than essential categories, as were also categories that feminism is predicated upon, namely 'woman' and 'man.' " Maynard, "Beyond the Big Three," 265–66.

69. I take the distinction between high and middle-range theory from Maynard, "Beyond the Big Three," 276, who herself was drawing on the work of Robert Merton. My examples are borrowed from Hall, "Politics," 209.

70. David Herlihy, *Women, Family, and Society in Medieval Europe: Historical Essays, 1978–1991* (Providence, R.I.: Berghahn Books, 1995); Stanley Chojnacki, *Women and Men in Renaissance Venice: Twelve Essays on Patrician Society* (Baltimore, Md.: Johns Hopkins University Press, 2000); P. J. P. Goldberg, *Women, Work, and Life Cycle in a Medieval Economy: Women in York and Yorkshire, c. 1300–1520* (Oxford: Clarendon Press, 1992).

71. See, in this regard, Berenice A. Carroll, "The Politics of Originality: Women and the Class System of the Intellect," *Journal of Women's History* 2:2 (1990): 136–63.

72. Natalie Zemon Davis, " 'Women's History' in Transition: The European Case," *Feminist Studies* 3:3/4 (1976): 83–103, reprinted in *Feminism and History*, ed. Joan Wallach Scott (Oxford: Oxford University Press, 1996), 79–105, at 93.

73. Natalie Zemon Davis, *The Return of Martin Guerre* (Cambridge, Mass.: Harvard University Press, 1983).

74. Natalie Zemon Davis, *Women on the Margins: Three Seventeenth-Century Lives* (Cambridge, Mass.: Harvard University Press, 1995). See also Kathleen Berry, "The New Historical Synthesis: Women's Biography," *Journal of Women's History* 1:3 (1990): 75–105; a forum on biography in *Gender and History* 2:1 (1990): 17–78; Barbara Caine, "Feminist Biography and Feminist History," *Women's History Review* 3:2 (1992): 247–62; Nell Irvin Painter, "Writing Biographies of Women," *Journal of Women's History* 9:2 (1997): 154–63.

75. Gerda Lerner, "U.S. Women's History Past, Present, and Future," *Journal of Women's History* 16:4 (2004): 10–27.

76. Laurel Ulrich Thatcher, *A Midwife's Tale: The Life of Martha Ballard, Based on her Diary, 1785–1812* (New York: Knopf, 1990).

77. For an early discussion of the feminist implications of the cultural turn, see Sonya Rose et al., "Women's History/Gender History: Is Feminist History Losing Its Critical Edge?" *Journal of Women's History* 5:1 (1993): 89–128.

78. Gail Bederman, *Manliness and Civilization: A Cultural History of Gender and Race in the United States, 1880–1917* (Chicago : University of Chicago Press, 1995).

79. Lerner, "U.S. Women's History."

80. Scott, *Gender and the Politics of History*, 27.

81. Linda Gordon, "The Trouble with Difference," *Dissent* (Spring 1991): 41–47, at 46; Lise Vogel, "Telling Tales: Historians of Our Own Lives," *Journal of Women's History* 2:3 (1991): 89–101.

82. Compare, for example, Eileen Boris and Peter Bardaglio's "The Transformation of Patriarchy" (1983) to its much improved revision "Gender, Race, and Class" (1987). Eileen Boris and Peter Bardaglio, "The Transformation of Patriarchy: The Historic Role of the State," in *Families, Politics, and Public Policy,* ed. Irene Diamond and Mary Lyndon Shanley (New York: Longman, 1983), 70–93. Eileen Boris and Peter Bardaglio, "Gender, Race, and Class: The Impact of the State on the Family and the Economy, 1790–1945," in *Families and Work,* ed. Naomi Gerstel and Harriet Engel Gross (Philadelphia: Temple University Press, 1987), 132–51.

83. Jane E. Mangan, *Trading Roles: Gender, Ethnicity, and the Urban Economy in Colonial Potosí* (Durham, N.C.: Duke University Press, 2005).

84. Elizabeth D. Heineman, *What Difference Does a Husband Make? Women and Marital Status in Nazi and Postwar Germany* (Berkeley: University of California Press, 1999); Amy M. Froide, *Never Married: Singlewomen in Early Modern England* (Oxford: Oxford University Press, 2005).

85. Nancy Hewitt, *Southern Discomfort: Women's Activism in Tampa, Florida, 1880s–1920s* (Urbana, Ill.: University of Illinois Press, 2001).

86. Deborah Gray White, *Too Heavy a Load: Black Women in Defense of Themselves, 1894–1994* (New York: Norton, 1999).

87. Toby L. Ditz, "The New Men's History and the Peculiar Absence of Gendered Power: Some Remedies from Early American Gender History," *Gender and History* 16:1 (2004): 1–36, quotes at 2, 7, 11.

88. I welcome this broadening of feminist history, but I hope we will not thereby dilute the field. In her most recent statement on feminist history, Scott constructs a feminist history that is characterized by desire, restless inquiry, critical spirit, and a "radical refusal to settle down." I doubt that anyone can read her essay without wanting to join Scott as a "double agent" in the "passionate pursuit of the not-yet-known" and informed by "an active, future-oriented feminist critical desire." But in characterizing feminist history as "the constant undoing of conventional wisdom" and the "latest pursuit of what has not yet been thought," Scott runs the risk of washing women—and the central problem of women's subordination to men—out of feminist history. Joan W. Scott, "Feminism's History," *Journal of Women's History* 16:2 (2004): 10–29. For quotes, see 21, 24–26.

89. Kate Haulman, "Room in Back: Before and beyond the Nation in Women's and Gender History," *Journal of Women's History* 15:1 (2003): 167–71, at 169–70.

90. See particularly Kelly's "The Social Relations of the Sexes: Methodological Implications of Women's History," first published in 1976 and reprinted in Kelly, *Women, History, and Theory* (Chicago: University of Chicago Press, 1984), 1–18.

91. Louise Tilly, "Gender, Women's History, and Social History," *Social Science History* 13:4 (1989): 439–62.

92. Caroline Walker Bynum, *Holy Feast and Holy Fast: The Religious Significance of Food to Medieval Women* (Berkeley: University of California Press, 1987). For examples in U.S. history, see Elizabeth Faue's comments in Scott et al., "Women's History in the New Millennium," 205.

93. Joan Jacobs Brumberg, *Fasting Girls: The Emergence of Anorexia Nervosa as a Modern Disease* (Cambridge, Mass.: Harvard University Press, 1988). Bynum argues that medieval saints were not suffering from anorexia nervosa; for such an interpretation, see Rudolph M. Bell, *Holy Anorexia* (Chicago: University of Chicago Press, 1985).

94. Bynum, *Holy Feast*, 295.

95. Barbara Young Welke, *Recasting American Liberty: Gender, Race, Law, and the Railroad Revolution, 1865–1920* (Cambridge: Cambridge University Press, 2001); Amy Richter, *Home on the Rails: Women, the Railroad, and the Rise of Public Domesticity* (Chapel Hill: University of North Carolina Press, 2005).

96. Tilly, "Gender," 439.

97. Mary Ritter Beard, *Woman as a Force in History* (1946; reprint, New York: Collier Books, 1971).

98. Bonnie Smith, *The Gender of History: Men, Women, and Historical Practice* (Cambridge, Mass.: Harvard University Press, 1998), at 116 and 69.

Chapter 3

I thank Cynthia Herrup, Mary Dockray-Miller, and Maryanne Kowaleski for their early comments on this chapter, as well as those who commented on a related presentation at the August 2003 meeting of the International Federation for Research in Women's History (Belfast).

1. Press release from the Brooklyn Museum of Art, April 23, 2002. Available online at http://www.brooklynmuseum.org/press/2002.

2. Barbara Ehrenreich and Deirdre English, *Witches, Midwives, and Nurses: A History of Women Healers* (1973); Joan Kelly, "Did Women Have a Renaissance?" first published in 1977 and reprinted in her *Women, History, and Theory* (Chicago: University of Chicago Press, 1984), 19–50.

3. The first issues of *Feminist Studies* were considerably less accommodating to premodern topics: in 1972–73, there were nine articles on the modern era, one early modern, and one medieval. The focus was, however, less contemporary than it would become; of the nine modern articles, all focused on the nineteenth century to some extent, and only two extended substantively into the twentieth century.

4. At the Fifth Berkshire Conference on the History of Women in 1981, 110 sessions (74 percent) dealt with the nineteenth and twentieth centuries, 14 (13 percent) were focused on the early modern era, and another 14 (13 percent) discussed premodern history. This was the first Berkshire Conference I attended and the earliest for which I have a program, but I have been reliably informed by Jo Ann McNamara that at all the early Berkshire Conferences, every time slot had one session devoted to medieval topics and another to ancient topics. In making these calculations, I excluded some sessions that were impossible to categorize chronologically as well as others that dealt with theoretical or methodological issues.

5. For a similar assessment of U.S. history specifically, see Kate Haulman, "Room in Back: Before and beyond the Nation in Women's and Gender History," *Journal of Women's History* 15:1 (2003): 167–71.

6. Interview in *Chicago Tribune*, May 25, 1916.

7. The story broke in the *Guardian* and other British media on May 10,

2003; I have taken the quote from the online *Guardian* article by Jeevan Vasagar and Rebecca Smithers. Along similar lines, a Canadian MP in 2000 characterized as "a personal past-time and [of] no benefit to Canadian taxpayers" research in the fine arts, classics, philosophy, anthropology, modern literatures, and medieval studies. Ted White, as quoted in Rosemary Drage Hale, "Brilliant Constellations: History in the Presence of the Now," *Journal of the History of Sexuality* 10:2 (2001): 167–72, at 171.

8. These proportions seem fairly settled. In 2000, 74 percent of the papers at the CISH conference dealt with modern topics, 16 percent with early modern, and 10 percent with pre-1500 topics. At the 2003 meeting of the AHA, the proportions were 78 percent modern, 13 percent early modern, and 9 percent pre-1500.

9. CISH offers the best opportunity to assess history practices globally; the American Historical Association offers the same for the United States (the main alternative—the Organization of American Historians—focuses on U.S. history, so its conference program is ipso facto tilted toward modernity). Proportions will certainly vary for other historical societies, and I invite readers to undertake similar counts for meetings which they attend. I checked a few others: (a) at the 2005 meeting of the Canadian Historical Association, there were only a half-dozen or so pre-1800 presentations among more than two hundred papers; (b) at the 2005 meeting of the Anglo-American Conference of Historians, organized annually by the Institute of Historical Research in London, more than half the papers were modern, one-third early modern; the rest pre-1500 (by far the best balanced chronological spread); (c) at the 2005 meeting of the North American Conference of British Studies, two-thirds of the papers were modern, one-third early modern, and none pre-1500.

10. Lynn Hunt, "Against Presentism," *Perspectives*, May 2002. Available online at: http://www.historians.org/perspectives/issues/2002/0205/0205 pre1.cfm.

11. *Speculum* is the journal of the Medieval Academy of America. For the history of the journal's title and its curious encounters with feminism, see my "Medievalism and Feminism," *Speculum: A Journal of Medieval Studies* 68 (1993): 309–31.

12. For a trenchant discussion of such enclaves within medieval studies, see Lee Patterson, "On the Margin: Postmodernism, Ironic History, and Medieval Studies," *Speculum* 65 (1990): 87–108, quote from 87.

13. These proportions also seem fairly settled. At the 2002 Berkshire Conference, the proportions were as follows: 85 percent modern, 9 percent early modern, 6 percent pre-1500.

14. Gerda Lerner, *The Creation of Patriarchy* (New York: Oxford University Press, 1986).

15. Cynthia Eller, *The Myth of Matriarchal Prehistory: Why an Invented Past Won't Give Women a Future* (Boston: Beacon Press, 2000). See also Lauren E. Talalay, "A Feminist Boomerang: The Great Goddess of Greek Prehistory," *Gender and History* 6:2 (1994): 165–83.

16. Jennifer Manion, "Calling all Liberals: Connecting Feminist Theory, Activism, and History," in *Taking Back the Academy! History of Activism, History as Activism*, ed. Jim Downs and Jennifer Manion (New York: Routledge, 2004), 145–59, at 155.

17. Jane O. Newman, "The Present and Our Past: Simone de Beauvoir, Descartes, and Presentism in the Historiography of Feminism," in *Women's Studies on Its Own*, ed. Robyn Wiegman (2002), 141–76, quotes from 145 and 148. Only ten years earlier, Antoinette Burton offered a quite different view of the place of history as "virtually indispensable to feminist theorists" in "'History Is Now: Feminist Theory and the Production of Historical Feminisms," *Women's History Review* 1:1 (1992): 25–39, at 25. Burton's essay is also useful for correcting a vision of feminism that sees only the Western past—whether since 1945 or earlier—as relevant to the history of feminism.

18. Newman, "The Present," 144.

19. Haulman, "Room in Back," 168.

20. These figures derive from a study of the titles and abstracts of 295 substantive articles published in the *Journal of Women's History, Gender and History*, and *Women's History Review* in 2001, 2002, 2003, and 2004. I excluded some forums, archival reports, book reviews, and similar miscellanea. About a dozen of the articles counted in the survey did not provide abstracts.

21. Gerda Lerner's survey of recent work in U.S. women's history similarly revealed that 15 percent of books focused on race and ethnicity, 23 per cent of dissertations, and 27 percent of articles. Gerda Lerner, "U.S. Women's History: Past, Present, and Future," *Journal of Women's History* 16:4 (2004): 10–27.

22. Joanne Meyerowitz, "Sexual Geography and Gender Economy: The Furnished Room Districts of Chicago, 1890–1930," *Gender and History* 2 (1990): 274–96, and her *Women Adrift: Independent Wage Earners in Chicago, 1880–1930* (Chicago: University of Chicago Press, 1988); Jean Allman, "Rounding Up Spinsters: Gender Chaos and Unmarried Women in Colonial Asante," *Journal of African History* 37 (1996): 195–214; Janice E. Stockard, *Daughters of the Canton Delta: Marriage Patterns and Economic Strategies in South China, 1860–1930* (Stanford, Calif.: Stanford University Press, 1989), 70–89 (chapter on "Becoming a Sworn Spinster"); Laurel L. Cornell, "Why Are There No Spinsters in Japan?" *Journal of Family History* 9 (1984): 326–39.

23. The American Historical Association publishes annual analyses of jobs in history but does not break "Europe" down into temporally defined fields. In any case, new appointments are a poor guide to these trends, as numbers of new positions must be compared to retirements and resignations. Robert Townsend of the American Historical Association is currently working on an analysis of faculty specialties as listed in the AHA Directory of History Departments over the last thirty years; this analysis will give us firm figures about which fields are growing or contracting in the United States.

24. I cannot use the women's history journals to trace these trade-offs because the emphasis on history that is more global and more attuned to difference was well underway by the time they started in the late 1980s. For example, it was not until the fifth issue (2:2) of the *Journal of Women's History* that the editors published an article focused on an ethnic or racial majority in the West. The numbers for articles, review essays, and reports in *Signs* in 1975–78 are as follows: modern West, 18; early modern West, 4; premodern West, 4; transhistorical West 5; non-Western, 7 (2 transhistorical, 5 modern); global, 0. The numbers for 2001–4 are: modern West, 5; early modern West, 1; premodern West, 0; transhistorical West, 0; non-Western, 2; global, 1.

25. Hunt, "Against Presentism," 1.

26. For example, the UK's Quality Assurance Agency for Higher Educa-

tion opens its statement about history thus: "We take it as self-evident that knowledge and understanding of the human past is of incalculable value to both the individual and the society at large, and that the first object of education in History is to enable this is be to acquired." I thank Laura Gowing for directing me to this resource, available at http://www.qaa.ac.uk/academic infrastructure/benchmark/honours/history.asp.

27. Perhaps the major source for this myth is Philippe Aries, *Centuries of Childhood: A Social History of Family Life,* trans. Robert Baldick (published in French in 1960; New York: Vintage Books, 1962). Among the many rebuttals of this thesis, see Barbara A. Hanawalt, *Growing Up in Medieval London: The Experience of Childhood in History* (New York: Oxford University Press, 1993); James A. Schultz, *The Knowledge of Childhood in the German Middle Ages, 1100–1350* (Philadelphia: University of Pennsylvania Press, 1995); and Lorraine C. Attreed, "From Pearl Maiden to Tower Princes: Towards a New History of Medieval Childhood," *Journal of Medieval History* 9 (1983): 43–58.

28. See Lawrence Stone, *The Family, Sex, and Marriage in England, 1500–1800* (New York: Harper and Row, 1977) for the myth; for the contrary view, see, for example, Christopher Brooke, *The Medieval Idea of Marriage* (New York: Oxford University Press, 1989), and the summary rebuttal in Peter Fleming, *Family and Household in Medieval England* (New York: Palgrave, 2001), 53–59.

29. John M. Riddle, *Contraception and Abortion from the Ancient World to the Renaissance* (Cambridge, Mass.: Harvard University Press, 1992), and Peter Biller, "Birth Control in the West in the Thirteenth and Early Fourteenth Centuries," *Past and Present* 94 (1982): 3–26.

30. Ruth Mazo Karras, "Prostitution and the Question of Sexual Identity in Medieval Europe," *Journal of Women's History* 11 (1999): 159–77, and responses 178–98. See also Ruth Mazo Karras on chastity as a sexual identity in her *Sexuality in Medieval Europe: Doing unto Others* (New York: Routledge, 2005), 28–58.

31. Gerda Lerner, *The Creation of Feminist Consciousness: From the Middle Ages to Eighteen-Seventy* (New York: Oxford University Press, 1993), and Beatrice Gottlieb, "The Problem of Feminism in the Fifteenth Century," in *Women of the Medieval World,* ed. Julius Kirshner and Suzanne F. Wemple (Oxford: Blackwell, 1985), 337–64.

32. *Women's History Review,* 11:4 and 12:1.

33. *Journal of Women's History,* 13:4, at 6; *Gender and History,* 13:3, at 440. One article begins in the 1780s before focusing on the Napoleonic era: Steven D. Kale, "Women, Salons, and the State in the Aftermath of the French Revolution," *Journal of Women's History* 13:4 (2002): 54–80.

34. The phrase "passive citizen" was coined by G. K. Schmelzeisen, as quoted in Martha C. Howell, "Citizenship and Gender: Women's Political Status in Northern Medieval Cities," in *Women and Power in the Middle Ages,* ed. Mary Erler and Maryanne Kowaleski (Athens: University of Georgia Press, 1988), 37–60, at 40.

35. Kif Augustine-Adams, " 'She Consents Implicitly': Women's Citizenship, Marriage, and Liberal Political Theory in Late-Nineteenth- and Early-Twentieth-Century Argentina," *Journal of Women's History* 13:4 (2004): 8–30; Brigitte Studer, "Citizenship as Contingent National Belonging: Married

Women and Foreigners in Twentieth-Century Switzerland," trans. Kate Sturge, *Gender and History* 13:3 (2001): 622–53.

36. Studer, "Citizenship," 625.

37. Howell, "Citizenship."

38. Two articles deal with the political influence of well-born women, but both focus on public institutions—salons (Kale, "Women, Salons, and the State") or the press (James N. McCord, "Taming the Female Politician in Early-Nineteenth-Century England: *John Bull* versus Lady Jersey," *Journal of Women's History* 13:4 [2002]: 31–53).

39. Barbara J. Harris, "Women and Politics in Early Tudor England," *The Historical Journal* 33:2 (1990): 259–81, and *English Aristocratic Women, 1450–1550: Marriage and Family, Property and Careers* (New York: Oxford University Press, 2002).

40. Kale, "Women, Salons," 55.

41. Lerner, *Creation of Feminist Consciousness.*

42. Laura E. Nym Mayhall, "The Rhetorics of Slavery and Citizenship: Suffragist Discourse and Canonical Texts in Britain, 1880–1914," *Gender and History* 13:3 (2001): 481–97, at 485.

43. Sarah Hanley has developed this argument in numerous articles. See especially "Social Sites of Political Practice in France: Lawsuits, Civil Rights, and the Separation of Powers in Domestic and State Government, 1500–1800," *American Historical Review* 102:1 (1997): 27–52, and "Engendering the State: Family Formation and State Building in Early Modern France," *French Historical Studies* 16:1 (1989): 4–27.

44. Mary Maynard, "Beyond the 'Big Three': The Development of Feminist Theory in the 1990s," *Women's History Review* 4:3 (1995): 259–81, at 273.

45. Florence Griswold Buckstaff, "Married Women's Property in Anglo-Saxon and Anglo-Norman Law," *Annals of the American Academy of Political and Social Sciences* 4 (1893–94): 233–64, at 264.

46. Joan Scott, "Feminism's History," *Journal of Women's History* 16:2 (2004): 10–29, at 24.

47. Charlotte Bunch, "Not by Degrees: Feminist Theory and Education," in *Learning Our Way: Essays in Feminist Education*, ed. Charlotte Bunch and Sandra Pollack (Trumansburg, N.Y.: Crossing Press, 1983), 248–60, at 251–53.

48. For a recent summation of the challenges and possibilities of comparative history, see Deborah Cohen, "Comparative History: Buyer Beware," *German Historical Institute Bulletin* 29 (2001): 23–33.

49. See the NCPE's website at http://www.pay-equity.org.

50. Claudia Goldin, *Understanding the Gender Gap* (New York: Oxford University Press, 1990), 211–17.

51. Newman, "The Present," 144. Newman was describing attitudes toward any history before the 1960s; I suggest that the older the history, the more it might be so labeled.

52. Karma Lochrie, *Heterosyncrasies: Female Sexuality When Normal Wasn't* (Minneapolis: University of Minnesota Press, 2005).

53. Caroline Walker Bynum, *Holy Feast and Holy Fast: The Religious Significance of Food to Medieval Women* (Berkeley: University of California Press, 1987).

54. E. Jane Burns, *Bodytalk: When Women Speak in Old French Literature* (Philadelphia: University of Pennsylvania Press, 1993).

55. Ruth Mazo Karras, *Common Women: Prostitution and Sexuality in Medieval England* (New York: Oxford University Press, 1996).

56. There is a large and growing literature on aristocratic women, queens, and the institution of queenship. Some particularly useful titles are John Parsons, ed., *Medieval Queenship* (New York: St. Martin's Press, 1993); Marion F. Facinger, "A Study of Medieval Queenship: Capetian France 987–1237," *Studies in Medieval and Renaissance History* 5 (1968): 3–47; Louise Olga Fradenburg, ed., *Women and Sovereignty* (Edinburgh: Edinburgh University Press, 1992); Theresa M. Vann, ed., *Queens, Regents, and Potentates* (Dallas: Academia, 1993); Pauline Stafford, *Queen Emma and Queen Edith: Queenship and Women's Power in Eleventh-Century England* (Oxford: Blackwell, 1997); Marjorie Chibnall, *The Empress Matilda: Queen Consort, Queen Mother, and Lady of the English* (Oxford: Blackwell, 1992); Margaret Howell, *Eleanor of Provence: Queenship in Thirteenth-Century England* (Oxford: Blackwell, 1998); Jennifer C. Ward, *English Noblewomen in the Later Middle Ages* (London: Longman, 1992); Michael K. Jones and Malcolm G. Underwood, *The King's Mother: Lady Margaret Beaufort, Countess of Richmond and Derby* (Cambridge: Cambridge University Press, 1992); Peggy K. Liss, *Isabel the Queen: Life and Times* (rev. ed.; Philadelphia: University of Pennsylvania Press, 2004).

57. Howell, "Citizenship and Gender," 47.

58. Judy Chicago, *The Dinner Party* (Garden City, N.Y.: Anchor Books, 1979), 18.

Chapter 4

1. Jakob Bachofen, *Mother-Right* (1861); see *Myth, Religion, and Mother Right: Selected Writings of J. J. Bachofen*, trans. Ralph Manheim (Princeton, N.J.: Princeton University Press, 1967). Friedrich Engels, *The Origins of the Family, Private Property, and the State* (1884); see English translation (New York: Pathfinder Press, 1972). Gerda Lerner, *The Creation of Patriarchy* (New York: Oxford University Press, 1986).

2. Robert Filmer, *Patriarcha and Other Writings* (Cambridge: Cambridge University Press, 1991); the introduction by Johann P. Sommerville lays out Filmer's intellectual antecedents.

3. Adrienne Rich, *Of Woman Born* (New York: Norton, 1976), 57.

4. Allan G. Johnson, *The Gender Knot: Unraveling Our Patriarchal Legacy*, rev. ed. (Philadelphia: Temple University Press, 2005), 5. In a footnote, Johnson further elaborates on "male privilege" by noting that "[p]rivilege refers to any unearned advantage that is available to members of a social category while being systematically denied to others."

5. Sylvia Walby, *Theorizing Patriarchy* (Oxford: Blackwell, 1990), 20.

6. For one study of the different patriarchal investments of men, see Stanley Chojnacki, "Subaltern Patriarchs: Patrician Bachelors in Renaissance Venice," in *Medieval Masculinities: Regarding Men in the Middle Ages*, ed. Clare A. Lees (Minneapolis: University of Minnesota Press, 1994), 73–90.

7. Shelley Feldman, "Exploring Theories of Patriarchy: A Perspective from Contemporary Bangladesh," *Signs: A Journal of Women in Culture and*

Society 26:4 (2001): 1097–1127; Tahera Aftab, "Negotiating with Patriarchy: South Asian Muslim Women and the Appeal to Sir Syed Ahmed Khan," *Women's History Review* 134:1 (2005): 75–97.

8. Michele Mitchell, *Righteous Propagation: African Americans and the Politics of Racial Destiny after Reconstruction* (Chapel Hill: University of North Carolina Press, 2004), 11. Mitchell's use of "patriarchy" draws on the domestic definition.

9. Chandra Talpade Mohanty, " 'Under Western Eyes' Revisited: Feminist Solidarity through Anticapitalist Struggles," *Signs: A Journal of Women in Culture and Society* 28:2 (2002): 499–535, at 505.

10. Ida Blom, "Global Women's History: Organizing Principles and Cross-Cultural Understandings," in *Writing Women's History: International Perspectives*, ed. Karen Offen, Ruth Roach Pierson, and Jane Rendall (Basingstoke: Macmillan, 1991), 135–49.

11. Zillah Eisenstein, *The Radical Future of Liberal Feminism* (New York: Longman, 1981); Heidi Hartmann, "Capitalism, Patriarchy, and Job Segregation by Sex," *Signs: A Journal of Women in Culture and Society* 1:3, part 2 (1976): 137–70, and "The Unhappy Marriage of Marxism and Feminism: Towards a More Progressive Union," in *Women and Revolution*, ed. Lydia Sargent (London: Pluto Press, 1981), 1–42, and critiques in the rest of the volume.

12. Walby, *Theorizing Patriarchy*.

13. Patricia Hill Collins, *Black Feminist Thought* (New York: Routledge, 1990).

14. Sylvia Walby might be right in arguing that "patriarchy is never the only mode in a society but always exists in articulation with another, such as capitalism." See *Patriarchy at Work: Patriarchal and Capitalist Relations in Employment* (Cambridge: Polity Press, 1986), 50. Yet we can only establish the systems with which patriarchy articulates through historical and comparative study.

15. John Tosh, *The Pursuit of History: Aims, Methods, and New Directions in the Study of History* (London: Longman, 1991), 236. Tosh is hard on the concept of patriarchy, but all his objections could be equally leveled at the study of "gender," of which Tosh approves. What Tosh says about "gender" on 286, I would say about "patriarchy": "Gender is now something to be explained, instead of being invoked as a ready-made explanation for everything else."

16. This sense that the study of patriarchy is equivalent to the study of men was expressed by Carroll Smith-Rosenberg in 1980 when she reported that "an exclusive emphasis on male oppression of women had transformed me into a historian of men." See "Politics and Culture in Women's History: A Symposium," *Feminist Studies* 6:1 (1980): 26–64, at 61. In *Gender Knot*, 4–5, Johnson talks about patriarchy "as a code word for 'men.' "

17. Margaret J. M. Ezell, *The Patriarch's Wife: Literary Evidence and the History of the Family* (Chapel Hill: University of North Carolina Press, 1988), 163.

18. See, for example, Anna Clark's study of an ideology that linked vulnerability to rape with movement in public, in *Women's Silence, Men's Violence: Sexual Assault in England, 1770–1845* (London: Pandora, 1987).

19. Deniz Kandiyoti, "Bargaining with Patriarchy," *Gender and Society* 2:3 (1988): 274–90, at 285.

20. See, for example, Feldman, "Exploring Theories of Patriarchy."

21. Eisenstein, *Radical Future*, 21.

22. Lawrence Stone, "The Use and Abuse of History," *The New Republic,* May 2, 1994, 31–37, at 34.

23. See, for example, two sets of exchanges: (1) Sheila Rowbotham, "The Trouble with 'Patriarchy'," and reply by Sally Alexander and Barbara Taylor, "In Defence of 'Patriarchy'," from 1979, reprinted in *People's History and Socialist Theory,* ed. Raphael Samuel (London: Routledge, 1981), 364–73; (2) Bridget Hill, "Women's History: A Study in Change, Continuity, or Standing Still?" *Women's History Review* 2:1 (1993): 5–22, and reply by Judith M. Bennett, "Women's History: A Study in Continuity and Change," *Women's History Review* 2:2 (1993): 173–84.

24. Deborah Valenze, *The First Industrial Woman* (New York: Oxford University Press, 1995), 181; Deborah Simonton, *A History of European Women's Work, 1700 to the Present* (London: Routledge, 1998), 261; see also Daryl M. Hafter, ed., *European Women and Preindustrial Craft* (Bloomington: Indiana University Press, 1995).

25. In recent years, the dynamic and productive tension between continuity and change has been discussed by some historians of women. See, for examples, the Hill-Bennett exchange cited above in n.23; Amanda Vickery, "Golden Age to Separate Spheres? A Review of the Categories and Chronology of Women's History," *Historical Journal* 36 (1993): 383–414, and response by Leonore Davidoff, "Gender and the 'Great Divide,' *Journal of Women's History* 15:1 (2003): 12–27; Pamela Sharpe, "Continuity and Change: Women's History and Economic History in Britain," *Economic History Review,* 2nd ser., 48 (1995): 353–69; Steve J. Stern, *The Secret History of Gender: Women, Men, and Power in Late Colonial Mexico* (Chapel Hill: University of North Carolina Press, 1995), 320–44.

26. I use "ways of seeing" advisedly, for I think that history-as-transformation might well wield a paradigmatic force over the field of women's history. See Thomas S. Kuhn, *The Structure of Scientific Revolutions,* 2nd ed. (Chicago: University of Chicago Press, 1970).

27. Kelly's essays were posthumously reprinted in *Women, History, and Theory* (Chicago: University of Chicago Press, 1984), and I use this edition of her work. See "The Social Relations of the Sexes: Methodological Implications of Women's History," 1–18, quote from 2. See also "Did Women Have a Renaissance?" 19–50. I would like to acknowledge the difficult slipperiness of the concept of the "status of women," which I nevertheless consider to be essential for the project of historicizing patriarchy. For Kelly's definitions of women's status, see pp. 2 and 20.

28. Sandra E. Greene, "A Perspective from African Women's History: Comment on 'Confronting Continuity'," *Journal of Women's History* 9:3 (1997): 85–104, at 98.

29. Valerie Traub, *The Renaissance of Lesbianism in Early Modern England* (Cambridge: Cambridge University Press, 2002), 331.

30. In addition to the work of Valenze and Simonton (on the Industrial Revolution) and Kelly (on the Renaissance) cited above, see, for example, Jo Ann McNamara, "Women and Power through the Family Revisited," in *Gendering the Master Narrative: Women and Power in the Middle Ages,* ed. Mary C. Erler and Maryanne Kowaleski (Ithaca, N.Y.: Cornell University Press, 2003), 17–31; Susan Cahn, *Industry of Devotion: The Transformation of Women's Work in England, 1500–1660* (New York: Columbia University Press, 1987); Lyndal

Roper, *The Holy Household: Women and Morals in Reformation Augsburg* (Oxford: Clarendon Press, 1989); Joan B. Landes, *Women and the Public Sphere in the Age of the French Revolution* (Ithaca, N.Y.: Cornell University Press, 1988); Richard Stites, "Women and the Revolutionary Process in Russia," in *Becoming Visible: Women in European History*, ed. Renate Bridenthal, Susan Mosher Stuard, and Merry E. Wiesner, 3rd ed. (Boston: Houghton Mifflin, 1998), 417–437.

31. Walby, *Theorizing Patriarchy*. For examples of assessments that avoid judgments of "better" or "worse," see Elizabeth A. Clark, "Devil's Gateway and Bride of Christ: Women in the Early Christian World," in her *Ascetic Piety and Women's Faith: Essays in Late Ancient Christianity* (Lewiston, N.Y.: E. Mellen Press, 1986), 23–60, and Julia M. H. Smith, "Did Women Have a Transformation of the Roman World?" *Gender and History* 12:3 (2000): 552–71. See also Anthony Fletcher's attempt to trace changing forms of patriarchy in his *Gender, Sex and Subordination in England 1500–1800* (New Haven, Conn.: Yale University Press, 1995).

32. Karen Offen, "A Comparative European Perspective: Comment on 'Confronting Continuity'," *Journal of Women's History* 9:3 (1997): 105–18, at 105–6. Of course, the very concept of "modernity" is built on highly questionable assumptions about a radical break in European history with a premodern past. See, for example, Lee Patterson, "On the Margin: Postmodernism, Ironic History, and Medieval Studies," *Speculum* 65 (1990): 87–108.

33. The actual moment of putative transformation is perhaps clearest in English history where the Norman conquest has been seen as a critical turning point (for the worse) for women. See Florence G. Buckstaff, "Married Women's Property in Anglo-Saxon and Anglo-Norman Law," *Annals of the American Academy of Political and Social Science* 4 (1893–94): 233–64; Doris Mary Stenton, *The English Woman in History* (London: Allen and Unwin, 1957); Betty Bandel, "The English Chroniclers' Attitude toward Women," *Journal of the History of Ideas* 16 (1955): 113–18; and Christine Fell, with Cecily Clark and Elizabeth Williams, *Women in Anglo-Saxon England and the Impact of 1066* (London: British Museum Publications, 1984). For dissent, see Anne Klinck "Anglo-Saxon Women and the Law," *Journal of Medieval History* 8 (1982): 107–21, and Pauline Stafford, "Women and the Norman Conquest," *Transactions of the Royal Historical Society*, 6th ser., 4 (1994): 221–49.

34. Jo Ann McNamara and Suzanne Wemple, "The Power of Women through the Family in Medieval Europe, 500–1100," in *Women and Power in the Middle Ages*, ed. Mary Erler and Maryanne Kowaleski (Athens: University of Georgia Press, 1988), 83–101, quote from 90; David Herlihy, "Life Expectancies for Women in Medieval Society," in *The Role of Woman in the Middle Ages*, ed. Rosmarie Thee Morewedge (Albany: State University of New York Press, 1975): 1–22, quote from 16. For more recent formulations that trace a transformation in gender relations in the central Middle Ages, see Susan Stuard, "The Dominion of Gender: Women's Fortunes in the High Middle Ages," in *Becoming Visible*, ed. Bridenthal et al., 129–50; Jo Ann McNamara, "The *Herrenfrage*: The Restructuring of the Gender System, 1050–1150," in *Medieval Masculinities: Regarding Men in the Middle Ages*, ed. Clare A. Lees (Minneapolis: University of Minnesota Press, 1994), 3–29, and "Women and Power through the Family Revisited."

35. The two major textbooks in modern European women's history both

emphasize change over continuity. Merry E. Wiesner's *Women and Gender in Early Modern Europe*, 2nd ed. (Cambridge: Cambridge University Press, 2000) adopts a nonchronological approach and regularly weighs evidence of continuity but invariably determines that some degree of transformation in women's status had occurred. The very title of Bonnie G. Smith's *Changing Lives: Women in European History since 1700* (Lexington, Mass.: D. C. Heath, 1989) speaks to its emphasis on change. Gianna Pomata's critique of women's history textbooks has dwelt on the problems feminist historians face that "[stem] from the historiographic tradition itself: from its periodizations, categories, narrative plots, and the way these resist the introduction of women into our field of vision." Gianna Pomata, "History, Particular and Universal: On Reading Some Recent Women's History Textbooks," *Feminist Studies* 19 (1993): 7–50, quote from 10–11. One textbook has emphasized continuity: Bonnie S. Anderson and Judith P. Zinsser, *A History of Their Own: Women in Europe from Prehistory to the Present* (New York: Harper and Row, 1988). Yet the emphasis on continuity in *A History of Their Own* has been much criticized; Pomata, for example, noted that it was "oversimplified" and "profoundly nonhistorical" (see Pomata, "History," 41). In a similar way, a survey of women in early modern Europe—Olwen Hufton's *The Prospect before Her: A History of Women in Western Europe, I: 1500–1800* (London: HarperCollins, 1995)—has also been criticized for its emphasis on continuity. See Lynn Hunt, *New York Times Book Review*, December 15, 1996, 11, and Anthony Fletcher, *Times Literary Supplement*, December 15, 1995, 8.

36. Elizabeth Gould Davis, *The First Sex* (New York: Putnam, 1971); Barbara Ehrenreich and Deirdre English, *Witches, Midwives, and Nurses: A History of Women Healers* (Detroit: Black and Red, 1973).

37. An underlying tension still divides "popular" and more "professional" histories of women. The study of women in religion provides a good example. On the one hand, many feminists are trying to reconstruct or create woman-centered religions, and their efforts have driven a vibrant movement in goddess-focused spiritualities. On the other hand, many other feminists seek to reinterpret existing traditions—especially Jewish and Christian—to better accommodate gender equality, and their efforts have revitalized the practices of many traditional religions. Both groups include feminists trained and employed in academia, as well as those who are self-taught, but it is striking how rarely the two interact. Moreover, when "professional" scholars of religion comment on "popular" trends, their comments are studiously respectful, carefully unengaged, and slightly dismissive. See, for example, Rosemary Radford Ruether, "The Feminist Critique in Religious Studies," *Soundings* 64 (1981): 388–402, and Caroline Walker Bynum, "Introduction: The Complexity of Symbols," in *Gender and Religion: On the Complexity of Symbols*, ed. Caroline Walker Bynum, Stevan Harrell, and Paula Richman (Boston: Beacon Press, 1986), 1–20.

38. Kelly, "Social Relations," 4.

39. Louise Tilly, "Gender, Women's History, and Social History," *Social Science History* 13:4 (1989): 439–462.

40. G. R. Elton, *The Tudor Revolution in Government: Administrative Changes in the Reign of Henry VIII* (Cambridge: Cambridge University Press, 1953).

41. Patterson, "On the Margin," esp. 93–95. See also chapters 5 and 6 in his *Negotiating the Past: The Historical Understanding of Medieval Literature* (Madi-

son: University of Wisconsin Press, 1987). David Aers, *Community, Gender, and Individual Identity: English Writing 1360–1430* (London: Routledge, 1988), quote from 17.

42. Alan Macfarlane, *The Origins of English Individualism: The Family, Property, and Social Transition* (Oxford: Blackwell, 1978). For one critique, see Stephen White and Richard Vann, "The Invention of English Individualism: Alan Macfarlane and the Modernization of Pre-Modern England," *Social History* 8 (1983): 345–63.

43. For examples, see Christopher Dyer, *Making a Living in the Middle Ages: The People of Britain, 850–1520* (New Haven, Conn.: Yale University Press, 2002), and Richard Britnell, *Britain and Ireland, 1050–1530: Economy and Society* (Oxford: Oxford University Press, 2004).

44. D. C. Coleman, *The Economy of England, 1450–1750* (London: Oxford University Press, 1977), 91.

45. See particularly Bonnie Smith, "Gender and Historical Understanding," in *Learning History in America: Schools, Cultures, and Politics,* ed. Lloyd Kramer, Donald Reid, and William L. Barney (Minneapolis: University of Minnesota Press, 1994), 107–19; "Gender and the Practices of Scientific History: The Seminar and Archival Research in the Nineteenth Century," *American Historical Review* 100 (1995): 1150–76; and *The Gender of History: Men, Women, and Historical Practice* (Cambridge, Mass.: Harvard University Press, 1998).

46. Peter Burke, *The Renaissance Sense of the Past* (New York: St. Martin's, 1970).

47. For an early response to the seeming "timelessness" of women's history, see Ann D. Gordon, Mari Jo Buhle, and Nancy Schrom Dye, "The Problem of Women's History," in *Liberating Women's History: Theoretical and Critical Essays,* ed. Berenice A. Carroll (Urbana: University of Illinois Press, 1976), 75–92.

48. For black feminism, see especially Patricia Hill Collins, *Black Feminist Thought: Knowledge, Consciousness, and the Politics of Empowerment* (Boston: Unwin Hyman, 1990). Collins rightly emphasizes that an ongoing dialectic between oppression and activism renders the matrix of domination "responsive to human agency" (237). A good guide to other sorts of feminisms is Rosemarie Tong, *Feminist Thought: A More Comprehensive Introduction,* 2nd ed. (Boulder, Colo.: Westview Press, 1998).

49. For an example of an interpretation influenced by liberal feminism, see Caroline Barron, "The 'Golden Age' of Women in Medieval London," in *Medieval Women in Southern England,* Reading Medieval Studies 15 (1989): 35–58. For an example of an interpretation influenced by socialist feminism, see Cahn, *Industry of Devotion.*

50. Carolyn Steedman, "La théorie qui n'en est pas une, or Why Clio Doesn't Care," in *Feminists Revision History,* ed. Ann-Louise Shapiro (New Brunswick, N.J.: Rutgers University Press, 1994), 73–94, quote from 77.

51. Caroline Walker Bynum, "Women's Stories, Women's Symbols: A Critique of Victor Turner's Theory of Liminality," in her *Fragmentation and Redemption: Essays on Gender and the Human Body in Medieval Religion* (New York: Zone Books, 1991), 27–51. Bynum herself explicitly eschews any broader implications of her specific observations. I thank Robert Stein for drawing this essay to my attention.

52. Amy Hollywood, "Inside Out: Beatrice of Nazareth and her Hagiographer," in *Gendered Voices: Medieval Saints and their Interpreters,* ed. Catherine M. Mooney, Philadelphia: University of Pennsylvania Press, 1999), 78–98.

53. Georges Duby, "The Courtly Model," in *A History of Women in the West,* vol. 2: *Silences of the Middle Ages,* ed. Christiane Klapisch-Zuber (1990, French ed., Cambridge, Mass.: Harvard University Press, 1992), 250–66, quote from 266.

54. Olwen Hufton, "Women in History: Early Modern Europe," *Past and Present* 101 (1983): 125–41, quote from 126.

55. Susan Staves, *Married Women's Separate Property in England, 1660–1833* (Cambridge, Mass.: Harvard University Press, 1990); Vickery, "Golden Age."

56. I am grateful to Sandy Bardsley for suggesting the term "patriarchal equilibrium." I discuss brewing more fully in my *Ale, Beer, and Brewsters in England: Women's Work in a Changing World, 1300–1600* (New York: Oxford University Press, 1996).

57. Alice Clark, *Working Life of Women in the Seventeenth Century* (London: Routledge, 1919), 230.

58. Marjorie McIntosh has recently taken issue with this assessment, arguing that married brewsters in the later Middle Ages enjoyed "unusual economic and social autonomy"; see her *Working Women in English Society, 1300–1620* (Cambridge: Cambridge University Press, 2005), 181. I am troubled by much of her evidence and not persuaded by her position. McIntosh and I agree that brewing was relatively good work among the options available to medieval women, that women from many social strata engaged in commercial brewing, that the success of a married brewster relied on her "husband's backing" (86; see also 39), and that this by-industry was one way in which many women contributed to household income. These characteristics do not, to my mind, translate into an unusual "degree of independent authority held by some late medieval women" that was then lost (253). See Chapter 5 for further comments on McIntosh's book.

59. I have taken the phrase "descent from paradise," from Cahn, *Industry of Devotion,* 9.

60. Offen, "Comparative European Perspective," 110–12, quote from 111. The dangers of such assumptions are perhaps best illustrated in Offen's comment that children today "take the same amount of time to mature physically" as in the past. As has been documented repeatedly, the age of menarche has declined in the West during the last century.

61. Elsa Barkley Brown, "Polyrhythms and Improvization: Lessons for Women's History," *History Workshop Journal* 31 (1991): 85–90.

62. Greene, "A Perspective," 101–2.

63. For institutions, see Raymond Williams, *Keywords: A Vocabulary of Culture and Society* (London: Fontana, 1976), 169. In the case of brewsters, I found that almost all patriarchal institutions served other purposes that were not patriarchal in intention or effect, but one of their effects was to assist in the maintenance of a patriarchal equilibrium. In a similar way, I would argue that the U.S. military before desegregation in the late 1940s was a racist institution because it helped to maintain racial asymmetry.

64. Sharpe, "Continuity and Change," and Stafford "Women and the Norman Conquest."

65. For anthropology, see the discussion of anthropological debates in

DuBois et al., *Feminist Scholarship*, 91–101, and for one example, Karen Sacks, *Sisters and Wives* (Westport, Conn.: Greenwood Press, 1979). For examples from social and political theory, see Walby's summary of current theories in *Patriarchy at Work*, 5–49, and Johnson, *Gender Knot*. For literature, see the survey of scholarship on the ideology of women's oppression in DuBois et al., *Feminist Scholarship*, 101–13.

Chapter 5

1. For the medieval data, see Sandy Bardsley, "Women's Work Reconsidered: Gender and Wage Differentiation in Late Medieval England," *Past and Present* 165 (1999): 3–29. See also John Hatcher, "Debate: Women's Work Reconsidered: Gender and Wage Differentiation in Late Medieval England," *Past and Present* 173 (2001): 191–98, and Bardsley, "Reply," *Past and Present* 173 (2001): 199–202. For contemporary Britain, see Wendy Olsen and Sylvia Walby, "Modelling Gender Pay Gaps," Equal Opportunities Commission Working Paper Series 17 (2004): esp. 8–11 (available online at www.eoc.org.uk).

2. Part-payment in kind was in decline by the late fourteenth century because workers preferred cash wages; nevertheless, the quality of the food was improving, and workers often received more food than they could have themselves consumed. I know of no studies—or sources—that distinguish the food offered to female and male workers. See Christopher Dyer, *Everyday Life in Medieval England* (London: Hambledon Press, 1994), 77–99, 185–6.

3. Jacob Burckhardt, *The Civilization of the Renaissance in Italy* (1860), 3rd. ed. (Oxford: Phaidon 1995), 87.

4. Lee Patterson, "On the Margin: Postmodernism, Ironic History, and Medieval Studies," *Speculum* 65 (1990): 87–108.

5. For a summary, see Janet Thomas, "Women and Capitalism: Oppression or Emancipation? A Review Article," *Comparative Studies in Society and History* 30:3 (1988): 534–49.

6. Martha C. Howell, *Women, Production, and Patriarchy in Late Medieval Cities* (Chicago: University of Chicago Press, 1986); Merry E. Wiesner, *Working Women in Renaissance Germany* (New Brunswick N.J.: Rutgers University Press, 1986); Caroline Barron, "The 'Golden Age' of Women in Medieval London," *Medieval Women in Southern England*, Reading Medieval Studies 15 (1989): 35–58, and further comments in *Medieval London Widows, 1300–1400* (London: Hambledon Press, 1994), xiv; P. J. P. Goldberg, *Women, Work, and Life Cycle in a Medieval Economy: Women in York and Yorkshire, c. 1300–1520* (Oxford: Clarendon Press, 1992); Joan Kelly, "Did Women Have a Renaissance?," 1977 essay reprinted in her *Women, History and Theory* (Chicago: University of Chicago Press, 1984), 19–51; Margaret King, "Book-Lined Cells: Women and Humanism in the Early Italian Renaissance," in *Beyond Their Sex: Learned Women of the European Past*, ed. Patricia H. Labalme (New York: New York University Press, 1984), 66–90, and, with Albert Rabil Jr., ed., *Her Immaculate Hand* (Binghampton N.Y.; Center for Medieval and Early Renaissance Studies, 1983); Linda Woodbridge, *Women and the English Renaissance* (Urbana: University of Illinois Press, 1984); Catherine Belsey, *The Subject of Tragedy* (London: Methuen, 1985); Katharina M. Wilson and Elizabeth M.

Makowski, *Wykked Wyves and the Woes of Marriage*, (Albany: State University of New York Press), 1990.

7. Alice Clark, *Working Life of Women in the Seventeenth Century* (1919: rpt London: Routledge and Kegan Paul, 1982); Kelly, "Did Women Have a Renaissance?"; Friedrich Engels, *The Origins of the Family, Private Property, and the State* (1884).

8. Annie Abram, "Women Traders in Medieval London," *Economic Journal* 26 (1916): 276–85; Marian K. Dale, "The London Silkwomen of the Fifteenth Century," *Economic History Review* 4 (1933): 324–25; Eileen Power, "The Position of Women," in *The Legacy of the Middle Ages*, ed. C. G. Crump and E. F. Jacob (Oxford: Clarendon Press, 1926), 401–33, at 410.

9. Barron, "Golden Age"; Peter Franklin, "Peasant Widows' 'Liberation' and Remarriage before the Black Death," *Economic History Review*, 2nd ser. 39 (1986): 186–204; Goldberg, *Women, Work*; Barbara A. Hanawalt, "Peasant Women's Contribution to the Home Economy in Late Medieval England," in *Women and Work in Preindustrial Europe*, ed. B. A. Hanawalt (Bloomington: Indiana University Press, 1986), 3–19; Simon A. C. Penn, "Female Wage-earners in Late Fourteenth-Century England," *Agricultural History Review* 37 (1987): 1–14; Kay. E. Lacey, "Women and Work in Fourteenth and Fifteenth-Century London," in *Women and Work in Pre-Industrial England*, ed. Lindsey Charles and Lorna Duffin (London: Croon Helm, 1985), 24–82. David Herlihy has posited a similarly dramatic and negative transition but has dated it much earlier (in the high Middle Ages); see *Opera Muliebria: Women and Work in Medieval Europe* (New York: McGraw-Hill, 1990). For a challenge to this chorus, see Chris Middleton, "Women's Labour and the Transition to Pre-Industrial Capitalism," in *Women and Work*, ed. Charles and Duffin, 181–206.

10. Roberta Hamilton, *The Liberation of Women: A Study of Patriarchy and Capitalism* (London: George Allen and Unwin, 1978); Bridget Hill, *Women, Work, and Sexual Politics in Eighteenth-Century England* (Oxford: Blackwell, 1989); K. D. M. Snell, *Annals of the Laboring Poor* (Cambridge: Cambridge University Press, 1985), 270–319; Michael Roberts, "Sickles and Scythes: Women's Work and Men's Work at Harvest Time," *History Workshop Journal* 7 (1979): 3–29, and "Sickles and Scythes Revisited: Harvest Work, Wages, and Symbolic Meanings," in *Women, Work, and Wages in England, 1600–1850*, ed. Penelope Lane, Neil Raven, and K. D. M. Snell (Woodbridge, Suffolk: Boydell, 2004), 68–101; W. Thwaites, "Women in the Market place: Oxfordshire, c. 1690–1800," *Midland History* 9 (1984): 23–42; Margaret George, "From 'Goodwife' to 'Mistress': The Transformation of the Female in Bourgeois Culture," *Science and Society* 37 (1973): 152–77; Susan Cahn, *Industry of Devotion: The Transformation of Women's Work in England, 1500–1660* (New York: Columbia University Press, 1987), at 9. For a more nuanced view, see Pamela Sharpe, "Introduction," in *Women's Work: The English Experience, 1650–1914* (London: Arnold, 1998), 1–20. For objections, see Bardsley, "Women's Work Reconsidered"; Judith M. Bennett, "'History that Stands Still': Women's Work in the European Past," *Feminist Studies* 14 (1988): 269–83, and "Medieval Women, Modern Women: Across the Great Divide," in *Culture and History, 1350–1600: Essays on English Communities, Identities, and Writing*, ed. David Aers, (London: Harvester Wheatsheaf, 1992), 147–175; Maryanne Kowaleski, "Women's Work in a Market Town: Exeter in the Late Fourteenth Century," in *Women and Work in Preindustrial Europe*, ed. Hana-

walt, 145–64; Mavis Mate, *Women in Medieval English Society* (Cambridge: Cambridge University Press, 1999).

11. Marjorie Keniston McIntosh, *Working Women in English Society, 1300–1620* (Cambridge: Cambridge University Press, 2005), 252. As McIntosh notes on 20, the book "relies heavily" on equity court petitions from 1470. Of the five market centers that also feature in the study, two have archives that begin in the 1280s, but the records of the other three start in 1362, 1379, and 1382; this makes it difficult to prove the earlier part of McIntosh's thesis that women between 1350 and 1500 took "a more active and independent part in the public economy than before or after" (40).

12. McIntosh, *Working Women*, 252. McIntosh's evidence of substantive change is thin, usually relying on either assertion or unconvincing evidence. For an example of an undocumented assertion of transformation, see the discussion of import/export trade, 125; for anecdotal evidence, see the discussion of baking, 184; for overlooked evidence, see 135, where Nancy Adamson's finding of seventy-three apprentices in Elizabethan records, available in print since 1992, is not mentioned; for misconstrued evidence, see also 135 (both male and female apprentices disappear from the main source—the London mayor's court—after c. 1450 because of changes in recording customs) and 158 (I do not argue, as said there, that opposition to brewsters "became more heated across the later fifteenth and sixteenth centuries"). McIntosh scarcely considers the evidence now available on women's wages and the status of women in craft guilds.

13. Eileen Power, "The Position of Women," in *The Legacy of the Middle Ages,* ed. Crump and Jacob, 401–33, at 410; Hanawalt, "Peasant Women's Contribution," in *Women and Work in Preindustrial Europe,* ed. Hanawalt, 3–19; Hill, *Women, Work, and Sexual Politics in Eighteenth-Century England,* 46; Louise Tilly and Joan Scott, *Women, Work, and Family* (New York: Holt, Rinehart and Winston, 1978), 230.

14. Olivia Harris, "Households as Natural Units," in *Of Marriage and the Market,* ed. Kate Young et al., 2nd ed. (London: Routledge and Kegan Paul, 1984), 136–55; Rayna Rapp et al., "Examining Family History," *Feminist Studies* 5 (1979): 174–200; Tessie P. Liu, "*Le Patrimoine Magique*: Reassessing the Power of Women in Peasant Households in Nineteenth-Century France," *Gender and History* 6:1 (1994): 13–36.

15. Medieval notions of *familia* easily embraced such persons, but our "family" does not. Richard Smith has noted from the 1377 poll tax listings that about 15 percent of rural households had servants, that 20–33 percent of urban households included servants, and that these figures underestimate the presence of servants because the poll taxes did not list persons under age fourteen and underlisted females. See Smith, "Geographical Diversity in the Resort to Marriage in Late Medieval Europe: Work, Reputation, and Unmarried Females in the Household Formation Systems of Northern and Southern Europe," in *Woman is a Worthy Wight: Women in English Society, c. 1200–1500,* ed. P. J. P. Goldberg (Stroud: Alan Sutton, 1992), 16–59, 35–36. Basing her estimate on a more extensive set of records, Maryanne Kowaleski found that at least 40 percent of households in Exeter in 1377 had servants. See Kowaleski, *Local Markets and Regional Trade in Medieval Exeter* (New York: Cambridge University Press, 1995), 168. These "snapshot" estimates suggest, of

course, that even more households would have been incorporating servants over time.

16. Edmund Tilney, *A Brief and Pleasant Discourse of Duties in Marriage, called the Flower of Friendshippe* (1571), as quoted in Susan Amussen, *An Ordered Society: Gender and Class in Early Modern England* (Oxford: Blackwell, 1988), 43–44. I have modernized the punctuation.

17. "Ballad of a Tyrannical Husband," in *Reliquiae Antiquae*, vol. 2, ed. Thomas Wright and James O. Halliwell (London: J. R. Smith, 1845), 196–99.

18. *Statutes of the Realm*, vol. 1 (London: Record Commission, 1810), 379–80.

19. Kowaleski, "Women's Work in a Market Town," 157–58.

20. L. F. Salzman, *English Industries of the Middle Ages* (Oxford: Clarendon Press, 1923), 328–29. See, for example, the Southwark poll tax for 1381: The National Archives, PRO, E179 184/30. The tendency to record only the occupations of husbands continues well into the modem era: see Peter H. Lindert, "English Occupations, 1670–1811," *Journal of Economic History* 40 (1980): 691–92; Paul Glennie, *"Distinguishing Men's Trades": Occupational Sources and Debates for Pre-Census England*, Historical Geography Research Series 25 (1990): esp. 12–13.

21. Kathryn Kelley Staples is completing a dissertation at the University of Minnesota on the inheritance of daughters in medieval London; her data suggest that daughters did receive considerable assets from their parents, but not as much as did sons.

22. Richard M. Smith, "Coping with Uncertainty: Women's Tenure of Customary Land in England, c. 1370–1430," in *Enterprise and Individuals in Fifteenth-Century England*, ed. Jennifer Kermode (Stroud: Alan Sutton, 1991), 43–67, at 49.

23. Derek Keene, *Survey of Medieval Winchester* (Oxford: Oxford University Press, 1985), 387. Keene found that 18 percent of property holders were women, of whom some 40 percent had acquired their land by inheritance. Despite the limitations that couverture imposed on married women, a few heiresses continued to hold their properties in their own right, but most did not.

24. Sian Eleri Jones, "Keeping Her in the Family: Women and Gender in Southampton, c. 1400–1600" (Ph.D. diss., University of Southampton, 1997), 142–52.

25. *The Treatise on the Law and Customs of the Realm of England Commonly Called Glanvill*, ed. G. D. G. Hall (London, Nelson, 1965), book 6, no. 3, p. 60.

26. Richard Smith, "Women's Property Rights under Customary Law: Some Developments in the Thirteenth and Fourteenth Centuries," *Transactions of the Royal Historical Society*, 5th ser., 36 (1986): 165–94, and "Coping with Uncertainty." Smith also notes an increase in "conjoint tenures" (that is, land held jointly by a husband and wife) by the early fifteenth century, although the social meanings of this legal shift are hard to assess (see especially his comments on 63 in "Coping with Uncertainty" and 166 in "Women's Property Rights"). In assessing the social meanings of legal changes to married women's property rights, Susan Staves's comment that "the same struggles appear to be repeated over and over again with only minor variations in vocabulary" provides an important caution; see her *Married Women's*

Separate Property in England, 1660–1833 (Cambridge, Mass.: Harvard University Press, 1990), 229.

27. Ada Elizabeth Levett, *Studies in Manorial History* (Oxford: Clarendon Press, 1938), 335. The transaction went ahead despite the wife's tear-stained consent but was voided when a jury intervened.

28. Mavis Mate, *Daughters, Wives and Widows after the Black Death: Women in Sussex, 1350–1535* (Woodbridge: Boydell Press, 1998), 78–79.

29. Northamptonshire Record Office, Montagu Collection, Box X364B, court for 20/3/1315. The jurors stated *"vendicio illa nulla est de uxore in absentia mariti sui."* Marjorie McIntosh has recently explored the legal maneuvers that *femme couverte* status offered to husbands and wives, concluding that "femme couverte status must have had some relative advantages in practice"; see McIntosh, "The Benefits and Drawbacks of Femme Sole Status in England, 1300–1630," *Journal of British Studies* 44:3 (2005): 410–39, at 430. I agree. A woman could accrue a variety of legal, social, and personal benefits from marriage, but in economic terms, it is hard to construe *femme couverte* status in a positive light.

30. Diane Hutton, "Women in Fourteenth Century Shrewsbury," in *Women and Work in Pre-Industrial England,* ed. Charles and Duffin, 83–99, at 86; Sue Wright, " 'Churmaids, huswyfs and hucksters': The Employment of Women in Tudor and Stuart Salisbury," in *Women and Work,* ed. Charles and Duffin, 100–121, at 107.

31. See especially McIntosh, "The Benefits and Drawbacks of Femme Sole Status." See also Kay Lacey, "Women and Work in Fourteenth and Fifteenth Century London," *Women and Work,* ed. Charles and Duffin, 24–82, esp. 41–45; Barron, "Golden Age," esp. 39–40; Mary Bateson, ed., *Borough Customs,* 2 vols., Selden Society 18 (London: B. Quaritch, 1904), esp. 222–28, and 21 (London: B. Quaritch, 1906), c-cxv, 102–29. In the surviving Mayor Court Bills for London, several cases involved women, noted as trading as *femmes soles,* who were nevertheless impleaded with their husbands. See, for examples, Corporation of London Record Office, Mayor Court Bills 1/123, 3/210, 3/373, 3/377. 1 would like to thank Caroline Barron for directing me to this source. Bateson notes that husbands joined their wives in such cases in London "for conformity"; see *Borough Customs,* 2: cxiv.

32. If there were no children of the marriage, a widow got half the lands and tenements and half the movable goods and chattels.

33. Caroline M. Barron and Anne F. Sutton, eds., *Medieval London Widows, 1300–1500* (London: Hambledon Press, 1994), xvii–xxi.

34. See Louise Mirrer, ed., *Upon My Husband's Death: Widows in the Literatures and Histories of Medieval Europe* (Ann Arbor: University of Michigan Press, 1992), and Sue Sheridan Walker, ed., *Wife and Widow in Medieval England* (Ann Arbor: University of Michigan Press, 1993).

35. On flexibilities within couverture specifically, see Amy Louise Erickson, "Coverture and Capitalism," *History Workshop Journal* 59:1 (2005): 1–16.

36. John Stuart Mill, *The Subjection of Women* (1869), esp. chap. 11.

37. R. H. Helmholz, *Marriage Litigation in Medieval England* (Cambridge: Cambridge University Press, 1974), 102.

38. I have treated the household economy in a static fashion in order to demonstrate that it never offered an ideal situation for women—in either medieval or early modem Europe. The full history of its development and

evolution are beyond the purposes of this chapter. Maxine Berg has raised substantial doubts about the supposedly negative effects of the decline of the household economy on women's work. See "Women's Work, Mechanization, and the Early Phases of Industrialization in England," in *On Work: Historical, Comparative and Theoretical Approaches*, ed. R. E. Pahl (Oxford: Blackwell, 1988), 61–94. See also Carole Shammas, *A History of Household Government in America* (Charlottesville: University of Virginia Press, 2002).

39. Jeremy Goldberg has characterized this comparison as "deeply flawed" on three counts, all of which I acknowledged from my first use of it in 1992 and, again, in my discussion here: the comparison of Southwark and London; the focus on singlewomen and widows (although Goldberg mentions only singlewomen); and the long time span. See P. J. P. Goldberg, *Medieval England: A Social History, 1250–1550* (London: Arnold, 2004), 216. In light of Goldberg's comments, I would like to emphasize two points. First, these two snapshots are not arbitrarily chosen; despite the challenges of their comparison, they remain the best data for a long-term comparison of female occupations over these centuries that anyone has been able to locate. Second, I use these snapshots in ways appropriate to their flaws—that is, I look for general trends, not precise patterns.

40. In the Southwark poll tax, for example, numerous skilled occupations were identified with men alone, including spicer, vintner, goldsmith, marshal, armiger, weaver, cooper, and smith.

41. "Assessment Roll of the Poll-Tax for Howdenshire, etc. in the Second Year of the Reign of King Richard II (1379)," *Yorkshire Archaeological and Topographical Journal* 9 (1886): 129–61; Peter Fleming, *Women in Late Medieval Bristol*, Bristol Branch of the Historical Association Local History Pamphlets 103 (2001): 10.

42. Peter Earle, "The Female Labor Market in London in the Late Seventeenth and Early Eighteenth Centuries," *Economic History Review*, 2nd ser., 42 (1989): 328–53.

43. Kowaleski, "Women's Work," 156–58.

44. For Oxford, see the transcription of the 1381 poll tax in *Oxford City Documents, 1268–1665*, ed. J. E. Thorold Rogers (Oxford: Oxford University Press, 1891). For Howdenshire, see "Assessment Roll." For Bristol, see Fleming, *Women in Bristol*. For Exeter, see Kowaleski, "Women's Work."

45. Goldberg, "Female Labour, Service, and Marriage in the Late Medieval Urban North," *Northern History* 22 (1986): 18–38, at 30.

46. Bennett, *Women in the Medieval English Countryside*; Kowaleski, "Women's Work"; Hutton, "Women"; Goldberg, "Female Labor, Service"; Sue Wright, "Churmaids"; Mary Prior, "Women and the Urban Economy: Oxford, 1500–1800," in *Women in English Society, 1500–1800*, ed. Mary Prior (London: Methuen, 1985), 93–117; Carole Shammas, "The World Women Knew: Women Workers in the North of England during the Late Seventeenth Century," in *The World of William Penn*, ed. R. Dunn (Philadelphia: University of Pennsylvania Press, 1986), 99–115; Jane Whittle, "Housewives and Servants in Rural England, 1440–1650: Evidence of Women's Work from Probate Documents," *Transactions of the Royal Historical Society* 6th series, 15 (2005): 51–74; Earle, "Female Labor Market."

47. Earle compared his data to the 1851 census, noting that "the general structure of occupations is very similar" in both periods, that the top four

employments of women remained unchanged, and that "there is certainly little evidence of a narrowing of women's employment opportunities as a result of the industrial revolution"; see "Female Labour Market," 341–42.

48. The literature on guilds is vast and often contentious. A general introduction can be found in Steven A. Epstein, *Wage Labor and Guilds in Medieval Europe* (Chapel Hill: University of North Carolina Press, 1991). For English materials specifically, start with Heather Swanson, *Medieval Artisans: An Urban Class in Later Medieval England* (Oxford: Blackwell, 1989), and "The Illusion of Economic Structure: Craft Guilds in Late Medieval English Towns," *Past and Present* 121 (1988): 29–48; Gervase Rosser, "Crafts, Guilds, and the Negotiation of Work in the Medieval Town," *Past and Present* 154 (1997): 3–31. Classic studies include George Unwin, *The Gilds and Companies of London* (London: George Allen and Unwin, 1938); Stella Kramer, *The English Craft Gilds* (New York: Columbia University Press, 1927); Charles Gross, *The Gild Merchant* (Oxford: Clarendon Press, 1890); Joshua Toulmin Smith and Lucy Toulmin Smith, eds., *English Gilds*, Early English Text Society 40 (London: Oxford University Press, 1870).

49. The literature on women and guilds was surveyed in Judith M. Bennett and Maryanne Kowaleski, "Crafts, Gilds, and Women in the Middle Ages: Fifty Years after Marian K. Dale," *Signs: A Journal of Women in Culture and Society* 14 (1989): 474–88. Among studies published since 1989, see especially Caroline Barron, "The Education and Training of Girls in Fifteenth-Century London," in *Courts, Counties, and the Capital in the Later Middle Ages*, ed. Diana E. S. Dunn (Stroud: Sutton, 1996), 139–53, at 144; Ingrid Batori, "Frauen in Handel und Handwerk in der Reichsstadt Nördlingen im 15. und 16. Jahrhundert," in *Frauen in der Ständegesellschaft*, ed. Barbara Vogel and Ulrike Weckel (Hamburg: R. Krämer, 1991), 27–47; Cécile Béghin, "Donneuses d'ouvrages, apprenties et salariées aux XIVe et XVe siècles dans les sociétés urbaines languedociennes," *Clio* 3 (1996): 31–54; Ilana Krausman Ben-Amos, "Women Apprentices in the Trades and Crafts of Early Modern Bristol," *Continuity and Change* 6:2 (1991): 227–52; Carol L. Loats, "Gender, Guilds, and Work Identity: Perspectives from Sixteenth-Century Paris," *French Historical Studies* 20:1 (1997): 15–54; Simone Roux, "Les Femmes dans les Métiers Parisiens: XIIIe-XVe siècle," *Clio* 3 (1996): 13–30; Margret Wensky, "Frauen im Handwerk," *Europäische Technik im Mittelalter, 800–1400*, ed. Utz Lindgren (Berlin: Gebr. Mann, 1996), 509–18.

50. Sheilagh Ogilvie, "How Does Social Capital Affect Women? Guilds and Communities in Early Modern Germany," *American Historical Review* 109:2 (2004): 325–59.

51. Bridget Hill, "Women's History: A Study in Change, Continuity, or Standing Still?" *Women's History Review* 2:1 (1993): 5–22, at 14–15.

52. Merry E. Wiesner, "Guilds, Male Bonding, and Women's Work in Early Modern Germany," *Gender and History* 1:2 (1989): 125–37, at 127; Herlihy, *Opera Muliebria*, 179; Maria R. Boes, "'Dishonourable Youth, Guilds, and the Changed World View of Sex, Illegitimacy, and Women in Late-Sixteenth-Century Germany," *Continuity and Change* 18:3 (2003): 345–73, at 352; Katrina Honeyman and Jordan Goodman, "Women's Work, Gender Conflict, and Labour Markets in Europe, 1500–1900," *Economic History Review* 44:4 (1991): 608–28, at 611.

53. Francis B. Bickley, ed., *The Little Red Book of Bristol, 2* (Bristol: W. C.

Hemmons, 1900), 127–28. For an example of an argument based entirely on ordinances, see Herlihy, *Opera Muliebria*, 177–79.

54. For the short-term purposes of such ordinances, see Wright, "Churmaids," 106, and Steven Rappaport, *Worlds within Worlds: Structures of Life in Sixteenth-Century London* (Cambridge: Cambridge University Press, 1989), 38–39.

55. Barron, "Golden Age," 46 and 48.

56. Stephanie Hovland, "Girls as Apprentices in Later Medieval London," paper presented at Harlaxton conference (2004). I thank Stephanie Hovland for giving me a copy of this paper and allowing me to cite it. Nancy Adamson, "Urban Families: The Social Context of the London Elite, 1500–1603" (Ph.D. diss., University of Toronto, 1983), 245–50.

57. Vivien Brodsky Elliott, "Single Women in the London Marriage Market: Age, Status, and Mobility, 1598–1619," in *Marriage and Society: Studies in the Social History of Marriage*, ed R. B. Outhwaite (London: Europa, 1981), 81–100, at 91. See, for other cites of this data, Ilana Krausman Ben-Amos, *Adolescence and Youth in Early Modern England* (New Haven, Conn.: Yale University Press, 1994), 135, and McIntosh, *Working Women*, 135 (mistakenly citing Ben-Amos as the source).

58. Unfortunately, Adamson does not list all seventy-three apprentices, but I have checked her references to several specific cases. Although the references are flawed (she miscites the Haberdasher's freeman's register instead of their apprentice binding books), the cases do exist (in Guildhall Library, MS 15860/1 and 2).

59. Derek Keene, "Tanners' Widows, 1300–1350," in *Medieval London Widows, 1300–1500*, ed. Caroline M. Barron and Anne F. Sutton (London: Hambledon, 1994), 1–28, at 4. Hovland found that virtually all the girl apprentices mentioned in the London Letter Books were orphans: seventeen of nineteen girls, as compared to thirty-nine of ninety-six boys. She found more equivalent ratios in the plea rolls and mayor's bills: two of twenty-five girl apprentices and thirty of 237 boys. The changeable meaning of apprenticeship for girls can confound attempts to trace secular trends. See, for example, Ben-Amos, *Adolescence*, 133–55.

60. Hovland, "Girls as Apprentices."

61. Toulmin Smith, *English Gilds*, xxx.

62. The distinction between parish guilds (also known as "fraternities" and "confraternities") and craft guilds was not always firm, as some craft guilds emerged from parish guilds and almost all craft guilds incorporated some of the religious practices of parish guilds. See Elspeth Veale, "The 'Great Twelve': Mistery and Fraternity in Thirteenth-Century London," *Historical Research* 64 (1991): 237–63. It has been recently argued not only that parish guilds were "markedly feminine" but also that, because these religious associations afforded medieval townspeople informal venues in which to negotiate work, craft, and trade, therefore "the strong female presence in most fraternities gave women, no less than men, opportunities to present themselves as credit-worthy and to benefit from the material resources of these societies." See Caroline M. Barron, "The Parish Fraternities of Medieval London," *The Church in Pre-Reformation Society*, ed. Caroline M. Barron and Christopher Harper-Bill (Woodbridge, Suffolk: Boydell, 1985), 13–37, at 30; and Gervase Rosser, "Workers' Associations in English Medieval Towns," in

Les Métiers au Moyen Age, ed. Pascal Lambrechts and Jean-Pierre Sosson (Louvain-la-Neuve: Université Catholique de Louvain, 1994), 283–305, at 291. Yet it seems likely to me that parish guilds—as much sites of "social capital" as the craft guilds examined by Ogilvie—might have disadvantaged women in equivalent ways. Virginia Bainbridge has suggested, for example, that in Cambridge "these organizations might have been rather like the gentlemen's or working men's clubs which still exist today; male clannish affairs with ladies in attendance only on high days or holidays, at feasts and funerals." See Bainbridge, *Gilds in the Medieval Countryside: Social and Religious Change in Cambridgeshire, c. 1350–1558* (Rochester, N.Y.: Boydell, 1996), 47. For the male tilt of fraternities on the Continent, see especially Giovanna Casagrande, "Women in Confraternities between the Middle Ages and the Modern Age: Research in Umbria," *Confraternitas* 5:2 (1994): 3–13; and Nicholas Terpstra, "Women in the Brotherhood: Gender, Class, and Politics in Renaissance Bolognese Confraternities," *Renaissance and Reformation/Renaissance et Réforme* 26:3 (1990): 193–212. There were, however, parish guilds for women alone, and these have been discussed extensively by Katherine French: "Women in the Late Medieval English Parish," in *Gendering the Master Narrative: Women and Power in the Middle Ages*, ed. Mary C. Erler and Maryanne Kowaleski (Ithaca N.Y.: Cornell University Press, 2003), 156–73; "Maidens' Lights and Wives' Stores: Women's Parish Guilds in Late Medieval England," *Sixteenth Century Journal* 29 (1998): 399–425; and " 'To free them from binding': Women in the Late Medieval English Parish," *Journal of Interdisciplinary History* 27 (1997): 387–412.

63. Guildhall Library, MS 5440.

64. Quarterage lists are rare for late medieval London. For the Grocers, see John A. Kingdon, *Facsimile of the First Volume of the Ms. Archives of the Worshipful Company of Grocers of the City of London, A.D. 1345–1463* (London: Richard Clay, 1886), 45–47. For the Coopers, see Guildhall Library, MS 5614a. For the Weavers, see Frances Consitt, *The London Weavers' Company*, vol. 1 (Oxford: Clarendon, 1933), 90. By the sixteenth century, extant quarterage lists are common; for the minimal involvement of women in guilds at that time, see Rappaport, *Worlds*, 36–42.

65. For more on women in the Brewers' guild of London, see Judith M. Bennett, "Women and Men in the Brewers' Gild of London, c. 1420," in *The Salt of Common Life: Individuality and Choice in the Medieval Town, Countryside, and Church*, ed. Edwin B. DeWindt (Kalamazoo, Mich.: Medieval Institute Press, 1995), 181–232, and *Ale, Beer, and Brewsters in England: Women's Work in a Changing World, 1300–1600* (New York: Oxford University Press, 1996), 60–76.

66. Keene, "Tanners' Widows," 26.

67. Rappaport has found, for example, that women (mostly widows) constituted less than 2 percent of those who engaged apprentices in sixteenth-century London; *Worlds*, 41. Widows constituted some 5 percent of the membership of York's Bakers' and Weavers' guilds, c.1560–1700; see Diane Willen, "Guildswomen in the City of York, 1560–1700," *The Historian* 46 (1984): 204–18.

68. For the prevalence of this type of work in medieval English towns, see Rodney Hilton, "Women Traders in Medieval England," in *Class Conflict and the Crisis of Feudalism* (London: Hambledon, 1985), 205–15; Kowaleski, "Women's Work." See also Judith Brown's theories about the Florentine sex-

ual division of labor (which placed women in less-skilled occupations), in "A Woman's Place Was in the Home: Women's Work in Renaissance Tuscany," in *Rewriting the Renaissance,* ed. Margaret Ferguson, Maureen Quilligan, and Nancy J. Vickers (Chicago: University of Chicago Press, 1986), 206–24.

69. Monica Green, "Women's Medical Practice and Health Care in Medieval Europe," *Signs: A Journal of Women in Culture and Society* 14:2 (1989): 434–73, at 449–50.

70. For the silkworkers of London, see Marian K. Dale, "The London Silkwomen of the Fifteenth Century," *Economic History Review* 4 (1933): 324–35; Kay Lacey, "The Production of 'Narrow Ware' by Silkwomen in Fourteenth and Fifteenth Century England," *Textile History* 18:2 (1987): 187–204; Walter B. Stem, "The Trade, Art or Mistery of Silk Throwers of the City of London in the Seventeenth Century," *The Guildhall Miscellany* 1:6 (1956): 25–30.

71. Howell, *Women, Production, and Patriarchy,* 130.

72. The only suggestion of a female guild in England (and a weak one at that) is a set of ordinances enacted by Southampton for its female woolpackers in 1503. See typescript available from the Southampton City Archives of text found in the Second Book of Remembrance, SC2/1/4 f. 26v-8r. The ordinances are discussed in Jones, "Keeping Her in the Family," 115–23.

73. These guilds are discussed in detail in Bennett and Kowaleski, "Crafts, Gilds, and Women," 18–20. For their postmedieval histories, see especially Daryl M. Hafter, "Female Masters in the Ribbonmaking Guild of Eighteenth-Century Rouen," *French Historical Studies* 20:1 (1997): 1–14; Claire Crowston, *The Seamstresses of Old Regime France, 1675–1791* (Durham, N.C.: Duke University Press, 2001); Cynthia Maria Truant, "Parisian Guildswomen and the (Sexual) Politics of Privilege: Defending their Patrimonies in Print," in *Going Public: Women and Publishing in Early Modern France,* ed. Elizabeth C. Goldsmith and Dena Goodman (Ithaca, N.Y.: Cornell University Press, 1995), 46–61, and "La maîtrise d'une identité? Corporations féminines à Paris aux XVIIe et XVIIIe siècles," *Clio* 3 (1996): 55–69.

74. Ogilvie, "Social Capital," 343. For an example of a recent golden-hued interpretation, see Boes, "Dishonourable Youth," 352.

75. M. M. Postan, *The Famulus: The Estate Laborer in the XIIth and XIIIth Centuries,* Economic History Review Supplements 2 (1954); Chris Middleton, "The Familiar Fate of the Famulae: Gender Divisions in the History of Wage Labour," in *On Work: Historical, Comparative and Theoretical Approaches,* ed. R. E. Pahl (Oxford: Blackwell, 1988), 21–47.

76. James E. Thorold Rogers, *Six Centuries of Work and Wages* (New York: G. P. Putnam, 1884), 329; Lord Beveridge, "Westminster Wages in the Manorial Era," *Economic History Review,* 2nd ser., 8 (1955): 18–35, at 34; Simon Penn, "Female Wage-Earners in Late Fourteenth-Century England," *Agricultural History Review* 35 (1987): 1–14, at 9.

77. Bardsley, "Women's Work Reconsidered," 14.

78. Mate, *Daughters, Wives, and Widows,* 55–58; L. R. Poos, *A Rural Society after the Black Death: Essex, 1350–1525* (Cambridge: Cambridge University Press, 1991), 217.

79. John Hatcher, "Women's Work Reconsidered," 191.

80. Penelope Lane, "A Customary or Market Wage? Women and Work in the East Midlands, c. 1700–1840," in *Women, Work and Wages in England,* ed. Lane, et al., 102–18.

81. For apt data, see Deborah Simonton, *A History of European Women's Work: 1700 to the Present* (London: Routledge, 1998), 35.

82. Dorothea Oschinsky, ed., *Walter of Henley and Other Treatises on Estate Management and Accounting* (Oxford: Oxford University Press, 1971), 427.

83. Joyce Burnette, "An Investigation of the Female-Male Wage Gap during the Industrial Revolution in Britain," *Economic History Review* 50:2 (1997): 257–81; Hatcher, "Women's Work Reconsidered."

84. Lane, "A Customary or Market Wage?"

85. Fleming, *Women in Bristol,* 21.

86. Rappaport, *Worlds,* 38–39. See also Sue Wright's observation that the 1461 Bristol weavers' order against the work of women was followed two years later by an ordinance urging women to work in support of their husbands; "Churmaids," 106.

87. Our estimates about the numbers of wage-earning persons in the late medieval population are expanding, but even our highest estimates indicate that only a minority of persons were so engaged; perhaps as much as one-third of the populace worked for wages at least occasionally. Only a minority of these wageworkers would have been women, perhaps one in every four (or fewer). See Simon A. C. Penn and Christopher Dyer, "Wages and Earnings in Late Medieval England: Evidence from the Enforcement of the Labor Laws," *Economic History Review,* 2nd ser., 43 (1990): 356–76. Similarly, our estimates of the urban population, although also growing, still suggest a largely rural population; perhaps as many as one in six persons lived in towns. See Christopher Dyer, "The Past, the Present and the Future in medieval rural history," *Rural History* 1 (1990): 47. See also Paul Bairoch, "Urbanization and the Economy of Preindustrial Societies: The Findings of Two Decades of Research," *Journal of European Economic History* 18 (1989): 239–90.

88. Goldberg, "Female Labour, Service," 35. Goldberg estimates that the population of York in 1377 was perhaps 12,000 and that sustained growth did not occur until the middle of the next century: "Mortality," 49–50. Between 1400 and 1449, 4,870 persons were admitted to the freedom of York: see E. Miller, "Medieval York," in *The Victoria History of the Counties of England: City of York,* ed. P. M. Tillott (London: Oxford University Press, 1961), 86.

89. Barron, in "Golden Age," n. 76, dismisses bleak assessments of women's work status by noting that "working conditions were rarely golden for men in the middle ages."

90. For figures cited here, see the NCPE website, http://www.pay-equity .org/index.html.

91. Amy Richlin, "How Putting the Man in Roman Put the Roman in Romance," in *Talking Gender: Public Images, Personal Journeys, and Political Critiques,* ed. Nancy Hewitt, Jean O'Barr, and Nancy Rosebaugh (Chapel Hill: University of North Carolina Press, 1996), 14–35, at 14.

92. One telling suggestion of patriarchal equilibrium at work might be that, as the NCPE reports, the wage gap has peaked at 77 percent (in 2002) and is now narrowing (76 percent in 2004).

Chapter 6

1. Judith C. Brown, *Immodest Acts: The Life of a Lesbian Nun in Renaissance Italy* (New York: Oxford University Press, 1986), 9. Ruth Vanita has similarly

commented on the tendency of South Asian scholars to "ignore materials on same-sex love or to interpret them as heterosexual." See *Queering India: Same-Sex Love and Eroticism in Indian Culture and Society* (New York: Routledge, 2002), xxiv.

2. Adrienne Rich, "Compulsory Heterosexuality and Lesbian Existence," 1977, reprinted with 1980 foreword in *Journal of Women's History* 15:3 (2003): at 11. For a more recent account of how lesbianism is obscured within feminist scholarship, see Cheshire Calhoun, "The Gender Closet: Lesbian Disappearance under the Sign 'Women,'" *Feminist Studies* 21:1 (1995): 7–34.

3. My numbers are vague because some articles or papers were difficult to categorize. I must confess that I expected to find more coverage of lesbian topics in these venues than I did (less than 5 percent in both instances). But the problem these low numbers suggest—that is, an exceedingly *small* safe haven for lesbian topics within women's history—is not my subject here.

4. Gerda Lerner, *The Creation of Feminist Consciousness* (New York: Oxford University Press, 1993), 179. This phrase is applied to female writers before the mid-nineteenth century, a group that implicitly includes the medieval nuns and mystics discussed earlier in the book. Lerner also describes medieval mystics in terms of "sacrifices" (65) and "insecurity, sickness" (83). On p. 30, she concludes that the single, cloistered, or widowed status of many learned women suggests that women were "forced to choose between the life of a woman and the life of the mind."

5. Jo Ann Kay McNamara, *Sisters in Arms: Catholic Nuns through Two Millennia* (Cambridge, Mass.: Harvard University Press, 1996). McNamara speaks briefly about emotional attachments between women on pp. 76 and 113, and she cursorily mentions medieval fears of same-sex attractions between women on pp. 144 and 380. As best I can tell, these are McNamara's only considerations of the possibility of emotional and/or sexual intimacy between medieval nuns. For a fuller view, see Ann Matter, "My Sister, My Spouse: Woman-Identified Women in Medieval Christianity," *Journal of Feminist Studies in Religion* 2:2 (1986): 81–93. For material published since McNamara's book, see especially Karma Lochrie, "Mystical Acts, Queer Tendencies," in *Constructing Medieval Sexuality*, ed. Karma Lochrie et al. (Minneapolis: University of Minnesota Press, 1997), 180–200; Susan Schibanoff, "Hildegarde of Bingen and Richardis of Stade: The Discourse of Desire," in *Same Sex Love and Desire among Women in the Middle Ages*, ed. Francesca Canadé Sautman and Pamela Sheingorn (New York: Palgrave, 2001), 49–84; Rosemary Drage Hale, "Brilliant Constellations: History in the Presence of the Now," *Journal of the History of Sexuality* 10:2 (2001): 167–72.

6. Judith M. Bennett, *Women in the Medieval English Countryside: Gender and Household in Brigstock before the Plague* (New York: Oxford University Press, 1986).

7. For discussions about the obfuscation of lesbianism within other branches of women's history, see Mattie Udora Richardson, "No More Secrets, No More Lies: African American History and Compulsory Heterosexuality," *Journal of Women's History* 15:3 (2003): 63–76, and Jennifer Manion, "Calling All Liberals: Connecting Feminist Theory, Activism, and History," in *Taking Back the Academy! History of Activism, History as Activism*, ed. Jim Downs and Jennifer Manion (New York: Routledge, 2004), 145–59.

8. Acknowledging the fantasy of "reality" (see Joan Scott, "The Evidence

of Experience," *Critical Inquiry* 17 [1991]: 773–97) does not, I think, reduce history to fiction; historians can still seek out the "actual" and "plausible." In this regard, I am indebted to Charles Zita, who introduced me to Greg Dening's distinction between the possibilities of "actuality" and the reductionism of "reality." See especially Greg Dening, *Performances* (Melbourne: Melbourne University Press, 1996), 60.

9. Jacqueline Murray, "Twice Marginal and Twice Invisible: Lesbians in the Middle Ages," in *Handbook of Medieval Sexuality*, ed. Vern L. Bullough and James A. Brundage (New York: Garland, 1996), 191–223; Karma Lochrie, "Mystical Acts"; Kathleen M. Blumreich, "Lesbian Desire in the Old French *Roman de Silence*," *Arthuriana* 7:2 (1997): 47–62; Robert L. A. Clark and Claire Sponsler, "Queer Play: The Cultural Work of Crossdressing in Medieval Drama," *New Literary History* 28:2 (1997): 319–44.

10. Karen V. Hansen, "'No *Kisses* is Like Youres': An Erotic Friendship between Two African-American Women during the Mid-Nineteenth Century," *Gender and History* 7:2 (1995): 153–82; Elizabeth Lapovsky Kennedy and Madeline D. Davis, *Boots of Leather, Slippers of Gold: The History of a Lesbian Community* (New York: Routledge, 1993); Nan Alamilla Boyd, *Wide Open Town: A History of Queer San Francisco to 1965* (Berkeley: University of California Press, 2003).

11. Unlike historians of more modern eras who can find information about the same-sex relations of ordinary women in letters, diaries, and other personal memorabilia or even through oral interviews, medievalists must rely on criminal accusations. These allow us to see lesbians in scripted contexts that emphasize deviance, disorder, and danger and that usually portray one woman as "normal" and the other as "abnormal" (the former asserts her innocence by accusing the latter of unnatural aggression toward her). There are precious few of even these. CASE 1: Bertolina, nicknamed Guercia, accused in the civic court of Bologna in 1295 of courting women with a silk dildo (*virilis sete*); she was banished. See Carol Lansing, "Donna con Donna? A 1295 Inquest into Female Sodomy," *Studies in Medieval and Renaissance History*, 3rd ser., 2 (2005): 109–22. CASES 2–3: two women cited in a French royal register of 1405. See Joan Cadden, *Meanings of Sex Difference in the Middle Ages: Medicine, Science, and Culture* (Cambridge: Cambridge University Press, 1993), 224, and Edith J. Benkov, "The Erased Lesbian: Sodomy and the Legal Tradition in Medieval Europe," in *Same-Sex Love and Desire*, ed. Sautman and Sheingorn, 101–23. CASES 4–5: two women charged with a "vice against nature which is called sodomy" in Rottweil in 1444. See Helmut Puff, "Localizing Sodomy: The 'Priest and Sodomite' in Pre-Reformation Germany and Switzerland," *Journal of the History of Sexuality* 8:2 (1997): 165–95, at 182–83. CASE 6: a reputed lesbian drowned in Speier in 1477. See Louis Crompton, "The Myth of Lesbian Impunity: Capital Laws from 1270 to 1791," *Journal of Homosexuality* 6:1/2 (1980–81): 11–25, at 17, and Helmut Puff, "Female Sodomy: The Trial of Katherina Hetzeldorfer (1477)," *Journal of Medieval and Early Modern Studies* 30 (2000): 41–61. CASES 7–13: seven women executed in Bruges in 1482–83. See Marc Boone, "State Power and Illicit Sexuality: The Persecution of Sodomy in Late Medieval Bruges," *Journal of Medieval History* 22:2 (1996): 135–53, at 151, n. 62 (Boone also cites some early sixteenth–century cases). CASES 14–15: two women who were "joined together like a man and a woman" (*vsaban en vno commo onbre e mugger*) in San Sebastián

(Spain) in 1497; one was executed by being hung by her feet. This case was posted to the Gay-Lesbian Medieval Studies listserve on behalf of Jesús Ángel Solórzano by Paul Halsall in October 2000. I have been unable to check the reference: Archivo de la Real Audiencia y Chancillería de Valladolid, SRE, legajo 181. Given these mere fifteen cases, it is no surprise that medievalists regularly forage beyond 1500 for more instances, using especially the early seventeenth-century case of the nun Benedetta Carlini discussed in Brown, *Immodest Acts*. But even absorbing "early modern" into "medieval" does not much help the problem, as few documented instances of lesbian behavior survive before the nineteenth century. See, for example, the relative paucity of female same-sex relations prosecuted in eighteenth-century Amsterdam: Theo Van der Meer, "Tribades on Trial: Female Same-Sex Offenders in Late Eighteenth-Century Amsterdam," *Journal of the History of Sexuality* 1:3 (1991): 424–45.

12. Blanche Wiesen Cook, "The Historical Denial of Lesbianism," *Radical History Review* 20 (1979): 60–65.

13. Martha Vicinus, "Lesbian History: All Theory and No Facts or All Facts and No Theory?" *Radical History Review* 60 (1994): 57–75; Alison Oram, "'Friends', Feminists and Sexual Outlaws: Lesbianism and British History," in *Straight Studies Modified: Lesbian Interventions in the Academy*, ed. Gabriele Griffin and Sonya Andermahr (London: Cassell, 1997), 168–83; Laura Gowing, "Lesbians and Their Like in Early Modern Europe," forthcoming from Thames and Hudson in *Gay History of the World*, ed. Robert Aldrich.

14. The development of queer studies is beyond the scope of this chapter, as is its complex relationship to lesbian/gay studies. Queer studies partakes of the cultural and theoretical turn of academic inquiry in the 1990s. In some venues today, "queer" is just a new name for "lesbian/gay" or LGBTQ (Lesbian, Gay, Bisexual, Transgender, and Queer) studies; in other contexts, strong contrasts are drawn between the two—that queer studies are ahistorical and lesbian/gay studies too materialist; that queer studies are so broad as to efface sexual practices and that lesbian/gay studies are too mired in identity politics; that queer studies are relentlessly male-focused and that lesbian studies are too separatist. I consider it most productive to focus on their shared project of interrogating the heteronormativity of scholarship and knowledge. For examples of queer studies in medieval scholarship, see *Queering the Middle Ages*, ed. Glenn Burger and Steven F. Kruger (Minneapolis: University of Minnesota Press, 2001); Anna Klosowska Roberts, *Queer Love in the Middle Ages* (New York: Palgrave Macmillan, 2005); and Carolyn Dinshaw, *Getting Medieval: Sexualities and Communities, Pre- and Postmodern* (Durham, N.C.: Duke University Press, 1999).

15. John Boswell, *Same-Sex Unions in Premodern Europe* (New York: Villard Books, 1994), xxvii–xxx.

16. As Murray phrases it on p. 199 of "Twice Marginal," for medieval people, "[s]exual activity without a penis was difficult to imagine."

17. Harry J. Kuster and Raymond J. Cormier, "Old Views and New Trends: Observations on the Problem of Homosexuality in the Middle Ages," *Studi Medievali*, ser. 3, 25 (1984): 587–610, esp. 600–601, 609.

18. Joan Cadden, *Meanings of Sex*, 224.

19. Hence, for example, Jacqueline Murray writes about "the devaluation of physical relations across medieval society" ("Twice Marginal," 206). This

was perhaps true for theologians, philosophers, and other clerics, but it was certainly *not* true for ordinary medieval people—peasants, laborers, artisans, merchants—whose appreciation of physical relations is manifestly clear in their bawdy tales and songs. For just two examples of such alternative discourses, see two songs copied into the commonplace book of an Oxford student in the fifteenth century, "Led I the Dance a Midsummer's Day" and "All this Day I have Sought," both printed in Richard Leighton Greene, *The Early English Carols*, 2nd ed. (Oxford: Clarendon Press: 1977), items 453 and 452 respectively.

20. Catharine MacKinnon, "Does Sexuality Have a History?" in *Discourses of Sexuality: From Aristotle to AIDS*, ed. Domna C. Stanton (Ann Arbor: University of Michigan Press, 1992), 117–36 at 121.

21. Bernadette J. Brooten has similarly observed that the "highly gendered, social arrangements" of same-sex love in ancient Rome distinguished male homosexuality and lesbianism. See her *Love between Women: Early Christian Responses to Female Homoeroticism* (Chicago: University of Chicago Press, 1996), at 14. For the greater physicality of elite understandings of lesbianism, see Helen Rodmite Lemay, "William of Saliceto on Human Sexuality," *Viátor* 12 (1981): 165–81, at 178–79; for latter versions of the same, see Katharine Park, "The Rediscovery of the Clitoris: French Medicine and the Tribade, 1570–1620," in *The Body in Parts: Fantasies of Corporeality in Early Modern Europe*, ed. David Hillman and Carla Mazzio (New York: Routledge, 1997), 170–93, and Emma Donoghue, "Imagined More than Women: Lesbians as Hermaphrodites, *Women's History Review* 2:2 (1993): 199–216. There is some evidence that the bodies of male homosexuals were occasionally also seen as marked by their acts. See Steven F. Kruger, "Racial/Religious and Sexual Queerness in the Middle Ages," *Medieval Feminist Newsletter* 16 (Fall 1993): 32–36, esp. 34 (to me, his evidence suggests physical revulsion on the part of medieval commentators, not an attribution of physical deformity to male homosexuals); Joan Cadden, "Sciences/Silences: The Natures and Languages of 'Sodomy' in Peter of Abano's *Problemata* Commentary," in *Constructing Medieval Sexuality*, 40–57; Mark D. Jordan, *The Invention of Sodomy in Christian Theology* (Chicago: University of Chicago Press, 1997), esp. 114–35. See also Joseph Ziegler, "Sexuality and the Sexual Organs in Latin Physiognomy Texts," *Studies in Medieval and Renaissance History*, 3rd ser., 2 (2005): 83–108.

22. As Judith Butler has made very clear, it would be a mistake to overlook matters of gender difference when studying sexuality. See her "Against Proper Objects," *differences: A Journal of Feminist Cultural Studies* 6:2/3 (1994): 1–26.

23. Not surprisingly, some critics have worked just as hard to erase the lesbian possibilities of medieval texts. See, for example, Angelica Rieger's argument that Bieris de Romans, author of a love song addressed to another woman, was not, in fact, expressing same-sex desire. Angelica Rieger, "Was Bieris de Romans Lesbian? Women's Relations with Each Other in the World of the Troubadours," in *The Voice of the Trobairitz: Perspectives on Women Troubadours*, ed. William D. Paden (Philadelphia: University of Pennsylvania Press, 1989), 73–94. Because of the heteronormativity of modern scholarship and the homophobia of some modern scholars, almost all citations to lesbian or gay practices can, of course, be interpreted out of existence—and done so in

ways that suit academic culture particularly well. For a brief critique of Rieger's argument, see Francesca Canadé Sautman and Pamela Sheingorn, "Introduction: Charting the Field," in *Same Sex Love*, ed. Sautman and Sheingorn, 1–49, at 30–31. See also Karma Lochrie, *Heterosyncrasies: Female Sexuality When Normal Wasn't* (Minneapolis: University of Minnesota Press, 2005).

24. Bruce Holsinger, "The Flesh of the Voice: Embodiment and the Homoerotics of Devotion in the Music of Hildegarde of Bingen (1098–1179)," *Signs: A Journal of Women in Culture and Society* 19:1 (1993): 92–125; Matter, "My Sister, My Spouse"; Ulrike Wiethaus, "Female Homoerotic Discourse and Religion in Medieval Germanic Culture," in *Difference and Genders in Medieval Society and Culture*, ed. Sharon Farmer and Carol Pasternak (Minneapolis: University of Minnesota Press, 2003), 288–322; Mary Anne Campbell, "Redefining Holy Maidenhead: Virginity and Lesbianism in Late Medieval England," *Medieval Feminist Newsletter* 13 (1992): 14–15; Kathy Lavezzo, "Sobs and Sighs between Women: The Homoerotics of Compassion in *The Book of Margery Kempe*," in *Premodern Sexualities*, ed. Louise Fradenburg and Carla Freccero (New York: Routledge, 1996), 175–98; Susan Crane, "Clothing and Gender Definition: Joan of Arc," *Journal of Medieval and Early Modern Studies* 26:2 (1996): 297–320.

25. Wiethaus, "Female Homoerotic Discourse."

26. This maternal interpretation runs throughout Bynum's *Holy Feast and Holy Fast: The Religious Significance of Food to Medieval Women* (Berkeley: University of California Press, 1987), but see also her explicit statement in *Fragmentation and Redemption: Essays on Gender and the Human Body in Medieval Religion* (New York: Zone, 1992), 86. For Karma Lochrie's critique, see "Mystical Acts" and "Desiring Foucault," *Journal of Medieval and Early Modern Studies* 27:1 (1997): 3–16.

27. Lochrie, "Mystical Acts." In public discussion at the 1998 conference on the Queer Middle Ages, Lochrie indicated her willingness to entertain the possibility that medieval nuns did, in fact, venerate Christ's wound in ways that spoke to their own same-sex desires and actions.

28. Karma Lochrie, "Between Women," in *The Cambridge Companion to Medieval Women's Writing*, ed. Carolyn Dinshaw and David Wallace (Cambridge: Cambridge University Press, 2003), 70–90. See also Lochrie's critique of my original formulation of "lesbian-like": "Doing Lesbians 'History-Like'" in the *SSHMA Newsletter*, n.s. 2 (Spring 2001): 2. (SSHMA is the acronym for the Society for the Study of Homosexuality in the Middle Ages.)

29. For "bosom sex," see Hansen, "No *Kisses*." For the "erotic in female terms," see Rich, "Compulsory Heterosexuality," 28 (in 2003 reprint). For an interesting examination of who defines lesbianism, see Donna Penn, "The Meanings of Lesbianism in Post-War America," *Gender and History* 3:2 (1991): 190–204.

30. We need no longer stumble on a distinction between sex acts (premodern) and sexual identities (modern). Even David Halperin—perhaps the most fervent of social constructionists—now agrees that there were, indeed, sexual *identities* before the nineteenth century; our job is to try to understand the very different constituents of these past sexual identities. See David Halperin, "Forgetting Foucault: Acts, Identities, and the History of Sexuality," *Representations* 63 (1998): 93–120, revised as chapter 1 in *How To Do the History*

of Homosexuality (Chicago: University of Chicago Press, 2002). This project is brilliantly illustrated by Anna Clark's essay on Anne Lister which shows how, long before sexologists like Havelock Ellis or Richard von Krafft-Ebing could have provided her with a ready-made identity, Anne Lister fashioned one for herself, from her "inherent desires," from her "material circumstances," and from the "cultural representations" available to her. See Anna Clark, "Anne Lister's Construction of Lesbian Identity," *Journal of the History of Sexuality* 7:1 (1996): 23–50, at 27.

31. For an example, see Hansen, "No *Kisses*," 173.

32. Bernadette Brooten, *Love between Women*, 5. For the original modern reference, see Albio Cesare Cassio, "Post-Classical λέσβίαί," *The Classical Quarterly*, n.s., 33:1 (1983): 296–97. Scholars debate Arethas's precise meaning—he might, for example, have used "lesbian" more as an eponym than as a classification—but the link between "lesbian" and "female same-sex relations" seems clear.

33. Louise Labé, *Oeuvres complètes*, ed. Enzo Giudici (Geneva: Droz, 1991), 129 (Elegie I, l. 15).

34. Emma Donoghue, *Passions between Women: British Lesbian Culture, 1668–1801* (London: Scarlet Press, 1993), 3.

35. Medievalists murmur continuously about both terms but cannot do without them. See Elizabeth A. R. Brown, "The Tyranny of a Construct: Feudalism and Historians of Medieval Europe," *American Historical Review* 79:4 (1974): 1063–88.

36. See especially Ruth Mazo Karras, *Sexuality in the Middle Ages: Doing unto Others* (London: Routledge, 2005), 28–58; also Lisa Weston, "Queering Virginity," *Medieval Feminist Forum* 36 (2003): 22–24, and Jo Ann McNamara, "Chastity as a Third Gender in the History and *Hagiography* of Gregory of Tours," in *The World of Gregory of Tours*, ed. Kathleen Mitchell and Ian Wood (Leiden: Brill, 2002), 199–210. For an alternative view of medieval sexualities, see Glenn Burger, who proposes that they developed around masculinity, on the one hand, and feminine, effeminate, and sodomitical, on the other: Glenn Burger, *Chaucer's Queer Nation* (Minneapolis: University of Minnesota Press, 2003), xviii. And yet another alternative has been proposed by Francesca Sautman and Pamela Sheingorn—that whereas there may have been no sexual identities in the Middle Ages, there was certainly sexual consciousness or self-perception; see *Same Sex Love*, 12–13.

37. They could disappear, as well, in history-writing that seeks out lesbianism as pervasive, natural, and ideal. Although little ink has been spilt on the heteronormativity of women's history, entire inkwells have been thrown over its equivalent in gay and lesbian history—that is, in the dispute between so-called essentialists and constructionists. For a measured commentary on this debate, see John Boswell, "Concepts, Experience, and Sexuality," *differences: A Journal of Feminist Cultural Studies* 2:1 (1990): 67–87.

38. Along similar lines, Eve Kosofsky Sedgwick has argued against the assumption "that 'homosexuality as we conceive of it today' itself comprises a coherent definitional field rather than a space of overlapping, contradictory, and conflictual definitional forces." See *Epistemology of the Closet* (Berkeley: University of California Press, 1990), 45.

39. Carol J. Clover, "Regardless of Sex: Men, Women, and Power in Early

Northern Europe," in *Studying Medieval Women*, ed. Nancy F. Partner (Cambridge, Mass.: Medieval Academy of America, 1993), 61–87.

40. Cadden, *The Meanings of Sex Difference*, esp. 221–27.

41. E. Jane Burns, "Refashioning Courtly Love: Lancelot as Ladies' Man or Lady/Man?" in *Constructing Medieval Sexuality*, ed. Lochrie et al., 111–34. See also Cary J. Nederman and Jacqui True, "The Third Sex: The Idea of the Hermaphrodite in Twelfth-Century Europe," *Journal of the History of Sexuality* 6:4 (1996): 497–517.

42. Valerie Traub, *The Renaissance of Lesbianism in Early Modern England* (Cambridge: Cambridge University Press, 2002), 16.

43. I am grateful to Sarah Ferber for explicating for me the useful instabilities of this term.

44. Carol Smith-Rosenberg, "The Female World of Love and Ritual: Relations between Women in Nineteenth-Century America," as reprinted in her *Disorderly Conduct: Visions of Gender in Victorian America* (New York: Oxford University Press, 1985), 53–76.

45. Rich, "Compulsory Heterosexuality."

46. Vicinus, "Lesbian History," 57.

47. Greta Christina, "Loaded Words," *Pomosexuals: Challenging Assumptions about Gender and Sexuality*, ed. Carol Queen and Lawrence Schimel (San Francisco: Cleis Press, 1997), 29–35.

48. I am grateful to David Halperin for this example. Paul Halsall offered me another: lesbian potlucks, which might lead us, ad absurdum, to characterize church potlucks as lesbian-like.

49. Sarah L. Delaney and A. Elizabeth Delaney, *Having Our Say: The Delany Sisters' First 100 Years* (New York: Delta, 1993). My example is deliberately provocative. I am not accusing the Delany sisters of incest, nor am I suggesting that they were lesbians. I am suggesting, however, that in both their singleness and their emotional partnership, the Delany sisters behaved in ways that offer affinities with certain modern lesbian behaviors and that are, therefore, lesbian-like.

50. The exception to positive treatment is, of course, Joan of Arc, once she fell into the hands of the English. Yet since she cross-dressed but never hid her female sex, she is an exception in other ways, too.

51. Michael Shank, "A Female University Student in Late Medieval Krakow," *Signs: A Journal of Women in Culture and Society* 12:2 (1987): 373–80. Shank notes that this might just be a literary tale, but he also adduces good evidence to suggest its historicity.

52. Unlike modern historians who have readily linked cross-dressing with homosexual or lesbian practices, most medievalists have rejected or avoided this link. Vern Bullough argues vigorously against a link between cross-dressing and homosexual practices in "Cross Dressing and Gender Role Changes in the Middle Ages," in Bullough and Brundage, *Handbook*, 223–42. Valerie R. Hotchkiss, *Clothes Make the Man: Female Cross Dressing in Medieval Europe* (New York: Garland, 1996), similarly underplays lesbian possibilities (see her brief discussion, 113–14). For a different view, see Crane, "Clothing."

53. See, for examples, van der Meer, "Tribades on Trial," esp. 439, and the case of Catharine Linck (guilty of religious inconstancy as well as same-sex relations) as reported in Brigitte Eriksson, "A Lesbian Execution in Ger-

many, 1721: The Trial Records," *Journal of Homosexuality* 6:1/2 (1980–81): 27–40.

54. The excerpted text can be found in Charles du Fresne du Cange, *Glossarium mediae et infimae Latinitatis* (Paris: Didot, 1844), 3:663–64, s.v. "hermaphroditus." I am grateful to Phillipe Rosenberg for his help in reading this text. I have not consulted the full letter (found in Archives Nationales de France, JJ 160:112) but have relied on Benkov's summary in "Erased Lesbian."

55. Leah Lydia Otis, *Prostitution in Medieval Society: The History of an Urban Institution in Languedoc* (Chicago: University of Chicago Press, 1985), esp. 73–75.

56. Joan Nestle, *A Restricted Country* (Ithaca, N.Y.: Firebrand Books, 1987), 157–77.

57. Brooten, *Love between Women*, 4–5.

58. Boswell, *Same-Sex Unions*, xxix, n. 31.

59. Ruth Karras, *Common Women: Prostitution and Sexuality in Medieval England* (New York: Oxford University Press, 1996), 185, n. 9, reports that she has found one "shred of evidence" linking prostitution and lesbianism, but she dismisses it as a clerical error on 175, n. 67. Both Otis (*Prostitution in Medieval Society*) and Karras discuss how prostitution was socially tolerated, in part, because of anxieties about male same-sex relations.

60. Mary Martin McLaughlin, "Creating and Recreating Communities of Women: The Case of Corpus Domini, Ferrara, 1406–1452," *Signs: A Journal of Women in Culture and Society* 14:2 (1989): 293–320.

61. For these and other demographic estimates of the presence of singlewomen, see Maryanne Kowaleski, "Singlewomen in Medieval and Early Modern Europe: The Demographic Perspective," in *Singlewomen in the European Past, 1250–1800*, ed. Judith M. Bennett and Amy M. Froide (Philadelphia: University of Pennsylvania Press, 1999), 38–81 and 325–44.

62. As Margaret Hunt has noted, however, marriage did not preclude lesbian relations; see "The Sapphic Strain: English Lesbians in the Long Eighteenth Century," in *Singlewomen*, ed. Bennett and Froide, 270–96.

63. I have taken this quote from a reprint of the 1928 translation of a handbook for witch hunting, written in 1486 by Heinrich Kramer and Jacob Sprenger: *The Malleus Maleficarum*, trans. Montague Summers (New York: Dover Publications, 1971), 43. The Latin reads: *Mulier cum sola cogitat, mala cogitat.*

64. Margaret Hunt, "Afterword," in *Queering the Renaissance*, ed. Jonathan Goldberg (Durham, N.C.: Duke University Press, 1994), 359–77, at 372. Lesbian history is replete with attempts to connect to the past while recognizing that such connections will be incomplete, fragile, and contingent. Thus, Carolyn Dinshaw has sought to create an "affective history" that moves between the poles of "mimetic identification with the past or blanket alterism"; see Dinshaw, *Getting Medieval*, 24. Valerie Traub has similarly urged us to search for a past that is neither "a mirror image of ourselves" nor "utterly alien"; see Traub, *Renaissance*, 32.

65. Traub, *Renaissance*, 220, italics in original.

66. Ibid., 350.

67. For discussions of this issue in another context, see Leila J. Rupp, "'Imagine My Surprise': Women's Relationships in Mid-Twentieth-Century

America," reprinted in *Hidden from History: Reclaiming the Gay and Lesbian Past*, ed. Martin Duberman, Martha Vicinus, and George Chauncey Jr. (New York: New American Library, 1989), 395–410; Estelle B. Freedman, "'The Burning of Letters Continues': Elusive Identities and the Historical Construction of Sexuality," *Journal of Women's History* 9:4 (1998): 181–200. Self-identification is, of course, important, but it is not determinative; see, for example, John Boswell's revised position in "Revolutions, Universals, and Sexual Categories," in *Hidden from History*, Duberman et al., 17–36, at 35. The term "lesbian-like" provides a good compromise between respecting the self-identifications of such women and rejecting their own homophobic, elitist, and racist ideas about what a "lesbian" was.

68. For a fascinating example of lesbian sexuality understood as incidental by the women so involved, see Elizabeth Lapovsky Kennedy, "'But We Would Never Talk about It': The Structures of Lesbian Discretion in South Dakota, 1928–1933," in *Inventing Lesbian Culture in America*, ed. Ellen Levin (Boston: Beacon Press, 1996), 15–39.

69. Bennett and Froide, eds., *Singlewomen*, and Amy M. Froide, *Never Married: Singlewomen in Early Modern England* (Oxford: Oxford University Press, 2005).

70. Lerner, *Creation of Feminist Consciousness*, 179.

71. Calhoun, "Gender Closet."

Chapter 7

1. Bonnie G. Smith, *The Gender of History: Men, Women, and Historical Practice* (Cambridge, Mass.: Harvard University Press, 1998), 238–39, italics in original. See also Billie Melman, "Gender, History and Memory: The Invention of Women's Past in the Nineteenth and Early Twentieth Centuries," *History and Memory* 5:1 (1993): 5–41; Nicholas B. Dirks, "History as a Sign of the Modern," *Public Culture* 2:2 (1990): 25–32.

2. Gerda Lerner, *The Creation of Feminist Consciousness: From the Middle Ages to Eighteen-Seventy* (New York: Oxford University Press, 1993), 220, 166.

3. Leila Rupp, "Is Feminism the Province of Old (or Middle Aged) Women?" *Journal of Women's History* 12:4 (2001): 164–73, at 170.

4. Interview by Liz Hoggard in *The Observer*, March 13, 2005. Available online at http://observer.guardian.co.uk/review/story/0,6903,1436296,00.html.

5. See, especially, Stacy Gillis and Rebecca Munford, "Genealogies and Generations: The Politics and Praxis of Third Wave Feminism," *Women's History Review* 13:2 (2004): 165–82.

6. Gerda Lerner, "Placing Women in History: Definitions and Challenges," in *The Majority Finds Its Past* (New York: Oxford University Press, 1979), 145–59, quotes at 159. First published in *Feminist Studies* 3:1–2 (Fall 1975): 5–14.

7. Joan Kelly, "The Social Relation of the Sexes: Methodological Implications of Women's History," *Signs: A Journal of Women in Culture and Society* 1:4 (Summer 1976): 809–23; the version used here was reprinted in her *Women, History, and Theory* (Chicago: University of Chicago Press, 1984), 1–18, quote at 1. See 19–50 for "Did Women Have a Renaissance," first published in

Becoming Visible: Women in European History, ed. Renate Bridenthal and Claudia Koonz (Boston: Houghton Mifflin, 1977).

8. Elsa Barkley Brown, "Polyrhythms and Improvization: Lessons for Women's History," *History Workshop Journal* 31 (1991): 85–90.

9. Gianna Pomata, "History, Particular and Universal: On Reading Some Recent Women's History Textbooks," *Feminist Studies* 19:1 (1993): 7–50.

10. Jane Austen, *Northanger Abbey,* chap. 14 in vol. 1.

11. Mary Beth Norton, "Rethinking American History Textbooks," in *Learning History in America: Schools, Cultures, and Politics,* ed. Lloyd Kramer, Donald Reid, and William L. Barney (Minneapolis: University of Minnesota Press, 1994), 23–33, at 29.

12. Denys Hay, *Europe in the Fourteenth and Fifteenth Centuries,* 2nd ed. (London: Longman, 1989), xii.

13. C. Warren Hollister and Judith M. Bennett, *Medieval Europe: A Short History,* 9th ed. (Boston: McGraw-Hill, 2002); Barbara H. Rosenwein, *A Short History of the Middle Ages* (Peterborough, Ontario: Broadview Press, 2002); Clifford R. Backman, *The Worlds of Medieval Europe* (New York: Oxford University Press, 2003); William R. Cook and Ronald B. Herzman, *The Medieval World View: An Introduction,* 2nd ed. (New York: Oxford University Press, 2004); Jo Ann H. Moran Cruz and Richard Gerberding, *Medieval Worlds: An Introduction to Medieval History, 300–1492* (Boston: Houghton Mifflin, 2004).

14. For more on this particular master narrative, see Lester K. Little, "Cypress Beams, Kufic Script, and Cut Stone: Rebuilding the Master Narrative of European History," *Speculum* 79 (2004): 909–28.

15. Carol Berkin, "'Dangerous Courtesies' Assault Women's History," *Chronicle of Higher Education* 38:16 (December 11, 1991): A44.

16. Cook and Herzman, *Medieval World View,* 131.

17. See their website at http://nchs.ucla.edu/guide.html.

18. Barbara A. Moss, "Getting Our Feet Wet: Women of Color and the National *Standards* for World History," *Journal of Women's History* 9:3 (1997): 143–53. This essay was part of a general forum found on 140–76.

19. I am relying here on Lester Little's description of Bitel's unpublished assertion of the "impossibility of teaching a medieval feminist history." See Little, "Cypress Beams," 917. See also Lisa Bitel, *Women in Early Medieval Europe, 400–1100* (Cambridge: Cambridge University Press, 2002).

20. Joan W. Scott, "Comment on 'Women's History and the *National History Standards*,'" *Journal of Women's History* 9:3 (1997): 172–76.

21. The critical revisions occurred between the 8th (1998) and 9th (2002) editions; a 10th (2005) edition is now available. The 9th edition is included among the five textbooks surveyed in this chapter.

22. Medieval textbooks are rarely reviewed, so I am afraid that this assessment is mine alone.

23. Jane Schulenburg, *Forgetful of Their Sex: Female Sanctity and Society, ca. 500–1100* (Chicago: University of Chicago Press, 1998), 176–209.

24. Bonnie G. Smith, "Gender and Historical Understanding," in *Learning History in America,* ed. Kramer, et al., 107–19, at 109.

25. C. Warren Hollister, *Medieval Europe: A Short History,* 8th ed. (Boston: McGraw-Hill, 1998), 296. Hollister does not give a source for the advice, so I have been unable to check the authorial perspective of the original.

26. One short-lived U.S. project took a tack not far different from the one

I advocate here: in the early 1980s, FIPSE (Fund for the Improvement of Post-Secondary Education) produced packets to help teachers integrate women in their teaching of survey courses in history. These packets guided my first efforts at feminist teaching, as they did for many others at the time.

27. As cited in Anne Clark Bartlett, "Defining the Terms: Postfeminism as an Ideology of Cool," *Medieval Feminist Forum* 34 (Fall 2002): 25–29, at 28. For further comments on the truncated historical vision of today's students, see Susan K. Freeman et al., "Perspectives on Teaching Women's History: Views from the Classroom, the Library, and the Internet," *Journal of Women's History* 16:2 (2004): 143–76.

28. Jane O. Newman, "The Present and Our Past: Simone de Beauvoir, Descartes, and Presentism in the Historiography of Feminism," in *Women's Studies on its Own*, ed. Robyn Wiegman (Durham, N.C.: Duke University Press, 2002), 141–73.

29. See above for the early influence of Lerner and Kelly. Mary Ritter Beard, *Woman as Force in History: A Study in Traditions and Realities* (New York: Macmillan, 1946).

30. Florence Griswold Buckstaff, "Married Women's Property in Anglo-Saxon and Anglo-Norman Law," *Annals of the American Academy of Political and Social Sciences* 4 (1893–94): 233–64, quote from 263; Mary Bateson, "History of the Double Monasteries," *Transactions of the Royal Historical Society*, n.s., 13 (1899): 137–98, quote from 150; Elizabeth Dixon, "Craftswomen in the Livre des Métiers," *Economic Journal* 5 (1895): 209–28, at 227.

31. For more on early female medievalists, see Jane Chance, ed., *Women Medievalists and the Academy* (Madison: University of Wisconsin Press, 2005).

32. Linda Kerber, "On the Importance of Taking Notes (and Keeping Them)," in *Voices of Women Historians: The Personal, the Political, the Professional,* ed. Eileen Boris and Nupur Chaudhuri (Bloomington: Indiana University Press, 1999), 45–60, at 45.

33. Judith M. Bennett, "Medievalism and Feminism," *Speculum* 68 (1993): 309–31, at 312.

34. The Society for Medieval Feminist Scholarship produces the *Medieval Feminist Forum* and cooperates with the electronic discussion group medfem-l and the online bibliographic resource *Feminae* (http://www.haverford-.edu/library/reference/mschaus/mfi/mfi.html).

35. A. Abram, "Women Traders in Medieval London," *The Economic Journal* 26 (1916): 276–85, quote at 285.

36. Power, "Position of Women," quote at 410.

37. Margaret Wade Labarge, *A Small Sound of the Trumpet: Women in Medieval Life* (Boston: Beacon Press, 1986), 238.

38. Jo Ann McNamara, "The *Herrenfrage*: The Restructuring of the Gender System, 1050–1150," in *Medieval Masculinities: Regarding Men in the Middle Ages*, ed. Clare A. Lees (Minneapolis: University of Minnesota Press, 1994), 3–29, quote from 15; see also McNamara's "Women and Power through the Family Revisited," in *Gendering the Master Narrative: Women and Power in the Middle Ages*, ed. Mary C. Erler and Maryanne Kowaleski (Ithaca, N.Y.: Cornell University Press, 2003), 17–31. Susan Mosher Stuard, "The Dominion of Gender, or How Women Fared in the High Middle Ages," in *Becoming Visible: Women in European History*, ed. Renate Bridenthal et al. (Boston: Houghton Mifflin, 1998), 129–50.

39. David Herlihy, "Land, Family, and Women in Continental Europe, 701–1200," *Traditio* 18 (1962): 89–120. Marion F. Facinger, "A Study of Medieval Queenship: Capetian France, 987–1237," *Studies in Medieval and Renaissance History* 5 (1968): 3–47. Jo Ann McNamara and Suzanne Wemple, "The Power of Women through the Family in Medieval Europe, 500–1100," in *Women and Power in the Middle Ages*, ed. Mary Erler and Maryanne Kowaleski (Athens: University of Georgia Press, 1988), 83–101. This article can also be found in *Feminist Studies* 1 (1973): 126–41, and *Clio's Consciousness Raised: New Perspectives on the History of Women*, ed. Lois Banner (New York: Harper and Row, 1974), 103–18; see also McNamara's 2003 retrospective in "Women and Power through the Family Revisited." Jane Tibbetts Schulenburg, "Female Sanctity: Public and Private Roles, ca. 500–1100," in *Women and Power in the Middle Ages*, ed. Erler and Kowaleski, 102–25.

40. Pauline Stafford, "Women and the Norman Conquest," *Transactions of the Royal Historical Society*, 3rd ser., 4 (1994): 221–50.

41. The research on regional differences is summarized in Maryanne Kowaleski, "Singlewomen in Medieval and Early Modern Europe: The Demographic Perspective," in Judith M. Bennett and Amy M. Froide, eds., *Singlewomen in the European Past, 1250–1800* (Philadelphia: University of Pennsylvania Press, 1998), 38–81.

42. Lisa M. Bitel, *Land of Women: Tales of Sex and Gender from Early Ireland* (Ithaca, N.Y.: Cornell University Press, 1996); Jenny Jochens, *Women in Old Norse Society* (Ithaca, N.Y.: Cornell University Press, 1995).

43. Richard Abels and Ellen Harrison, "The Participation of Women in Languedocian Catharism," *Mediaeval Studies* 41 (1979): 215–51; Peter Biller, "The Common Woman in the Western Church in the Thirteenth and Early Fourteenth Centuries," in *Women in the Church*, ed. W. J. Sheils and Diana Wood (Oxford: Blackwell, 1990), 127–57, and his "Cathars and Material Women," in *Medieval Theology and the Natural Body*, ed. Peter Biller and Alastair J. Minnis, York Studies in Theology and the Natural Body 1 (1997): 61–107; Shannon McSheffrey, *Gender and Heresy: Women and Men in Lollard Communities, 1420–1530* (Philadelphia: University of Pennsylvania Press, 1995). For a brief summary of McSheffrey's argument that works well with students, see her "Women and Lollardy: A Reassessment," *Canadian Journal of History* 26 (1991): 199–223.

44. Recent studies of the growth of persecutions in the central Middle Ages recognize that prostitutes were harassed alongside other minorities and also stress how often majority groups imagined rampant sexual deviance among reviled "others," but they generally ignore or downplay gender. Few scholars have yet linked the increasing virulence of misogynous ideas among Christians with expanding discourses against other groups, and even as magisterial a book as Robert Bartlett's study of medieval colonization is much weakened by its inattention to gender; Robert Bartlett, *The Making of Europe: Conquest, Colonization, and Cultural Change, 950–1350* (Harmondsworth: Penguin, 1993). See also R. I. Moore, *The Formation of a Persecuting Society: Power and Deviance in Western Europe, 950–1250* (Oxford: Oxford University Press, 1987); Jeffrey Richards, *Sex, Dissidence and Damnation: Minority Groups in the Middle Ages* (London: Routledge, 1991). For studies that have begun to address issues of gender, see Louise Mirrer, *Women, Jews, and Muslims in the Texts of Reconquest Castile* (Ann Arbor: University of Michigan Press, 1996);

Joan Young Gregg, ed., *Devils, Women, and Jews: Reflections of the Other in Medieval Sermon Stories* (Albany: State University of New York Press, 1997), more useful for its texts than for its analysis; David Nirenberg, *Communities of Violence: Persecution of Minorities in the Middle Ages* (Princeton, N.J.: Princeton University Press, 1996).

45. Nirenberg, *Communities of Violence*, esp. 129–65; see also his "Conversion, Sex, and Segregation: Jews and Christians in Medieval Spain," *American Historical Review* 107:4 (2002): 1065–93. For women in Castilian society, see Heath Dillard, *Daughters of the Reconquest: Women in Castilian Town Society, 1100–1300* (Cambridge: Cambridge University Press, 1984), and Mirrer, *Women, Jews, and Muslims.*

46. Sharon Kinoshita, "The Politics of Courtly Love: *La Prise D'Orange* and the Conversion of the Saracen Queen," *Romanic Review* 86 (1995): 265–87; Sarah Kay, "Contesting 'Romance Influence': The Poetics of the Gift," *Comparative Literature Studies* 32 (1995): 320–41; Jacqueline de Weever, *Sheba's Daughters: Whitening and Demonizing the Saracen Woman in Medieval French Literature* (New York: Garland, 1998); Mirrer, *Women, Jews, and Muslims*, 17–30 (Mirrer also discusses Christian representations of Jewish women, 31–44).

47. Susan Mosher Stuard, "Ancillary Evidence for the Decline of Medieval Slavery," *Past and Present* 149 (1995): 3–28. See also Ruth Mazo Karras, "Desire, Descendants, and Dominance: Slavery, the Exchange of Women, and Masculine Power," in *The Work of Work: Servitude, Slavery, and Labor in Medieval England*, ed. Allen J. Frantzen and Douglas Moffat (Glasgow: Cruithne Press, 1994), 16–29.

48. Alain Boureau, *The Lord's First Night: The Myth of the Droit de Cuissage*, trans. Lydia G. Cochrane (Chicago: University of Chicago Press, 1998). Donna Woolfolk Cross's novel *Pope Joan* (New York: Crown, 1996) includes a historical postscript that purports to prove that the story has a basis in truth, as does a new book by Peter Stanford, *The She-Pope* (London: William Heineman, 1998). Do not be fooled; the story is a myth and an antifeminist one at that. See Alain Boureau, *The Myth of Pope Joan*, trans Lydia G. Cochrane (Chicago: University of Chicago Press, 2001), and Valerie R. Hotchkiss, *Clothes Make the Man: Female Cross Dressing in Medieval Europe* (New York: Garland Publishing, 1991), 69–82. I know of no modern account that unpacks the myth of chastity belts, but I also know of no chastity belts that can be dated earlier than the sixteenth century.

49. An excellent summary of early Christian attitudes is Elizabeth A. Clark, "Devil's Gateway and Brides of Christ: Women in the Early Christian World," in *Ascetic Piety and Women's Faith* (Lewiston, N.Y.: E. Mellen, 1986), 23–60.

50. For a fascinating exploration of medieval ideology as it pertained to women and gender, see Dyan Elliot, *Fallen Bodies: Pollution, Sexuality, and Demonology in the Middle Ages* (Philadelphia: University of Pennsylvania Press, 1998). For a study that links certain representations of gender to specific literary genres, see Simon Gaunt, *Gender and Genre in Medieval French Literature* (Cambridge: Cambridge University Press, 1995).

51. See especially Marina Warner, *Alone of All Her Sex: The Myth and the Cult of the Virgin Mary* (New York: Knopf, 1976), and Jaroslav Pelikan, *Mary through the Centuries: Her Place in the History of Culture* (New Haven, Conn.: Yale University Press, 1996).

52. There is a vast literature on medieval nuns, but see especially Jane Tib-

betts Schulenburg, *Forgetful of their Sex: Female Sanctity and Society, ca. 500–1100* (Chicago: University of Chicago Press, 1998); Bruce L. Venarde, *Women's Monasticism and Medieval Society: Nunneries in France and England, 890–1215* (Ithaca, N.Y.: Cornell University Press, 1997); Jo Ann Kay McNamara, *Sisters in Arms: Catholic Nuns through Two Millennia* (Cambridge, Mass.: Harvard University Press, 1996); Penelope D. Johnson, *Equal in Monastic Profession: Religious Women in Medieval France* (Chicago: University of Chicago Press, 1991); Marilyn Oliva, *The Convent and the Community in Late Medieval England: Female Monasteries in the Diocese of Norwich, 1350–1540* (Woodbridge, Suffolk: Boydell Press, 1998). For Saint Francis's observation, see Shulamith Shahar, *The Fourth Estate: A History of Women in the Middle Ages* (London: Methuen, 1983), 36.

53. Sharon Farmer, "Persuasive Voices: Clerical Images of Medieval Wives," *Speculum* 61 (1986): 517–43. For discussion about the nature of women's power in the Middle Ages, see Erler and Kowaleski, eds., *Women and Power in the Middle Ages*, and its sequel, *Gendering the Master Narrative*.

54. For misogamy, see Katharina M. Wilson and Elizabeth M. Makowski, *Wykked Wyves and the Woes of Marriage: Misogamous Literature from Juvenal to Chaucer* (Albany: State University of New York Press, 1990).

55. Alcuin Blamires, ed., *Woman Defamed and Defended: An Anthology of Edited Texts* (Oxford: Clarendon Press, 1992), quote from 12. R. Howard Bloch, "Medieval Misogyny," *Representations* 20 (1987): 1–24, quote from 22, n. 15. Bloch's argument in this essay generated heated debate. See responses by eight feminist scholars in *Medieval Feminist Newsletter* 6 (December 1988): 2–15; and Bloch's response in *Medieval Feminist Newsletter* 7 (Spring 1989): 8–12. His opinions were somewhat moderated in his later *Medieval Misogyny and the Invention of Western Romantic Love* (Chicago: University of Chicago Press, 1991).

56. For brewsters, see Judith M. Bennett, *Ale, Beer, and Brewsters in England: Women's Work in a Changing World* (New York: Oxford University Press, 1996), 124–44. For prostitutes, see Ruth Mazo Karras, *Common Women: Prostitution and Sexuality in Medieval England* (New York: Oxford University Press, 1996), quote from 141.

57. For students, an especially accessible article is Kathryn Gravdal, "Chrétien de Troyes, Gratian, and the Medieval Romance of Sexual Violence," *Signs: A Journal of Women in Culture and Society* 17 (1992): 558–85. See also Kathryn Gravdal, *Ravishing Maidens: Writing Rape in Medieval French Literature and Law* (Philadelphia: University of Pennsylvania Press, 1991), and Anna Roberts, ed., *Violence against Women in Medieval Texts* (Gainesville: University of Florida Press, 1998).

58. Caroline Walker Bynum, *Holy Feast and Holy Fast: The Religious Significance of Food to Medieval Women* (Berkeley: University of California Press, 1987). For a brief summary that works well in the classroom, see Bynum, "Fast, Feast, and Flesh: The Religious Significance of Food to Medieval Women," *Representations* 11 (1985): 1–16. Rudolph M. Bell, *Holy Anorexia* (Chicago: University of Chicago Press, 1985).

59. John M. Riddle, *Contraception and Abortion from the Ancient World to the Renaissance* (Cambridge, Mass.: Harvard University Press, 1992), and *Eve's Herbs: A History of Contraception and Abortion in the West* (Cambridge, Mass.: Harvard University Press, 1997). For classroom use, try this article by Riddle:

"Oral Contraceptives and Early-Term Abortifacients during Classical Antiquity and the Middle Ages," *Past and Present* 132 (1991): 3–32.

60. See essays in Barbara A. Hanawalt, ed., *Women and Work in Preindustrial Europe* (Bloomington: Indiana University Press, 1986), and Lindsey Charles and Lorna Duffin, eds., *Women and Work in Pre-Industrial England* (London: Croom Helm, 1985). My biographical study of a peasant woman also works well: *A Medieval Life: Cecilia Penifader of Brigstock, c. 1297–1344* (McGraw-Hill, 1998).

61. For both "double monasteries" and virginity, see n. 52.

62. For an overview that generates vigorous classroom discussion, see Jacqueline Murray, "Twice Marginal and Twice Invisible: Lesbians in the Middle Ages," in *Handbook of Medieval Sexuality*, ed. Vern L. Bullough and James A. Brundage (New York: Garland, 1996), 191–223. For an introduction to Church efforts to regulate sexual behavior, see James A. Brundage, *Law, Sex, and Christian Society in Medieval Europe* (Chicago: University of Chicago Press, 1987).

63. Clarissa W. Atkinson, *The Oldest Vocation: Christian Motherhood in the Middle Ages* (Ithaca, N.Y.: Cornell University Press, 1991); Ann Marie Rasmussen, *Mothers and Daughters in Medieval German Literature* (Syracuse, N.Y.: Syracuse University Press, 1997); John Carmi Parsons and Bonnie Wheeler, eds., *Medieval Mothering* (New York: Garland Publishing, 1996). Lois Huneycutt's article in Parsons and Wheeler's collection works particularly well with students, "Public Lives, Private Ties: Royal Mothers in England and Scotland, 1070–1204," 295–311.

64. Ruth Mazo Karras, *From Boys to Men: Formations of Masculinity in Late Medieval Europe* (Philadelphia: University of Pennsylvania Press, 2003); Lees, ed., *Medieval Masculinities*; Jeffrey Jerome Cohen and Bonnie Wheeler, eds., *Becoming Male in the Middle Ages* (New York: Garland, 1997); D. M. Hadley, ed., *Masculinity in Medieval Europe* (London: Longman, 1999); Jacqueline Murray, ed., *Conflicted Identities and Multiple Masculinities: Men in the Medieval West* (New York: Garland, 1999).

65. Karras, *Common Women*, Leah Lydia Otis, *Prostitution in Medieval Society: The History of an Urban Institution in Languedoc* (Chicago: University of Chicago Press, 1985). For students, few things are as gripping as the case of a transvestite prostitute who worked in London and Oxford: see Ruth Mazo Karras and David Lorenzo Boyd, "'Ut Cum Muliere': A Male Transvestite Prostitute in Fourteenth-Century London," in *Premodern Sexualities*, ed. Louise Fradenburg and Carla Freccero (London: Routledge, 1996), 101–16.

66. Valerie R. Hotchkiss, *Clothes Make the Man*; Vern L. Bullough, "Cross Dressing and Gender Role Change in the Middle Ages," in *Handbook of Medieval Sexuality*, ed. Bullough and Brundage, 223–42. In addition to the case of the transvestite prostitute cited above, an excellent case for use in the classroom can be found in Michael H. Shank, "A Female University Student in Late Medieval Krakow," in *Sisters and Workers in the Middle Ages*, ed. Judith M. Bennett et al. (Chicago: University of Chicago Press, 1989), 190–97 (also in *Signs: A Journal of Women in Culture and Society* 12 [1987]: 373–80). See also Rudolf M. Dekker and Lotte C. van de Pol, *The Tradition of Female Transvestism in Early Modern Europe* (London: Macmillan, 1989).

67. Bynum, *Holy Feast and Holy Fast*, and her "Fast, Feast, and Flesh"; Bell, *Holy Anorexia*. For primary sources, see especially Elizabeth A. Petroff, ed.,

Medieval Women's Visionary Literature (New York: Oxford University Press, 1986), and Emilie Zum Brunn and Georgette Epiney-Burgard, eds., *Women Mystics in Medieval Europe* (New York: Paragon House, 1989).

68. Betty Radice, ed., *The Letters of Abelard and Heloise* (Harmondsworth: Penguin, 1974); Barbara Newman, "Authority, Authenticity, and the Repression of Heloise," *Journal of Medieval and Renaissance Studies* 22 (1992): 121–57.

69. For a brief overview, see Elizabeth A. R. Brown, "Eleanor of Aquitaine: Parent, Queen, and Duchess," in *Eleanor of Aquitaine: Patron and Politician*, ed. William W. Kibler (Austin: University of Texas Press, 1976), 9–34, but there are many book-length studies of which the best is probably Douglas D. R. Owen, *Eleanor of Aquitaine: Queen and Legend* (Oxford: Blackwell, 1993). For students, the liveliest biography is Marion Meade, *Eleanor of Aquitaine: A Biography* (New York: Penguin, 1977), but it interprets Eleanor in somewhat anachronistic ways. Amy Kelly, *Eleanor of Aquitaine and the Four Kings* (Cambridge, Mass.: Harvard University Press, 1950), is now old but responsible for the argument that places Eleanor at the center of the development of courtly love.

70. The best biography is Charity Cannon Willard, *Christine de Pizan: Her Life and Works* (New York: Persea Books, 1984). For the issue of Christine de Pizan's feminism (and an article that works very well with students), see Beatrice Gottlieb, "The Problem of Feminism in the Fifteenth Century," in *Women of the Medieval World*, ed. Julius Kirshner and Suzanne F. Wemple (Oxford: Blackwell, 1985), 337–64.

71. Sabina Flanagan, *Hildegard of Bingen: A Visionary Life*, 2nd ed. (London: Routledge, 1998); Barbara Newman, *Voice of the Living Light: Hildegard of Bingen and her World* (Berkeley: University of California Press, 1998). Among the many editions of the many writings of Hildegard of Bingen, her edited letters might be most accessible: *The Letters of Hildegard of Bingen*, vols. 1 and 2, trans. Joseph L. Baird and Radd K. Ehrmann (New York: Oxford University Press, 1994 and 1998).

72. See especially Marina Warner, *Joan of Arc: The Image of Female Heroism* (New York: Vintage, 1981), and Régine Pernoud, *Joan of Arc: By Herself and Her Witnesses* (New York: Stein and Day, 1982); set into a narrative format, this latter text provides documents from the many trials of Joan of Arc. For women warriors, see Megan McLaughlin, "The Woman Warrior: Gender, Warfare, and Society in Medieval Europe," *Women's Studies* 17 (1990): 193–209 (students respond well to this article), and Helen Nicholson, "Women on the Third Crusade," *Journal of Medieval History* 23 (1997): 335–49. See also brief comments in Jonathan Riley-Smith, *The First Crusaders, 1095–1131* (Cambridge: Cambridge University Press, 1997).

73. Thomas de Cantimpré, *The Life of Christina of St. Trond*, trans. Margot H. King (Saskatoon: Peregrina, 1985).

74. For Margery Kempe, the most straightforward historical study is Clarissa W. Atkinson, *Mystic and Pilgrim: The Book and the World of Margery Kempe* (Ithaca, N.Y.: Cornell University Press, 1983), and an accessible edition of her biography is *The Book of Margery Kempe*, trans. B. A. Windeatt (Harmondsworth, U.K.: Penguin, 1985).

75. Mary Wollstonecraft, *A Vindication of the Rights of Woman*, ed. Miriam Brody (1792: London: Penguin, 2004), 46–47.

76. Interview in the G2 section of *The Guardian*, April 4, 2005, available online at: http://www.guardian.co.uk/.

77. Amy Richlin, "How Putting the Man in Roman Put the Roman in Romance," in *Talking Gender: Public Images, Personal Journeys, and Political Critiques*, ed. Nancy Hewitt, Jean O'Barr, and Nancy Rosebaugh (Chapel Hill, N.C.: University of North Carolina Press, 1996), 14–35, at 31.

Chapter 8

1. Barbara Christian, "The Race for Theory," 1986 essay reprinted in *The Nature and Context of Minority Discourse*, ed. Adbul R. JanMohamed and David Lloyd (New York: Oxford University Press, 1990), 37–49, at 47. Christian asked her readers to consider "for whom are we doing what we are doing when we do literary criticism." She continued, "The answer to that question determines what orientation we take in our work, the language we use, the purposes for which it is intended."

2. Joan Scott, "Feminism's History," *Journal of Women's History* 16:2 (2004): 10–29, at 24.

3. Anne Firor Scott, Sara Evans et al., "Women's History in the New Millennium: A Conversation across Three Generations, Part 2," *Journal of Women's History* 11:2 (1999): 199–220, at 213.

4. Bonnie Smith, *The Gender of History: Men, Women, and Historical Practice* (Cambridge, Mass.: Harvard University Press, 1998), 69.

Index